PORTFOLIO

HOW TO MAKE MILLIONS IN REAL ESTATE
IN THREE YEARS STARTING WITH NO CASH

TYLER G. HICKS is president of International Wealth Success Inc. and director of a large New York–based full-service lender. A consultant to real estate wealth builders around the world, he is the author of numerous books on real estate, including *How to Make Big Money in Real Estate* and *How to Borrow Your Way to Real Estate Riches*.

HOW TO
MAKE MILLIONS
IN REAL ESTATE
IN THREE YEARS
STARTING WITH
NO CASH

FOURTH EDITION

COMPLETELY REVISED AND EXPANDED

TYLER G. HICKS

PORTFOLIO

PORTFOLIO
Published by the Penguin Group
Penguin Group (USA) Inc., 375 Hudson Street, New York, NY 10014, U.S.A.
Penguin Group (Canada), 10 Alcorn Avenue, Toronto, Ontario, Canada M4V 3B2
(a division of Pearson Penguin Canada Inc.)
Penguin Books Ltd, 80 Strand, London WC2R 0RL, England
Penguin Ireland, 25 St Stephen's Green, Dublin 2, Ireland
(a division of Penguin Books Ltd)
Penguin Group (Australia), 250 Camberwell Road, Camberwell, Victoria 3124, Australia
(a division of Pearson Australia Group Pty Ltd)
Penguin Books India Pvt Ltd, 11 Community Centre, Panchsheel Park,
New Delhi – 110 017, India
Penguin Group (NZ), cnr Airborne and Rosedale Roads, Albany, Auckland 1310, New Zealand
(a division of Pearson New Zealand Ltd)
Penguin Books (South Africa) (Pty) Ltd, 24 Sturdee Avenue, Rosebank,
Johannesberg 2196, South Africa

Penguin Books Ltd, Registered Offices: 80 Strand, London WC2R 0RL, England

First published in the United States of America under the title *How to Make One Million Dollars in Real Estate in Three Years Starting with No Cash* by Prentice-Hall, Inc. 1976
Second edition published 1989
Third edition published 2000
This fourth edition published by Portfolio, a member of Penguin Group (USA) Inc. 2005

1 3 5 7 9 10 8 6 4 2

Publisher's Note: This publication is designed to provide accurate and authoritative information in regard to the subject matter covered. It is sold with the understanding that the publisher is not engaged in rendering legal, accounting, or other professional services. If you require legal advice or other expert assistance, you should seek the services of a competent professional.

LIBRARY OF CONGRESS CATALOGING IN PUBLICATION DATA
Hicks, Tyler Gregory, 1921–
    How to make millions in real estate in three years starting with no cash / Tyler G. Hicks—
4th ed., completely rev. and expanded.
        p. cm.   Rev. ed. of: How to make millions in real estate in 3 years starting with no cash. 3rd ed., completely rev. and expanded. c2000.
    Includes bibliographical references and index.
    ISBN 1-59184-097-X
    1. Real estate investment. I. Hicks, Tyler Gregory, 1921– How to make millions in real estate in 3 years starting with no cash. II. Title.
HD1382.5.H54 2005
332.63'24—dc22   2004065480

Printed in the United States of America

To Real Estate Wealth Builders everywhere, with many thanks for your letters, telephone calls, faxes and e-mails describing your many accomplishments in providing shelter and work spaces for humanity. Your activities are an inspiration to Beginning Wealth Builders throughout the world and your author is grateful you share them with him.

Special Notice for All Readers

Business examples given in this book are based on: (a) letters, faxes, or e-mails voluntarily sent to the author by readers of his books, newsletters, or courses; (b) real estate investments studied by the author in various areas of the world using local media and similar sources; and (c) telephone calls voluntarily made to the author by readers describing their real estate investments and the financial results obtained with these investments. Letters, faxes, and e-mails from readers are available in their original form for inspection by any interested reader. The author requests that he be given several days' notice by any reader seeking to view the correspondence so he can arrange comfortable desk space in his office for the reader.

WHAT THIS BOOK DOES FOR YOU

READ THIS AND THE NEXT FOUR PAGES FIRST!

They tell you what this book will do for you. And these pages could lead you into a world of borrowed money that's available to almost anyone—especially you!

Between the time the third edition of this book was written and today—about eight years—a studio condo apartment a beginning wealth builder (BWB) paid $98,000 for, using borrowed money, was sold for $1.2 million! This means that he earned nearly $138,000 a year from the appreciation, or rise in value, of this studio apartment. And, of course, he had full use of the condo apartment during those years. This real-life example—just one of hundreds I can cite for you—shows you what you might do in real estate today.

During the several editions of this book, many readers wrote me to tell me how they're using the ideas in each edition to build their wealth in real estate. For instance, one delighted reader writes:

> In the past six months we bought four pieces of real estate totaling $2.6 million for $4 down payment—$1 on each deal. And we have just gained control of another piece of property (via option with no expiry date) valued at $5.8 million—again with no money down.

While I know that $4 down is not the "starting with no cash" in the title of this book, it's so close to "no cash" that I say to you:

> If you can equal the deals of the above reader, I'll be glad to supply 10 times the "no cash" to you free of any charge of any kind—that

is, no strings! Just write or fax me, giving all the facts about the property. I'll get back to you the same day I receive your letter, fax, or e-mail. Or you can call me toll-free on my 800 number and I'll give you an instantaneous answer.

And, as another gesture of my desire to help you, you're free to inspect any—and all—original copies of every letter quoted in this book. All I need is a few days' notice that you want to visit my office in New York City to look over the letters. I'll have them taken from the safe deposit box where they're kept and put on display for your inspection.

Now that you know where I'm coming from—as people so often say today—let's take a quick look at what this book does for *you*. To start, we'll look at our basic needs and how they're served.

Every person in the world has two basic needs—food and shelter. There are thousands of firms supplying the food that we all need every day of our lives. Likewise, there are thousands of organizations supplying the shelter, or real estate, needs of individuals and firms of all kinds.

But of the two basic needs, the shelter need is probably served less efficiently. There are many reasons for this lower efficiency, such as: poor tenant relations leading to controversies, neglected maintenance, delayed upgrading of heating and air-conditioning systems, and so on. *You* can help improve the efficiency of the shelter, or real estate, business and build riches for yourself, using the magic power of borrowed money. This book shows you, step by step, exactly how to build significant wealth in real estate ventures without investing a cent of your own, while giving your tenants superior housing.

Now what do we mean by shelter? In this book shelter means:

- Single-family homes

- Apartment houses

- Hotels and motels

- Factories

- Shopping centers

- Mobile homes

- Any other type of enclosure that provides protection for people and their possessions

Since every structure must be built on something, we'll also show you how to make significant profits from borrowed money that you invest in:

- Vacant land
- Developed land
- Air rights
- Wetlands
- Offshore waters

Yes, there's a fortune waiting for every serious beginning real estate builder who:

- Improves real estate
- Offers better values
- Capitalizes on his or her investments
- Takes "safe" risks
- Provides clean, neat, safe housing

So no matter what your background may be—inside or outside real estate—whether you're a:

- Beginner in property investments
- Widely experienced professional
- Real estate salesperson
- Doctor, lawyer, minister
- Bricklayer, plumber, plasterer
- Homemaker, secretary, widow
- Beginning wealth builder in any field

this book can help you get richer—faster—in real estate, using the gigantic leverage of borrowed money. I have seen so many big fortunes built in real estate of all types—from raw land to enormous residential-commercial complexes—that I'm completely convinced that you, too, can do the same if you apply the methods given in this book.

In just a few short, fact-filled pages you'll learn how to:

- Get 100% financing for real estate
- Put together zero-cash deals
- Mortgage out—that is, take over an income property and walk away with cash in your hand
- Sell air rights over property
- Build enormous tax-free income
- Live free of charge in the best part of town
- Take over property for pennies
- Borrow your way to a real estate fortune
- Build wealth using my tested methods
- Use options to control property with just a very small cash outlay

During my years of helping others build their real estate wealth, I've met plenty of people who use my methods successfully. I'll tell you about these people in this book. And I'll tell you about my own real estate deals, which are usually successful moneymakers.

Not only am I a real estate wealth builder with some years' experience, I'm also a director on the board of a multimillion-dollar real estate lending organization. And the board (my boss, really) is constantly after me, saying in effect, "How can we make more real estate loans? We've got millions of dollars sitting here 'looking for a home.' Why can't you, Mr. Director, find us some good loans so we can earn more for our depositors?"

Some board members even imply that they want to fire me if I don't get them more loans. Yet I remember a time when I had to almost slug them over the head to get them to make real estate loans running more than 12 years. Today we routinely make 30-year loans.

So I speak "from both sides of the desk"—as a real estate borrower and as a real estate lender. And I can tell you this, good friend, I've made a lot more money personally as a real estate wealth builder than I have as an officer of a lender! Top executives come to me at least once a week asking,

"How can I make some money in real estate, Ty?" This book tells you—and them—exactly how!

And let me say this right now. If you're a reader of any of my many books, my newsletter, or my courses, you're a friend of mine! That means I'll try to help you—personally—get rich in real estate. You can write me, fax me, or e-mail me; you can call me day or night, or you can visit me in my office. I'll be there to help. You have a good friend in Ty Hicks!

So come along with me, interested real estate wealth builder, to learn how *you* can get started on *your* riches program. I'm certain that you'll find our journey is interesting, challenging, and best of all, rewarding! And I'm nearly 100% certain your real estate profits will exceed any profits you try to earn in the unpredictable stock market! Let's start—here and now.

Tyler G. Hicks

CONTENTS

"New" Condo Methods • Get in on the "New" Condo Yourself • Take Over the Property You Want • Get Your Money Back Quickly • Another "New" Condo Idea • Use "Built-In" Financing to Get Your Condo • Be a Multi-condo Owner • Renting Condos to Sublet • Profit from the World's Condo Craze • Co-ops Also Make Money

Go the Borrowed-Money Road • Get All the Things You Want • Understand What Real Estate Can Do for You • Make Your Fortune as a Loan Originator • How to Get Business Money through Real Estate • Rented Property Can Earn You Big Profits • Profit While You Can • Combine the Stock Market and Real Estate • Make Theaters Your Fortune Source • Other Real Estate–Based Businesses for You • Try "Moving Real Estate" to Build Your Wealth • Get Others to Pay for Your Movable Real Estate • Make Your Fortune in Real Estate–Based Businesses

From Pennies to Millions in Real Estate in Three Years, Starting with *No* Cash • "Convincers" for the Disbelievers Everywhere

Real Estate Investment and Management Books • Real Estate Success Kits, Books, Reports, and Newsletters

HOW TO
MAKE MILLIONS
IN REAL ESTATE
IN THREE YEARS
STARTING WITH
NO CASH

ONE

WHY REAL ESTATE IS FINANCIALLY VALUABLE TO YOU

Most of us live in houses, apartments, mobile homes, motels, or hotels for years without sensing the importance, from a *money aspect,* of the space we occupy. If we live in a desirable area, the value of the shelter and space (land) we occupy is constantly rising. Time, as is proven again and again, is on the side of real estate. This means that time is on *your* side if you're a real estate owner.

For instance, one property that I paid $84,000 for recently was sought by a real estate broker who offered me $1.2 million for it. I'm sure that if I put this same property on the market myself I could get at least $1.3 million for it. The secret? The property is in a prime area that regularly attracts new investors. This leads me to an important law of real estate fortune building:

PRIME PROPERTIES PAY PROFITS

The law of the 4 Ps (which I developed) is at work 24 hours a day. This law is:

Prime properties pay profits.
Also, prime properties increase in value, year by year.

And why do prime properties rise in value steadily, year after year? Because some 70% of the population of the United States lives on about 2% of the land! This means that the 2% land area becomes more valuable as the population increases and larger numbers of people try to squeeze into a city or town of fixed area.

Further, the amount of land area available for real estate use rarely increases; if anything, this area often decreases. And when you have more people—homeowners, apartment dwellers, or factory owners—seeking a piece of a decreasing commodity (land or desirable shelter), the price of that commodity has nowhere to go but *up*! For this reason, land—and the shelter built on it—is one of the best investments you can ever make. Long experience shows that:

> **The best investment made by the average person, from the standpoint of eventual profit, is in real estate. The profits the average person earns from real estate far outpace his or her profits in the stock market, antiques, paintings, and similar investments.**

So you see, your chances of hitting the big money in real estate are much greater than in any other area of investment. And what's more important from a beginning wealth builder's (BWB) standpoint is that:

> **Real estate of all types is almost always financed with other people's money (OPM). So *you are expected to borrow* to buy real estate. Paying cash is the rare exception in real estate deals.**

For example, a woman subscriber to my *International Wealth Success* monthly newsletter writes:

> **We're off and running. Borrowed $407,000 as follows: $100,000 equity loan; $231,000 land acquisition loan; $76,000 signature loan; total $407,000. *You said it could be done!* Cost of property was $390,000. All money was borrowed from the savings and loan which has our home mortgage. Same bank is giving us construction money, too! When we found the right bank, *they* sold *us* on our own project.**

KNOW THE IMPORTANCE OF SHELTER

Today we all take shelter for granted and expect:

- Warmth in winter

- Coolness in hot summers

- Dryness in fog and rain
- Protection from winds and snow
- Graciousness to improve the quality of our lives
- Safekeeping for our belongings

With inflation a fact of life since the invention of money, shelter that provides all, or most of, these features is constantly increasing in value—just like the land on which the shelter is built. It is the combination of these two value increases that will help *your* real estate investments make *you* rich!

YOUR REAL ESTATE BUSINESS IS A SAFE BUSINESS

You can invest money in thousands of different businesses, such as:

- Manufacturing
- Services
- Leisure and sports
- Entertainment
- Computers, software, telecommunications, and the Internet

and lose your shirt in a few months. But invest in well-located real estate and it is usually almost impossible to lose money, because:

Well-located real estate is constantly increasing in value. There is almost nothing a sensible person can do that will permanently injure the value of well-located real estate.

So when I recommend real estate investments to you, I do so with the complete assurance that it is almost impossible for you to go wrong. Further, it is also almost impossible for you *not* to make money in real estate if you:

- Hold the property a few years
- Have the structures maintained properly
- Keep the property rented, if it is a rental holding

While it is true that real estate, like any other business, has its ups and downs, usually the swings are less severe than in other businesses—say retailing, like hardware, groceries, and so on. So your real estate business is a safe business—and a business that can make *you* wealthy in a relatively short time.

YES—YOU *CAN* GET RICH FASTER!

Do you believe what I just said: "A business that can make *you* wealthy in a relatively short time"? If you don't, then I hope to convince you with a series of real-life excerpts from letters that thousands of beginning wealth builders (BWBs) have written to me telling me how they built their wealth using my methods—starting (in general) with no cash of their own. Each letter was sent to me voluntarily and is so valuable that I keep it in a safe-deposit box. I'm sure you'll find these letters convincing, inspiring, and powerfully motivating.

In giving you excerpts from these letters, I'm following the practice I used in my many other money books, which are listed at the beginning of this book. What I did in each of those other books was to feature a special way *you* can get rich. And, I'm happy to say, I've helped make a number of people rich—quickly, easily, and happily.

From Debt to Millions

Here's another BWB who made it big in real estate. I call him "From Debt to Millions" BWB. Here's his story, as given in his letter to me.

> As I stated on the telephone, I was $12,500 in debt 24 months ago and have subsequently built a company with assets of approximately $2 million. Prior to building the company I visited our local library and read many books. All of the books offered some help. However, your book *How to Borrow Your Way to a Great Fortune* proved to furnish me with the ultimate plan. In this respect I owe you my deepest gratitude. . . . Again, I wish to thank you for everything you have done for me.

KNOW THE ADVANTAGES OF REAL ESTATE

Real estate has many advantages for *every* investor—including you. These advantages include:

- Income-tax savings (even with tax-law changes!)

- Capital growth

- Use of other people's money

- Multiple-loan financing

- Long life of property

- Constant rise in value

- Little management time required

- Zero-cash takeover of property *and* income

Let's take a look at each of these advantages to see how you can use them in your fortune-building program. You'll quickly learn how to get rich in real estate using borrowed money—that is, without putting up a penny of your own.

SAVE ON YOUR INCOME TAXES

All shelter-type income-producing real estate—except vacant land—can be *depreciated. Depreciation is the money set aside for income to pay for the replacement of the structure, equipment, or other items for which rental, leasing, or other fees are received.*

Let's say you take over a $600,000 income-producing building, which produces $75,000 annual total income to you. Your operating expenses are $40,000 per year and your accountant tells you the structure has a life of 40 years. You and he decide that you will depreciate the building over 40 years on the required *straight-line* basis under the revised tax law. This means you'll deduct an equal amount each year during the life of the building for depreciation.

So, for this building, you'll deduct $600,000 ÷ 40 years = $15,000 per year.

In a given year, therefore, your total expenses will be $40,000 + $15,000 = $55,000. So you'll pay income taxes on $75,000 − $55,000 = $20,000 even though the $15,000 depreciation "expense" is money in your pocket.

Current tax law requires you to use the straight-line method of depreciation. The shortest "life" for depreciation of apartment houses and other residential buildings is 27.5 years. For office buildings and warehouses, you must use 31.5 years. And you can, if you wish, use the 40-year life we chose above and reduce your alternative minimum tax, if you're subject to it. (*Note:* Be certain to check with a competent real estate certified public accountant [CPA] to learn if these tax rules still apply when you decide to buy an income-producing property.)

I know many real estate operators and they usually pay less in income taxes than any other business people. So you, too, can expect to pay lower income taxes on your real estate income than on almost any other kind of income. What's more, we'll show you how—when you have large real estate holdings—you can use your real estate depreciation to help you save income taxes on your other income.

GROW RICH ON CAPITAL GROWTH

A dollar you put into income real estate today may grow this way:

Year Number	Investment Value
1	$1
2	1.07
3	1.14
4	1.22
5	1.31

Thus, in five years your $1 investment has grown to $1.31 while you are:

- Receiving income

- Saving income taxes

- Using Other People's Money (OPM)

So you see, capital growth *can* be an important factor in the increase of your fortune. Real estate is truly the magic business because:

Real estate investments work for you 24 hours a day, seven days a week. You could say that real estate makes money for you while you sleep!

USE OTHER PEOPLE'S MONEY TO BUILD YOUR RICHES

Almost every real estate project you've ever seen is financed using other other people's money (OPM) instead of your own. Very few real estate structures are ever bought or built using your own money. So if you, as a typical BWB, don't have much money to start building your fortune, you can go into real estate without worrying about borrowing the money you need.

Why should you—a BWB with plenty of original ideas—have to put up your own money? You shouldn't have to if you're "putting up" the ideas. Plenty of banks, mortgage lenders, savings and loan associations, and other real estate financers are crying for good projects into which they can put the money that is overflowing their coffers.

Go into real estate if you want to:

- Build a fortune on OPM

- Borrow all the money you need with the greatest of ease

- Get more than one loan at the same time

A Fortune for the Price of Manhattan Island

Another happy reader who has gained success using OPM in real estate recently wrote saying:

> It is with greatest pleasure that I write to you and say *Thanks!* Nor am I forgetting Mr. Hicks who is kind enough to share his knowledge with the world. Four months ago I was beating my brains out trying to make ends meet. Now just the reverse; I am beating my brains out trying to spend my money wisely.
>
> It all started when I read Mr. Hicks's book *How to Borrow Your Way to a Great Fortune.* I suppose I have read this book a dozen times, and still refer to it from time to time. After subscribing to *International Wealth Success** I was on my way. I followed Mr. Hicks's instructions to the letter, capitalizing loans, obtaining leads for second mortgages from *IWS,* and then purchased my first apartment house. I now own four and am in the process of buying a shopping center. Just think. All that for $24! The same price as Manhattan Island [which the Dutch bought from the Native Americans for $24 in trinkets and beads].

---

*The BWBs' monthly newsletter of great wealth opportunities for you. To subscribe send $24 for 12 monthly issues to IWS Inc., P.O. Box 186, Merrick, NY 11566-0186.

GET MULTIPLE-LOAN FINANCING

Many people think that having more than one loan at a time is somehow indecent. Yet in real estate financing, multiple loans (mortgages)—that is, more than one loan on a single piece of income property—are very common. Many income-producing properties routinely have two loans on them. Some properties have as many as eight mortgages!

So go where the money is: the real estate income-property business. Earn big money using other people's money to finance still other people's property without investing a cent of your own! Get paid for your creative ideas and management ability.

Forget your fear of the multiple loan. Instead use multiple loans to finance your way to a real estate fortune!

Three Days to Wealth

A happy reader using multiple loans writes:

> I just got my loans. It took only three days to get $25,000. I capitalized five $5,000 property-improvement loans on a building I don't even own yet. I've taken over a $200,000 38-unit apartment building and borrowed the down payment. The cash flow pays all the loans, too. By carefully timing the close of escrow, prorations of rents, and payments, I walk away with $3,000 cash and a building for my trouble.
>
> I'm looking at three more buildings that are even better. Every bank in town and some out-of-town ones, too, are trying to lay more cash on me than I can ever spend. —— Bank and —— Bank PR people are taking me to lunch offering lines of credit, compensating balances, ballpoint pens, and blue-chip stamps.
>
> I'm putting students and recovering alcoholics to work as apartment managers, painters, carpet layers, and plumbers, and giving senior citizens a good place to live and doing a lot of really good things. I'm thrilled and delighted. I have all of Ty Hicks's books, and the *Starting Millionaire Success Kit* and *Financial Broker Success Kit*.* Many thanks for your ideas and assistance.

---

*Available from IWS Inc., P.O. Box 186, Merrick, NY 11566, for $99.50 each. See chapter 15 for more information.

Note that this reader used three of my wealth-building methods, namely:

1. Get your money fast—it took just three days here.

2. Use multiple loans—five here.

3. Mortgage out—he got $3,000 more cash than he needed.

You can learn how to do the same if you keep reading this book.

SEVEN WAYS TO GET YOUR REAL ESTATE DOWN-PAYMENT MONEY

The biggest hurdle to getting income real estate for most BWBs is the down-payment money needed to take over a property. I'm sure you've either run into this hurdle yourself or heard of other BWBs who have. Why is the down payment such a hurdle for most BWBs? Because:

- *Most BWBs* can find suitable income properties to buy.

- *The down payment* (10% to 25% of the property cost) rises with the price of the real estate you want to buy.

- *The higher the price* of the property you want to buy, the larger the down payment.

- *Lenders place limits* on the amount of down-payment money most BWBs can raise by borrowing.

There are seven types of loans you might use for your real estate down payment:

1. *Personal loan* from a bank, credit union, or finance company that you obtain for an acceptable use

2. *Credit-card lines of credit* on one or more credit cards you hold that offer you a cash line of credit you can borrow against

3. *Home-equity loan* or second mortgage on property you already own

4. *Second (purchase money)* mortgage from property seller that covers either all or part of your down payment

5. *Money from family members* using a "gift letter" in which a relative promises to give you enough money for the down payment on the property without requiring that the money ever be repaid

6. *Investor's loan* from people who like real estate deals and trust you to take good care of their investment by running the real estate in such a way that it regularly earns a profit for the investor and you

7. *Secured loan* using stocks, bonds, or savings accounts as "quick collateral" as contrasted with real estate, which takes longer (six to eight weeks usually) to be pledged as collateral

Let's look at some of these down-payment loans and how and where you might use them:

- *When your down payment* is $50,000 or less, use a personal loan. Most personal loans are in the $50,000 or less range.

- *With a down payment up to $25,000,* use credit-card lines of credit. Such lines can go up to $100,000.

- *Above $50,000 for your down payment* you'll often have to use a home-equity loan, or a second mortgage, on property you already own.

- *Purchase money (PM) mortgages* can run you up to $50,000; most are in the $10,000 to $25,000 range.

- *Family members* having excess funds can advance you money for a down payment using a gift letter.

- *Investors or business partners* can make loans to you for your down payment if they have enough ready cash.

- *Secured loans* using stocks and bonds as collateral can quickly get you the down-payment money you need. Such securities can be your own or can be borrowed from others.

Use one of these methods today. Just be sure to get your down-payment loan!

BUY LONG-LIFE PROPERTY

Buy the usual auto, TV, or computer and you'll wear it out in four years or less. Then you're faced with buying a replacement—usually at a higher price.

But buy a good real estate income property and it's profitable for 30, 50, or even 100 years. I've been in hotels in England that were more than 400 years old! Sure, the roof had been replaced a few times, candles were replaced by electric bulbs, and TV and the Internet provide more modern forms of entertainment. But the walls, floors, doors, and windows are still the same. Just imagine how many lives have been lived out in such a building, how much profit the building earned for its various owners over the years!

Yes real estate—at least most of it—is financially valuable because it has a long life. Repairs have to be made now and then but the cost of repairs is generally low compared to the value of the property. Yes you *can* add solid, lasting values to your life by taking over a well-kept piece of income property.

GET IN ON CONSTANTLY RISING VALUES

We've all heard of hitching our wagon to a star. In real estate you hitch your wagon to a magic money machine. This great money machine—24 hours a day—increases the value of the money you invest in real estate. Truly, in real estate you make money while you sleep!

I know of no other investment that rises in value like real estate. The stock market may go up in value for 12, 18, or 24 months. But just as surely as it goes up, so, too, may it go down. You *may* be able to make money in the stock market. If you can, I'm all for you. But plenty of people *don't* make money in the market while millions of people *do* make money in real estate.

Why do so many people make *big* money in real estate? Because they get in on the constantly rising value of well-located and well-built income real estate. You can, too, and I'll show you how.

WORK THE FEWEST HOURS POSSIBLE

Take over any kind of retail business—such as a travel agency, hardware store, or department store—and you'll put in at least eight hours a day, and more likely 12 hours. But in real estate you can get by on less than half an hour a day if you organize your income property well.

So why spend 40 to 60 hours a week struggling for an income when you can get the same return in dollars for less than five hours of work? Truly, real estate probably requires less time than any other business! So if you like to work short hours, income real estate is *your* business. What's more, you can make it your spare-time business while you hold down a job or run a business in some other field.

WALK AWAY WITH PROPERTY, CASH, AND INCOME

In real estate you can, with proper planning:

1. Take over property with other people's money (OPM)

2. Get extra cash

3. Own the property

4. Never invest a cent of your own

Real estate is one of the few businesses in which you can take over a valuable asset using borrowed money, own the asset, and have extra cash to put in your pocket! The reason for this is that:

- Real estate is an OPM business

- There's almost always money available for real estate

- Borrowing is "in" in real estate

If you want to borrow plenty of money without getting embarrassed over it, then real estate is for you. Keep in mind that real estate that provides our shelter is the *second* most important item in all our lives, food being first.

The No-Money-Down Way to Wealth

Another happy reader writes:

I'm buying my second apartment building with no money down. The first was 43 units for $185,000 with a $25,000 down payment. I got the $25,000 with five $5,000 capitalized loans from five different banks. I've been paying them out of the increased spendable.

My second building is 20 units for $90,000, $9,000 down, a new first loan of $60,000 and the owner will carry the balance of $26,000 plus the loan fee of 1.5 points will be added to the owner's note. On the down-payment money on this one, I'm getting the friendly real estate broker to loan me his 6% commission of $5,400 and getting a property improvement loan for $5,000 from a savings and loan as you recommended. I'm also carefully timing the close of escrow and prorations of rent to get the owner to make the payments the first month and give me the rent receipts, putting a little extra in my pocket. I plan to raise the rents.

I'm also becoming a business opportunity broker and learning an exciting new career. We charge a minimum $3,000 fee or 10% of the sale price, whichever is greater, on the sale of a business and a 6% fee on the sale of the real estate, or on a net basis. I recently found a drive-in dairy. Listed the business and real estate. The business sold for $16,000 with a $3,000 commission. We had a net listing on the real estate for $75,000 and sold it for $90,000. Business is very good. I very much enjoy the ideas in the *IWS* newsletter and other publications. Thanks.

GO WHERE THE MONEY IS

Real estate is financially important to you, me, our relatives, and our friends. To *you*, I want to make real estate as financially important as it has been to *me*. My goal in this book is to make you a real estate multi-millionaire in three years. If you want to stop anywhere short of this goal, that's your decision.

Just remember that everyone needs space—from the hospital bed on which we are born to the six-foot hole in which most of us are finally put to rest. In between we occupy apartments, homes, hotels, motels, and other real estate. And to date, there is not one human being who can do without real estate.

With the population of our world on its way to doubling, real estate has nowhere to go but up in value. To get in on this worldwide boom, come along with me to learn how *you* can get rich in the world's greatest OPM business.

Points to Remember

- Prime properties pay profits to *you*.
- Real estate is the best investment made by the average person.
- Real estate is one of the safest businesses known today.
- Your real estate can save you money on your income taxes.
- You can easily grow rich on capital growth in real estate.
- Real estate is a borrowed-money business, meaning that you can get started on zero cash.
- It is easy to get multiple loans on real estate property.
- In real estate you can work just a few hours a week and may become a multimillionaire in three years or less.

TWO

HOW TO FINANCE YOUR REAL ESTATE FORTUNE

There are dozens of ways for *you* to finance *your* real estate fortune. Many of these ways are well known—they're called *conventional financing*. Other ways are less well known. You might call these *nonconventional* or *creative financing*. But no matter which way you choose, it can put enormous wealth into *your* pocket. For example, recent deals using these methods:

- Built an $8.5-million real estate empire in two years with only a $4 down payment for the five properties the reader owns

- Obtained a $4-million loan with just three telephone calls, using a name supplied by an experienced real estate lender

- Took over about $800,000 in real estate less than a year ago, with zero money down, by a buyer who is 21

- Used credit cards to buy $300,000 worth of real estate in less than one year, giving the BWB $800 a month positive cash flow after *all* expenses and *all* credit-card loan payments

- Bought four properties in three months with zero cash down and received several thousands back at closing on each property. Now the buyer has assets totaling over $1 million, with a net worth of $360,000. Quit his job to stay home with his wife and teach his kids.

- Put a penniless disabled man into a rental real estate business in one month, raising his income from zero to $1,200 per month in 30 days

- Allowed purchase of a $300,000 estate for $546.

You'll learn about many more of these deals as you read this book. Let's look at conventional financing for new income real estate projects. Later we'll look at conventional financing for existing real estate projects.

MAKE CONVENTIONAL FINANCING WORK FOR YOU

Conventional real estate financing is the money you borrow from sources such as:

- Banks

- Insurance companies

- Mortgage lenders

- Government-backed sources

- Pension funds

- Profit-sharing plans

To make conventional mortgage-money sources work for you, try to:

- Negotiate to get the lowest interest rate.

- Avoid paying points (1% of the mortgage per point).

- Use conventional financing for newer income properties whenever possible.

- Never let the lender know you're *overfinanced*—that is, that you've borrowed more than 80% of the funds needed.

- Fight against *takeouts* and *sweeteners*, or deals in which a lender gets part of the profits (usually 1% or 2% for the life of the project), and perhaps a small piece of the ownership.

- Be a complete businessperson at all times.

Recognize that the people you deal with at sources of conventional funds, such as those listed above:

- May dislike wheeler-dealers
- Shun mavericks
- Avoid "roulette players"

This means that to get conventional financing for your real estate deal, you must:

1. Prepare neat, typed documents.
2. Present income and expense statements and a short (one- or two-page) business plan for each project.
3. Fill out all the blanks on the application form.
4. Never lose your temper.
5. Be ready to make concessions, if they'll make you money.
6. Never be afraid of a *no* answer.
7. Keep trying one source after another.

CONVENTIONAL MONEY CAN MAKE YOU RICH

A reader who got into rental real estate using my methods writes:

I have all your books and have just finished reading *Magic Mind Secrets for Building Great Riches Fast*. Also subscribe to *IWS* and have the *Starting Millionaire* and *Financial Broker* success kits.

I'm now driving a new Cadillac and enjoying the better things in life. —— Bank told me to bring them some more professional people with good statements and they would lend me down payments all day long. [This reader wrote this after getting multiple loans to finance his first zero-cash property.] I'm getting ready to buy my second $200,000 building across the street. Many thanks for a better way of life and an opportunity to put into practice principles that really work.

Another reader writes:

After reading *How to Borrow Your Way to Real Estate Riches* by Ty Hicks, we thought we'd give it a try. So we inquired at a local bank if they would give us a loan on a $6,000 rental property. One week later they loaned us $7,000. Tomorrow we're buying our second property with no money down, plus repair money. Not bad after having filed for bankruptcy three years ago. Your wealth-building ideas really work!

YOU CAN GET MILLIONS

Conventional mortgage money sources can furnish you millions of dollars for your real estate projects. Some such sources lend a minimum of $1 million for their loans; others set their minimum at $2 million or $5 million. So we're not talking about peanuts.

To latch onto these millions, in general you must:

- Have a new or relatively new income project in real estate

- Have a good income potential from this real estate

- Carry adequate insurance on the property

- Prepare a short (one- or two-page) business plan for the property

You can also say that, *in general,* some conventional loan sources:

- Dislike projects in slum or run-down areas

- May avoid way-out projects—like mobile homes, trailer parks, marinas, and so on

- Can make you sweat for your money longer than other sources of funds

But don't turn off conventional funds. Why? The answer is a five-letter word: *money*! Keep in mind at all times this Hicksism:

Be friendly, sweet, and engaging to every source of big money. You never know when you'll need big money—and having a friend at the bank costs you nothing!

LEARN THE VARIETY OF CONVENTIONAL LOANS

Most of the conventional money sources listed above usually prefer long-term mortgage loans, 15 years or more. But you'll find that at certain times, insurance companies will lend *short-term money* for:

- Building construction
- Interim financing
- Standby purposes

Knowing how each of these financing arrangements works can help make you rich.

Building-construction loans cover only constructing a structure. As such, these loans run for about three years or less. The money may be paid directly to you or to the contractor doing the work, after you've certified that the work is finished satisfactorily. On large jobs, you will usually have your lender make payments after completion of certain percentages of the work—20%, 40%, 60%, etc. Some banks dislike construction loans because too much can go wrong during construction to cause problems and the possible loss of the borrowed money. Construction funds are usually high cost—typically 12% interest or more.

To use these facts to make big money from conventional funds:

- Don't ask a bank for a loan for this purpose unless it specifically advertises the availability of construction funds.

- Remember that once you get off on the wrong foot with a bank, it takes a long time to set things right again.

- Keep an eye open for construction funds at all times.

Interim financing covers the time from the start of construction of a real-estate project until you get long-term financing. Thus, your interim financing can cover:

- Buying the land
- Breaking ground
- Construction
- First few months' operation

For a comprehensive list of construction lenders, see *Selected Lenders for Commercial and Residential Construction Loans* in chapter 15.

To show you how this method works for you, here's a beautifully profitable way to get started in real estate in multidwelling condominiums (condos for short) on 100% interim financing—that is, without investing a cent of your own. Here are the steps you can take:

1. Find a suitable piece of land for your proposed condo.

2. Get interim financing for the price of the land plus 10% to 25% or more to cover unforeseen costs.

3. Have plans prepared for the building you are planning to put up on the land. (You may need sketch plans to get the financing mentioned in step 2—the usual cost of such plans is $2,000 or less.)

4. Advertise the units for sale. (Typical prices range from $100,000 to as high as $1 million or more per unit, depending on the building, its location, the floor the unit is on, etc.)

5. Collect the down payments in cash from the buyers of the units.

6. Obtain from the lender or mortgagee (this is the organization that lends to you and is usually a bank) the credit for the balance of the sale price of each unit.

KNOW HOW CONVENTIONAL FINANCING WORKS IN REAL LIFE

Now let's look at a real-life example of this technique as it was used recently in a southern state condominium put up with 100% plus financing.* This 12-story building is to be built on a waterfront property that has a price of $240,000. You visit a local architect and have him prepare a sketch plan of a building containing 80 units (each of which is a complete apartment) having an average price of $70,000. The construction cost is estimated to be $4.8 million. A one-third, or $23,333, average down payment will be made by each purchaser of one unit or apartment in this condominium. The local bank agrees to finance the remainder of each unit.

You are required by the seller of the land to pay 60%, or $144,000 cash, with the remainder being financed by a five-year *purchase-money* (called PM) mortgage given to you by the seller. This means that he is willing to finance $96,000 of the $240,000 price of the land. So your

---

*To work a deal such as this, you *must* have an attorney and you *must* follow all federal (Securities and Exchange Commission) and state laws.

task is to come up with $144,000 cash to put down on the land. Once you do this, you can start selling units. So here's how you handle the deal:

1. You borrow $144,000 interim money from a bank or an insurance company to put down on the land. (This interim money is sometimes called a *development loan* when used for this purpose.)

2. At the same time, another bank or insurance company gives you a written promise to lend you 80% of the construction money you need, or 0.8 ($4.8 million) = $3.84 million. (The same bank or insurance firm that lends you the interim money might also make the construction loan.)

3. As soon as you have the land, you start advertising the units.

4. Within one week you sell 30 units, which gives you 30 ($23,333) = $699,990 in cash, plus the mortgages on these 30 units. (Note that the mortgages are *promises* by the bank or other lender to pay you, the owner, for the unit when the building is finished.)

5. You hold the $699,990 cash for use as operating capital while the building is being put up. Note that within a short time after taking over the land, you have cash in hand.

6. You now have $3,840,000 + $699,990 = $4,539,990 available to you from the construction loan and the cash down payments on the units you sold. Also, you'll receive $1,400,010 in cash from the units you sold, when they are occupied. Thus, your cash inflow will be $5,940,000. This compares with a total cost of $4,800,000 + $240,000 = $5,040,000. And remember that you still have 50 units available for sale!

This real-life deal shows you a number of facts about conventional money sources for real estate, namely, that such sources:

- Are loaded with potential wealth for you

- Can be tapped easily if you plan carefully

- Are excellent reservoirs of 100% financing of your real estate deal

- Have *billions* available for *your* deal—if you work hard

Hard Work Pays Off in Real Estate

Yes, hard work *does* pay off in real estate. As one reader writes:

> Approximately one year ago I purchased your book *How to Borrow Your Way to a Great Fortune.*
>
> The results speak for themselves.
>
> Three million dollars of properties "sales arranged" in ———.
>
> Thus far in ———, confirmed sales of $3.5 million of mobile-home parks...nursing homes, income property...plus $5 million of hospitals and $1 million of nursing homes on tap.
>
> After reading your book, my initial letterhead cost $6.50, and the present letterhead and other mailing pieces as developed are attached. Thus, anyone can do it.
>
> Other than your book we have had some great gifts from friends...real friends, that is...But the results speak... and, of course, lots of hard work...Four to eight letters a week...developing forms, etc....It was all worth it and plenty of prayers to a wife and family of sons willing to put up with it all....All of us a lot better for it....Keep up the good work.

GET AN INTEREST-ONLY CONVENTIONAL MORTGAGE

With an interest-only mortgage you pay just interest, not principal, each month. Today many real estate BWBs seek interest-only mortgages for the income properties they want to buy. Why is this? Because with an interest-only mortgage, you will find:

- Your monthly payments are lower.

- Your net rental income is higher for the term of the interest-only payments. And your net rental profit is also higher.

- Your chances of selling or refinancing the property before having to make principal payments may be greater.

"So how does the interest-only mortgage work?" you ask. Let's look at an apartment house you buy for $250,000. You work out an interest-only mortgage at 8% for 30 years, with the first 15 years being interest-only payments. Thus:

- Monthly interest-only payment for first 15 years = $1,667

- Monthly interest and principal payment for the next 15 years = $2,390

- Monthly payment savings for the first 15 years = $723

- Monthly savings × 12 = $8,676 per year, or $130,140 in 15 years

You save yourself over $130,000 during the first 15 years you own this property. And if you sell it during that time your profit from the sale will be higher because your cost was lower. Or:

- You could refinance the apartment house during the 15 years.

- If the building rose $175,000 in value during this time you could take $175,000 cash out of the apartment house, tax-free when you receive the money, and still own the building and its income!

So how do you get an interest-only mortgage? Here are easy steps for you to follow to get your interest-only mortgage:

1. Find a building or property you want to buy. Lenders are reluctant to talk in general terms; they want a specific property.

2. Know the full details of the property—its *price,* its *income,* its *expenses,* and the *down payment* being asked for. Know your numbers and the money needs!

3. Prepare a short (one- or two-page) business plan for the property showing how its income will allow you to make both the interest-only and the principal and interest (P&I) payments.

4. Contact mortgage lenders. Ask for a conventional mortgage for the longest term possible—at least 30 years. And get the longest possible interest-only term, at least 15 years. Hold, sell, or refinance according to your income needs!

EXPAND YOUR CONVENTIONAL FINANCING BY ONE-THIRD

The first deal above shows you an important aspect of modern real estate that most people never learn, namely:

The average value of a completed commercial real estate property today is often one-third more than its total cost, including

the land. This general rule applies to apartment houses, shopping centers, motels, hotels, office buildings, and similar structures. The reason why the value of a completed structure rises is because all of its component costs—land, materials, and labor—usually increase while construction is taking place.

Let's take a look at how this can work out for you if you put up structures having various total costs, including the land. You will, I'm sure, be impressed with the magic "grow power" of other people's money (OPM) available to you from conventional mortgage money sources.

Cost of Completed Project	Value of Completed Project (Rounded)
$900,000	$1,200,000
1,200,000	1,600,000
1,800,000	2,400,000
2,400,000	3,200,000
3,000,000	4,000,000
3,600,000	4,800,000
4,200,000	5,600,000
6,000,000	8,000,000
9,000,000	12,000,000
12,000,000	16,000,000
15,000,000	20,000,000

To find the probable sale value of any completed real estate project, just take one-third of the total cost of the completed project, including the land, and add this to the cost of the project. While this rule may vary a trifle from one area to another, you can be reasonably sure that the value of your project will rise:

- During the time of construction

- Because of your development efforts

- As a result of increased labor, material, and land costs

Thus, time and nature are on *your* side when you use OPM and 100% financing from conventional real estate money sources to put up a project. Further, you *can* wind up with 110% to 130% financing, meaning that:

- You walk away with tax-free cash in your pocket.

- You can (or may, if you wish) retain ownership of all, or some, of the property.

- You have the beginnings of a new real estate empire using OPM, the difference being that the second time around you need not be so hungry!

For the moment at least, let's glance away from conventional financing of real estate deals and look at nonconventional financing arrangements. But before we go, let's remember that conventional financing is usually:

- Persnickety—requiring many forms, long discussions, precise contracts, and so on

- The way to go when you have first-class projects

- Able to provide you with, and make you, a bundle of money

- Safe and seldom gets you into money troubles that may come with being overfinanced

Yes, conventional OPM is the dream way to riches in real estate. But don't buy it 100% until after you've looked at nonconventional sources of real estate funds.

Go All the Way in Your Wealth Building

Conventional real estate money sources can lead to all sorts of wealth. For instance, a reader wrote: "Your work has been an inspiration to me lately. Although I had the so-called 'academic fame' previously, now I am a donor (to academic causes), company president as well as everything else and feel pretty good about it. In less than a year after reading your book, I now have my own company, own 200 acres of land, two apartment houses which bring in rent, a co-op on Sutton Place,* and a computer! I am also going into the trading business in cosmetics and wigs."

USE ANY COLLATERAL YOU CAN TO GET PROPERTY YOU WANT

The biggest money problem faced by real estate BWBs using conventional financing is getting the down-payment money to take over income property that can make them rich. One novel approach that's becoming more popular with BWBs is to *use any collateral you can* to get the down-payment money for a profitable income property you want to buy. Such collateral can be: Actively traded stocks and bonds; equity (ownership) you have in other real estate (land, buildings, leases); assets your family, friends, or business associates own that they could pledge for your loan.

A few stock brokerage firms today offer 100% financing for real estate when stocks or bonds are pledged as collateral for the down payment on an income property. Here's how it can work for you, using either your own securities or those that you borrow from relatives, friends, or business associates:

1. You put securities having a market value of 40% of the price of the property into an account at a brokerage house.

2. You are loaned the down payment for the property by the brokerage house, which uses the securities as collateral for the loan. Thus, on a property priced at $500,000, you would be loaned 0.4 × $500,000 = $200,000 for the down payment and closing cost.

3. You avoid any income taxes on the down-payment loan because you are not selling the securities. The same is true if you use borrowed securities for the transaction.

4. You make regular monthly payments on your mortgages—the long-term first mortgage and your second mortgage (which can be long- or short-term, depending on your wishes). Your income from the property pays these monthly mortgage bills. *Note*: Some brokerage houses will make the entire loan for the property to you, using your securities and the real estate as

---

*One of the most expensive and most exclusive residential areas in the world in New York, NY.

collateral. Thus, you truly have 100% financing of your income property!

5. Your only downside risk with such a down-payment loan is a decline in the value of the securities you pledge for the loan. Thus, if the market value of your pledged securities falls below 33% of the amount of your loan, you'll have to add more securities to the account to cover your loan.

With almost any financial condition, you can get 100% financing for your real estate today! All you need to do is take a creative approach to raising the money you need.

GET YOUR MONEY FASTER BUT PAY MORE

Nonconventional sources of real estate funds include:

- Money brokers
- Private lenders
- Investment trusts
- Limited partnerships
- Finders
- Corporate lenders
- Finance companies
- Hard-money (high-interest rate) lenders

There are other nonconventional sources that we'll mention as we go along. For full coverage of the newest and most active nonconventional sources of real estate funds, be sure to regularly read the monthly newsletter for all wealth builders—beginning and experienced—*International Wealth Success,* which often presents:

- 100%, 110%, 115%, and more, financing (money) sources
- Compensating-balance loan sources
- New wealth ideas every month

- Many, many sources of business loans

- Part-time moneymaking ideas

- Mail-order riches opportunities

- Hundreds of finders' fee listings

- Worldwide international moneymaking ideas

- Fast-fortune, easy-money wealth deals

- Franchise-riches ideas and methods

- Capital available for borrowers of all types

- Monthly Ty Hicks page where I talk to *you*

- Financial broker opportunities

- Hundreds of other ideas, sources, and ways to earn big money and make your fortune today

- Ways to get money you need

- Unique methods to earn big money

- Techniques that put cash in your pocket

To order this excellent newsletter, send $24 to IWS Inc., P.O. Box 186, Merrick, NY 11566-0186.

Now let's look at how the usual nonconventional sources can put big amounts of OPM into your realty pocket. But first we'll take a quick look at how some folks get their loans.

Get the Loans You Need

Sometimes readers tell a simple, short story in two or three sentences, such as this one written to the editors of *IWS*. "Keep up the good work. I have already received one loan through your paper. I am on my way!"

Another reader writes:

> I have used your methods since I started reading your wonderful *International Wealth Success* newsletter. Using your methods I now have four apartment buildings worth about $450,000. Three years ago I had only a triplex. But by using your methods of borrowing to the hilt, I have been able to acquire these four larger buildings.

Still another writes:

> You are the gentleman who started us on the road to property ownership 14 years ago. My husband and I now have about 235 units, of which about 150 are single-family dwellings. Thank you very much!

And this last happy reader who says:

> I got a $6,000 home-improvement loan, a $10,000 second-mortgage loan, and a $4,000 loan to pay off our car. All my thanks go to you. Your newsletter is worth every cent I paid for it.

USE MONEY BROKERS TO THE HILT

Money brokers bring you and money sources together, just like a marriage broker brings people together to make a happy union. My observations of a number of money and marriage brokers is that people are usually happier with the results they obtain from their money brokers than from their marriage brokers!

You probably have a number of questions for me concerning money brokers and I'm ready to answer them. I hope that your questions are among those answered below.

Money-Broker Questions and Answers

Q. Why should I use a money broker?
A. There are several reasons why you should at least consider using a money broker, including:

- Easier loans
- Faster loans
- Less investigation
- Money for marginal properties
- Multiple loans possible
- Numerous sources
- Few geographical limitations

Q. Do money brokers charge higher rates?

A. Yes, you will usually have to pay higher interest rates for the real estate funds you borrow through money brokers. But the interest rate is unimportant if:

- You can make a profit on the money

- You attain your goals

- You're better off with the money than without the money

Keep in mind one fact about interest rates:

As long as you can make a profit on borrowed money, the rate of interest you pay is unimportant because the interest is both provable and tax deductible.

A further very important concept is this: You pay your bills with dollars, not with percent signs. So what you seek in real estate—if you use my methods—is spendable dollars, not low interest rates!

Q. Why are money brokers important to me?

A. With conventional financing you put up at least $1 for every $3 the mortgage lender puts up—in the usual deal. But with a money broker you will usually put up zero dollars for every dollar the broker finds for you. True, you have to pay more for the broker's money; but when a BWB is just starting, he or she is "hungry," and a hungry person will do almost anything honest for some food. So, too, the BWB, but for bucks.

Q. Where can I get the names and addresses of reliable money lenders and brokers with cash in hand for me?

A. The three best sources I know of are *International Wealth Success,* mentioned earlier, *Money Watch Bulletin* (which gives you 100 active lenders each month and their lending requirements for $95 per year), and the big money book, *Business Capital Sources,* available at $15 from IWS at the address given earlier. This book lists thousands of money sources from which you might borrow all of the money you need for profitable real-estate deals.

Q. Why is it easier for me to borrow through a money broker?

A. It is easier for you to borrow through a money broker because he or she:

- Will take greater risks

- Wheels and deals faster

- Requires little or no collateral

- Understands you better than the average bank loan officer

Of course, your money broker will charge you more for your loan. But if you can bank your profits, or put them into other, bigger real estate deals, who cares about a higher charge? Remember this:

When you borrow money to make money, the interest you pay is nothing more than "rent" for the use of money to make money!

So if you're paying 10% interest for a mortgage-broker-arranged loan (and this is a typical charge), you're paying 10¢ a year to rent $1. But if you can earn 20¢ or 25¢ a year on each borrowed dollar you put into real estate, then a money broker's charge is low, compared to your potential profit on the deal.

As a general guide you can say that there are few times when conventional financing beats the money broker. One is:

Most banks are usually legally allowed to give 100% financing on real estate when they have foreclosed (taken over because of lack of payments) on a property. The 100% financed property may be your best possible deal because you don't put a penny down.

There are, of course, 110%, 120%, 130%, and so on, financing deals in which you get more cash than you need at the moment. But you can't put these together just with conventional funds. You need the help of a money broker's or some other lender's bucks.

How do I know? Because I specialize in publishing data about the money end of such deals for people. The biggest *mortgaging out* or *windfall* deal I ever heard of was 162%—the buyer walked away with $620,000 in cash after taking over a $1 million building without a penny down! We'll talk more about that later. The buyer used a money broker to the hilt, just as we advised earlier.

SEARCH OUT PRIVATE LENDERS

If you could sit with me and listen to the money complaints I hear, you'd cry tears of joy. Why? Because the people I deal with are sometimes desperately looking for:

- Good investments for their millions of dollars of surplus cash
- Borrowers who will put other people's money (OPM) to work in a safe, creative, and profitable way

As director of an over $100-million asset money-lending organization, I have to listen to the monthly bellyaches of my board of directors saying:

- *When* will we make more loans?
- *How* can we make more loans?
- *Who* can we find to borrow our money?
- *How* can we get people to borrow more money from us?
- *Why* are we losing loans to competition?
- *What* kind of offers can we make to people to get them to give us their loan business?

Truly, this organization is loaded with money that we can lend to our members for all good deals, such as:

- Real estate
- Personal purchases
- Auto, boat, airplane, and equipment financing
- Debt consolidation
- Other—medical, dental, tax, vacation, education

Yet we worry and worry as to why we can't make more good loans! Each month we try to make more loans than the previous month. And each year we try to beat the previous year by making more loans to more people for more purposes for which more of our loan money is needed!

True, we grow each year—but not as fast as we'd like to. And why is this? Because our rate of growth is held down by the intense loan competition from:

- Private lenders

- Banks

- Finance companies

- Credit unions

- Other organizations—savings associations, real estate developers, government lenders

But for all the competition, the private lenders may, we think, give us the worst battle.

To show you that 100% financing really is available today, here's an excerpt from a recent letter I received from a reader of my newsletter, *International Wealth Success*, and one of my real estate books. This BWB plans to buy an apartment house in a western state priced at $695,000. Here's how he plans to arrange the financing:

> In five days my wife and I found a lender that can get me into a 30-unit apartment house in a first position [that is, *first mortgage*] for a $525,000 loan at 13.5% interest for up to three years, or 14% up to five years, with interest-only payments. The seller will carry back another $170,000 mortgage at 9.37% for seven years. With a total purchase price of $695,000, I can get in with no money down. Even though the interest rate is high, I could refinance the property in six months.
>
> Another lender is trying to work out a better deal for me. Since the existing mortgage of $360,000 is assumable at 9.37% and runs out its term in seven years, he is trying to get a second mortgage for $175,000 at a low rate and have the seller carry the remaining $160,000 in third position [a *third mortgage*].
>
> With either loan I would receive about $1,100 money in fist [MIF = positive cash flow] each month. But when I refinance I will get about $3,300 per month positive cash flow.

Another reader recently faxed me the following information under the general subject of financing using private lenders:

> When I first came across one of your books, I didn't even have the money to buy it. I would stand in the aisle [of the bookstore] reading it bit by bit. Now, a year later, after having purchased three of your books and subscribed to your newsletter, I own $500,000 [one-half million dollars] in assets. Thank you.

IDENTIFY THE PRIVATE LENDERS

And who are these private lenders? They are the wealthy and the not-so-wealthy people of this world who want to put their excess cash to work earning better than bank rates. For instance, the usual private lender receives 10% to 18% a year on his loans to corporations. Some smart private lenders even get a piece of the real estate action from an *equity kicker* during tight money times. (An equity kicker is a small share in the profits of a property, plus a small percentage of ownership and, possibly, a share in the capital-gains profit on the sale of the property.) Now for some questions.

Q. Where can I locate private lenders?

A. Here are a few publications that carry ads or notices of private lenders looking for a safe "home" for their funds:

- *International Wealth Success*

- *Money Watch Bulletin*

- *Wall Street Journal*

- *New York Times*

- The book *Business Capital Sources*

- The book *Worldwide Riches Opportunities,* volume 2 (lists foreign lenders)

Q. How do I approach a private lender?

A. There are various ways to approach a private lender. One of the best I know of—and one that has worked beautifully for numerous BWBs—is this:

> When a prospective lender asks you: "Where did you get our name?" reply: "You were recommended to me by an outstanding financial adviser," if you have consulted such an adviser.

Such a reply is a compliment to the lender and puts him or her on *your* side. Using such a reply:

- Gives you a greater chance of getting a loan

- Makes your dealings more cordial

- Reduces the possibility of arguments and hard feelings

Never, never tell a lender: "Oh, I found your name on a list of lenders." This is the surest way to turn off a lender. And it can lead to a *no* answer in situations where you might get a *yes* if you used the response given above.

Q. *Can private lenders* really *help me?*

A. Positively yes! The private lender can put you in the chips faster than you think. So don't overlook the private lender. He or she can be the difference between riches and poverty for you!

WILL AN INVESTMENT TRUST HELP YOU?

Real estate wealth builders like yourself are fortunate in many ways, including being able to use a proven money-raising approach (namely a real estate investment trust) to get:

- Plenty of other people's money

- High leverage on this money

- Fantastic appreciation in value

- Regular income to the owner

- A business serving a basic need

- Almost foolproof income

- An income that can be paid into a trust

A *real estate investment trust* (called REIT for short—which rhymes with "feet") can put bundles of money into your real estate pocket. What's more, a REIT pays *no* federal income taxes if it distributes 90% or more of its income, after expenses. And of course, one of the expenses of a REIT could be *your* annual salary.

REIT Questions and Answers

Q. What is a REIT?

A. A REIT is a trust set up to invest in real estate—either by operating, lending for, or otherwise earning a profit from real estate. A REIT is allowed to own real estate of any kind—apartment houses, hotels, motels, nursing homes, marinas, hospitals, mini-storage warehouses. And a REIT can earn large profits from its investments in real estate. A REIT can also lend money for first, second, third mortgages, instead of owning property. Or a REIT can be a *combination trust*—owning some properties and lending on others, if it wishes.

Q. How and where does a REIT get money?

A. A REIT sells shares of *beneficial* interest, much like stock shares, to the public. Thus, a REIT recently sold 1.2 million shares at $25 each giving a total cash inflow of nearly $30 million to the REIT. (The underwriting fees are paid out of the proceeds of the offering.) This REIT is a mortgage trust—that is, its funds will be invested in real estate mortgages at a profitable rate of interest. Other REITs raise $50, $100, $200 million, depending on their size and the amount of money they need for their operations.

Q. Must a REIT go for millions of dollars?

A. No; you can have a trust that takes in only a small amount of money—say $300,000 or $500,000. The amount of money sought depends upon the goals of the REIT.

Q. Can I form a REIT?

A. You certainly can! All you need is the know-how.

Q. Where can I get this know-how?

A. Later in this book you will find more information on the formation of a REIT. You can obtain additional information from the IWS *How to Build Your Real Estate Fortune Today in a Real Estate Investment Trust Kit* available from IWS. See chapter 15 for more information. Just keep in mind that a REIT can put millions of dollars of OPM into your bank for use in real estate ventures.

Luck Comes to Those Ready for It

Many BWBs think they are "unlucky." Yet my experience shows that luck comes to those who are ready for it. Like this reader who says:

> I started this shop with one ad in the paper for a 6% loan and a 5% finder's fee—got two $100,000 offers within one week. Was

scratching my head on which to take, and what to do with excess capital, when a relative left me enough to do the job comfortably. God helps those who help themselves, I guess—but things like this never happened to me before knowing you and venturing out with some of your ideas and suggestions.

MAKE A LIMITED PARTNERSHIP PAY OFF

The *limited partnership* (LP) is a popular way to finance real estate—from one building to an entire complex of structures. In an LP, two or more *general partners* operate the business. *Limited partners* contribute money to the LP (generally in amounts of $5,000 or more each) but do not take part in the business operation at all. Further, if there is a business failure or disaster of some sort, the liability of each limited partner is restricted to his or her contribution to the LP. Other advantages of the LP are:

- Fast raising of real estate funds
- Control of project is retained
- Easy legal requirements
- Few operating problems

To form an LP, all you need to do is prepare the LP agreement, register it with your county clerk or other responsible official, and take the necessary steps to sell participations in the LP. While this seems simple, remember this fact at all times:

You *must, must* have an attorney help you form and market an LP. If you do not use an attorney, you can get into serious business problems.

Now how much money might you raise with an LP? You can raise as little as $10,000 to as much as $50 million or more. What you can raise depends on:

- Number of participations offered
- Price per participation
- Number of participations sold
- Selling expenses involved

For a typical LP agreement and the type of ads used to promote such firms, see the IWS *Starting Millionaire Success Kit* described in chapter 15. You should also check with your attorney to have him or her show you what is required in an LP agreement. The *Starting Millionaire Success Kit* contains a full-length example of an LP agreement for a typical real estate venture. You will also find LP data in two other IWS kits, namely: *Fast Financing of Your Real Estate Fortune Success Kit* and the *Real Estate Riches Success Kit*. Each is priced at $99.50.

USE FINDERS TO GET YOUR MONEY

A *finder* is a person or firm who *finds* things that other people or firms seek, and for which they are willing to pay a finder's fee. Thus you can ask a finder to locate money that you can borrow and invest in real estate. You don't have to pay the finder's fee until *after* you obtain the money you seek.

Now where can you locate a finder? That's easy. Just run a free ad in the monthly newsletter *International Wealth Success*. Any one-year subscriber is entitled to run as many free ads as he or she wishes, and for which space is available. You will also get a lot of information on finders from the book *FINDERS International Network Directory*, priced at $25, and described in chapter 15.

The usual finder's fee will run between 1% and 5% of the money obtained for you. You pay a lower percentage as the amount of money obtained increases.

CORPORATE LENDERS ARE LOADED

Millions of corporations around the world are loaded with excess cash they'd like to invest. Certain corporations are willing to invest their money in real estate.

To locate corporate lenders, search the "Capital Available" and "Mortgages" columns of:

- *International Wealth Success*
- *Money Watch Bulletin*
- *The Wall Street Journal*
- *The New York Times*

- Large newspapers in your area

- The book *Business Capital Sources*

You must be constantly alert to find suitable corporate lenders. But these sources have so much money that the time you put in is well worth the effort. We'll talk some more about corporate lenders in later chapters.

FINANCE COMPANIES CAN HELP YOU, TOO

The finance company most of us know is the small firm that lends $800, $1,500, or some other pittance to people who need money to tide them over a few rough spots. Yet there are giant finance companies that lend millions for real estate. You can find many of these finance companies listed in the sources given earlier for corporate lenders.

You will usually pay higher interest rates to finance companies and corporate lenders. But if you're just getting started in real estate, you can't be too choosy about who offers his or her funds to you. Later, when you have your real estate empire, you can pick and choose among lenders who want your mortgage business. You may even complain to me that "people are trying to throw money at me that I don't want! How can I make them stop?" The day *you* come to me with such complaints, I'll be very happy for you.

GO WITH THE HOME-EQUITY MONEY FLOW

Today lenders are going "bonkers" over home equity loans. They just love these loans and the borrowers who take them out! Why don't you go with the money flow and get a home-equity loan for your real estate wealth building?

"But," you say, "I don't own a home. How can *I* get a home-equity loan if I don't own a home?" Easy—just try these methods:

- Borrow using a relative's home as your equity.

- Borrow using a partner's home as equity.

- Offer a fee to a person who will borrow his or her home equity and loan to you.

- Run a classified ad in your local paper to find homeowners who might help you.

The whole key to getting a home-equity loan is to have a home that can be put up as collateral. Once you get a suitable home, figure your loan amount thus:

1. *Find out the "equity"*—that is, how much the owner owns. Thus, on a $250,000 home where the owner still owes $50,000 on the mortgage, the owner's equity, or what is owned, is $250,000 − $50,000 = $200,000. You *must* know this number before you can do anything on a home-equity loan.

2. *Most lenders will lend 75% of the equity* in the home. Thus, for this home, you could borrow 0.75 × $200,000 = $150,000 on the equity. You may need more than this, but the $150,000 will certainly give you a start.

3. *You can even get home-equity loans* with *no* credit check, *no* income verification (checking of your salary or business income with employer), and *no* employment investigation. How? By paying a much higher interest rate and much higher points. Thus, as an example of current loans, rates, and points (which may change as rates rise and fall) for loans with and without checks:

With Checks
Interest rate 9.5% fixed,
10.8% variable
Points:* 2 to 2.5

Without Checks
14% fixed, no variable

*A point is 1% of the mortgage amount or $1,000 per $100,000 of mortgage amount.

The difference in payment is about $300 per month more for a no-check loan per $100,000 in loan. But some people feel the difference is worth the extra cost if they can get the loan!

By using a home-equity loan you're "going with the flow," making your loan much easier to get. Since 94% of the large banks offer home-equity loans today, you're in the money flow. How much money is loaned on home equity today? Over $100 billion a year!

Why fight with lenders when you can have them begging you to take their money? Be a hero to yourself and your lender! Get the loan you need quickly and easily.

GET MONEY WITH THE 125% LOAN

Real estate is so safe to lend on that lenders recently introduced the *125% loan*. "And what's that?" you ask.

The 125% loan is a home-equity loan that gives you 125% of your equity in a property, instead of the 75% described earlier. Thus, with the $200,000 in equity the owner has in the property listed earlier, you could borrow 1.25 × $200,000 = $250,000, instead of the $150,000 mentioned earlier.

Why are lenders willing to "go out on a limb" to lend this much on the equity in a home? Because real estate has proven so safe and so valuable that lenders believe the value of the property will "catch up" with the increased loan amount! And so far they haven't been wrong.

USE CREDIT-CARD LOANS TO GET STARTED

If you have a major credit card, you probably also have a line of credit on it. You can use this line of credit to get your down-payment loan for your first real estate property. Thousands of my readers are doing exactly that right now. Here's what two say:

> We're especially interested in obtaining more credit cards for down-payment dollars. So far we've bought eight converted apartment houses in this small college town (including one three-bedroom, single-family) with credit-card dollars—zero dollars out of pocket. A total of 20 units with a positive cash flow of over $800 per month. So our credit-card payments are made by renters! That's over $300,000 worth of property—all within one year. I have quit my job of truck driving to manage, maintain, and improve our houses.

The second reader writes:

> I started a year ago with an old but structurally sound four-family that had been run down. I purchased it for $35,000, the seller held a $30,000 first at 8.5% for 20 years. I borrowed the $5,000 down payment from my credit card and proceeded to take out home-improvement loans from five different banks to renovate the building. Now I have a three-family (obtained with $12,000 borrowed for the down payment), a beautiful 55-acre farm, a double

(two-family), and I'm in the process of buying another four-family and a six-family building. I am pretty well leveraged out and I have refinanced where possible.

Remember these facts about your credit-card line of credit:

- You're allowed to use the money for *any* purpose *you* choose.

- Monthly repayments on your line of credit will be made by the income from your real estate.

- The interest on your credit-card lines-of-credit real estate business loan is tax deductible.

- Buy only positive cash flow properties so your monthly repayments are made by your tenants!

USE BUSINESS CREDIT CARDS

Almost all major banks today issue *business credit cards.* These credit cards offer lines of credit up to and including $100,000 per card! Get ten such cards—which is relatively easy to do—and your total line of credit will be 10 × 100,000 = $1 million! Not bad for a BWB. At my company, IWS Inc., we specialize in researching and publishing the names of banks issuing such cards. Ask for a free list of such banks when you subscribe to my newsletter, *International Wealth Success,* for two years ($48) or longer. Some banks will even imprint your company name on your credit card. It really looks impressive when you see your firm's name on your own credit card.

When you get multiple credit cards, you must of course use them carefully so you do not go deeply into debt. Your credit is one of your most valuable assets. So treat it carefully at all times!

GET 0% CREDIT-CARD LOANS FOR YOUR REAL ESTATE

When thinking of using a credit-card line of credit as the down payment on income real estate, people often say, "The interest rate is too high!" This isn't true! Why? Because:

1. You can get 0% interest "introductory rates" on some credit cards for as long as nine months.

2. This 0% rate is good for cash advances, purchases, and balance transfers from other credit card issuers to your new credit card.

3. The 0% rate allows you to get interest-free money for your real estate down payment for as long as nine months. And you can use this money for any other real estate purpose you choose, including the rehabbing (fixing up) of income real estate you buy!

4. Some credit card issuers offer a line of credit (LOC) up to $20,000, with no annual fee, no balance-transfer fee, and no cash-advance fee.

So how do you get in on such deals for your real estate down payment or rehabbing? It's easy! You just take these quick steps:

1. Check your local papers every day for ads run by banks offering credit cards with special rates, balance-transfer options, and larger lines of credit.

2. Call or visit the bank and describe your credit situation, giving your credit (FICO) score, if you know it.* Ask if the banker thinks you'd be approved for the special offer. Say that you do *not* want your credit checked—you just want an opinion. This way you do not lower your FICO score. But you *do* get an opinion!

3. Apply for the credit card if you get a yes! Why? Because you'll be able to get the cash you need!

Once you get your new credit card, decide how you'll use your cash line of credit. Most people today:

• Use their credit card line of credit for the down payment on income real estate, or to improve a property they want to run for income purposes. Either pays off the loan.

• Many BWBs wait until the day of the closing before using their LOC. Why? Because the usage does not show on their credit report until after they've closed on the deal. Then the BWB works quickly to find a lender who will refinance the real estate or property improvement at a higher value, allowing the BWB to take

---

*A FICO score is part of a widely used credit rating system developed by Fair, Issac & Company of Minneapolis, MN. You will frequently hear the abbreviation FICO used when your credit score is discussed.

cash out of the deal and pay off the credit card LOC. Thus, your purchase will be financed at 0% interest if you can refinance during the grace period.

So stop thinking that credit card LOCs have interest rates that are too high! You really can't go lower than 0% interest, anywhere!

CHECK OUT INTERNET LENDERS

If you use, or have access to, the Internet, you may be able to find additional lenders on it for your real estate deals. If you don't have your own personal computer (PC) connected to the Internet, you can go to your local public library, Boy Scout troop, Girl Scout troop, or place of religious worship. Many such facilities have a PC connected to the Internet that you can use free of charge.

A number of Web sites offer residential loans; others offer commercial loans. Here are some Web sites you may wish to check out. (Warning: *If one or more of these Web sites ceases to offer loans, please do not call or write me threatening some sort of action against me. I cannot control the business activities of any firm except my own. So if a Web site is unavailable, just go on to the next one. However, all these Web sites were active at the time of the writing of this book.*)

Real Estate Lenders

www.LoopLender.com

www.nrfunding.com

www.swhfunding.com

www.commercialfinancing.com

www.johnsoncapital.com

www.orix.com

www.galaresources.com

www.nationalcitymortgage.com

www.peoplestrustmortgage.com

www.kennedyfunding.com

www.usa-lender.com

www.finova.com

Just be sure never, never to pay front money or an advance fee for any loan, including Internet loans! Front money and advance fees have long been a source of fraud in the loan business.

In a typical front money or advance fee scheme, a "lender" or "broker" asks you for $5,000, $10,000, even $100,000 up front to get you a loan. The money—according to what the lender tells you—could be for "legal fees, travel expenses, land surveys, etc." You pay the money and nothing happens.

Try to get a refund of your money (which is often promised for non-performance) and you'll rarely, if ever, get it! So, never, never pay front money or an advance fee for a loan. You'll regret it for the rest of your life. No legitimate lender or broker will ask you for large fees before the loan is made.

HOW, AND WHERE, TO GET A LOAN FOR REAL ESTATE WITH BAD CREDIT

Probably the most common question we get from beginners wanting to buy income real estate is: "My credit is bad. But I want to get started in income real estate. How can I get a loan for the real estate I want to buy? And how can I avoid making beginner's mistakes?" The clear, useful answer is:

1. When your credit is bad, you must get a partner with good credit to join you in your income real estate activities. Your partner's credit becomes "your" credit for the income real estate project you're in.

2. Give your partner a portion of the ownership of the real estate, usually 3% or 5%, depending on the size of the property and how strongly you need your partner's credit rating to get your real estate loan. This is called an "equity kicker" and is very popular.

3. You can also give your partner a small portion of the profit from your real estate when you sell or rehab the property. Again, the amount should be in the range of 3% or 5%, depending on how profitable your real estate project is.

4. Build your own credit rating while you work on your real estate project. In most deals you'll be the working partner and your "good credit" partner will be silent—he or she will supply the needed credit and nothing more to the deal. You build your credit rating by paying your bills on time, getting a "secured" credit card, and using it actively while paying it off fully each month of the year.

5. By owning an asset, such as income real estate, you immediately improve your FICO credit score. Then, when you pay off your credit cards each month, your score rises. All of this leads to a higher future credit rating for you!

6. Form a real estate company that will put you on the payroll, giving you a source of income, a W-2, and an employment history. This will again raise your credit rating because you have a traceable history that lenders love to cite when approving a real estate loan that you've applied for at their organization.

7. Become a "solid citizen" by joining respected real estate organizations. Being a member contributes to your credibility, making you more credit-worthy, while improving your real estate know-how! And the dues are provable and tax deductible. You will eventually be able to get loans on your own for your next income real estate deal.

YES, YOU CAN BORROW YOUR WAY TO WEALTH

Real estate has many "beauties" for the BWB. Probably the most important one is that borrowed money is the way of life in real estate. So if you're short of cash—and plenty of good people seem to be—consider using real estate as *your* way to great wealth.

This chapter has shown you a few sources of ready cash for financing *your* real estate fortune. Now let's get busy earning that fortune for you!

Points to Remember

- You *can* borrow your way to a real estate fortune quickly and easily.

- Conventional money sources (banks, insurance companies, etc.) can make you rich in real estate.

- The day you finish putting up a new real estate project, it may be worth 30% more than you paid for it with OPM.

- You may get real estate money faster from nonconventional sources but it may cost you more in interest.

- Money brokers, private lenders, finders, and corporations are a few other sources of real estate loans.

- Real estate is a borrowed-money business, which makes it easier for you to get the loans you need.

- I am available to *you* day and night to answer questions either by phone (you can use my 800 toll-free number if you subscribe to either of my newsletters, *International Wealth Success* or *Money Watch Bulletin*) or in person in my New York office. You *always* have a friend on the East Coast!

THREE

YOUR KEYS TO FIVE THOUSAND SOURCES OF READY REAL ESTATE MONEY

Real estate offers you many, many chances to get rich faster. One of the main reasons for this is:

As you now know, real estate is a *borrowed-money business*! Hardly any income real estate deals are ever closed for all cash.

This means that is it almost always easy for you to get the borrowed money you need to put a real estate deal together. But you *must* know *where* and *how* to get borrowed money! Knowledge is power!

GO THE WAY OF 100% FINANCING

Lots of real estate deals are closed with 100% financing. When this happens, the buyer:

- Puts up *no* money at all from his or her pocket
- Takes over valuable property for *no* cash from his or her pocket
- May *get* cash for taking over a valuable property
- Often gets a monthly income from the property
- Seldom has to pay cash for legal expenses (you should *always* have an attorney when buying real estate)

"Ty," you say, "this sounds too good to be true! How, and where, can *I* get the money to work such deals?"

I'll answer your questions this way:

1. Such deals may sound too good to be true, but they can and do happen every business day of the year in this great land of ours!

2. You can—I'm almost positive—get the money for these deals from one or more of the sources I'll give you in this chapter!

So forget all the negative talk about your not being able to get the money you need that you may have heard from people who'd rather "yack" than "do." For I'm telling *you* here and now that:

You *can* get the real estate money you need—if you use the hints I give you here.

REAL ESTATE MONEY IS EVERYWHERE

How can I be so sure *you* can get the money *you* need? That's easy. Thousands of my readers have written or told me—or both—that they got the real estate money they needed, using my methods. A few standout readers I remember include:

- A beginning wealth builder (BWB) who was $12,500 in debt and full of failure. Yet while reading one of my books he found the key to his future real estate wealth. Using the financing methods given in this book, he was able to build a garden-type apartment complex firm, starting with no cash of his own. In just 24 short months he went from $12,500 in debt to the ownership of a real estate firm worth nearly $2 million—starting with *no cash* of his own. His letter describing this wonderful experience, and thanking me for the help my books gave him, is in my reader letter file for anyone who wants to read it. "I owe you an eternal debt of gratitude for what you've done for me," the letter says, in part.

- Two BWBs from New England took over some 100 rental units for no cash down, no legal fee payout, no closing costs, and no other out-of-pocket expenses. These two young BWBs walked away from the closing (called the "passing" in their state) with $1,400 in their pockets and the income from the rental units starting to come in the *next* day. Also, they took over rent security deposits of several thousand dollars. While you are not allowed to spend such deposits, putting them into your business bank account will sure help you win friends at *your* bank! Try it and see for yourself!

I could continue with case after case. But these two should convince you that:

You *can* get started in real estate today on borrowed money without putting up a penny of your own!

But just in case I haven't convinced you (I worry about *you*), here's a letter that brings out the above point:

I will be acquiring two properties this week for a low down payment of $100 (borrowed!) because of the ad I placed in the *IWS* newsletter. Last month I bought two older doubles for zero down. The *IWS* newsletter and your books have been a tremendous help. I can now start working for myself and stop working for other people.

During a recent year of "tight money" (a period when it is more difficult than usual to find lenders), more than $100 billion was loaned for real estate, just in the United States. If you were to include loans in the rest of the world, more than $700 billion was loaned on real estate in just one tight-money year! That's a bundle of money. Remember, friend, that a billion is a thousand million, and *you* can easily make some of that *yours*—even in tight money times!

HOW TO FIND THE RIGHT REAL ESTATE LENDER

There are many types of real estate lenders. These include:

- Commercial banks
- Savings and loan associations (now called Savings Associations)
- Mutual savings banks

- Mortgage companies

- Insurance firms

- Federal and state lenders

- Real estate investment trusts

- Mortgage bankers

- Private lenders

- Pension funds

- Large corporations

These lenders may make all or some of the following types of real estate loans:

- First, second, third, etc., mortgage loans

- Construction loans

- Land loans

- Standby loans

- Takeout loans

- Property improvement loans

- Bridging loans

- Utility (sewer, sidewalks, electric) loans

- Takeover loans

- Refinancing loans

- Development loans

- Property expansion loans

- Permanent financing loans

You now know what types of lenders make real estate loans and the kinds of loans you can get for real estate use. The lenders you seek can be found:

- In this book

- In other books I'll recommend to you

- In real estate magazines

To help you out immediately, I'm listing in this chapter some 60 active real estate lenders. To give you a variety of sources, I've picked banks, insurance companies, real estate investment trusts, mortgage firms, and others that were actively making real estate loans at the time this book was written.

And as a further service to you, I've picked these lenders from a variety of geographical areas. Why did I do this? Because no matter what a lender tells you:

Many real estate lenders prefer to make local loans—at least for the first loan they make to a borrower.

So try a lender in your state or a nearby state first. You just may get the money you need on your first try, as some of my readers have. Where a statement appears after the name and address of a lender, the wording is that of the lender at the time of this writing—not my wording.

Important warning: Lenders, like other businesses, may change their policies, merge, go out of business, or alter their practices in other ways. I have *no* control of these events. The lenders listed here *are* making real estate loans as of the time of this writing. If for any reason this has changed when you check with the lenders, simply contact the next lender, and the one after that. But please do *not* blame me because a lender has changed policies. I'm trying to help you. I have *no* control over what a lender does about the direction of its future business!

Active Real Estate Lenders

Aegon USA Realty Advisors Inc., 4333 Edgewood Rd. NE, Cedar Rapids, IA 52499; (319) 369-2224; fax (319) 369-2188; www.aegonrealty.com

AFC Realty Capital Inc., 888 Seventh Ave., New York, NY 10106; (212) 245-2050; fax (212) 245-0025; www.afcrealtycapital.com

Allfirst Mortgage Corporation, 25 S. Charles St., Baltimore, MD 21202; (800) 737-2344; fax (410) 545-2395; www.allfirstmortgage.com

American Property Financing, 6 E. 43rd St., New York, NY 10017; (212) 850-4200; www.apfmultifamily.com

AmeriSphere Multifamily Finance, LLC, 1 Pacific Pl., Omaha, NE 68124; (402) 498-9184; fax (402) 498-9231

AMI Capital Inc., 7255 Woodmont Ave., Bethesda, MD 20814; (301) 654-0033; fax (301) 321-1300; www.amicapital.com

Apartment Lending Corporation, 10232 S. Jill Ave., Highlands Ranch, CO 80130; (303) 771-1031; fax (303) 290-6491; www.1031 income.com

Arbor Commercial Mortgage, LLC, 333 Earle Ovington Blvd., Uniondale, NY 11553; (516) 832-8002; fax (516) 832-8045

ARCS Commercial Mortgage, 26901 Agoura Rd., Calabasas Hills, CA 91301; (818) 880-3300; fax (818) 880-3333; www.askARCS.com

Berkshire Mortgage Finance, 1 Beacon St., Boston, MA 02108; (877) 523-7722; fax (617) 556-1507; www.berkshiremortgage.com

Boston Capital, 1 Boston Pl., Boston, MA 02108; (617) 624-8900; fax (617) 624-8999; www.bostoncapital.com

Business Loan Express, 645 Madison Ave., New York, NY 10022; (212) 751-5626; fax (212) 888-3949; www.businessloanexpress.net

Cambridge Realty Capital, 35 E. Wacker Dr., Chicago, IL 60601; (312) 357-1601; fax (312) 357-1611; www.cambridgecap.com

CapitalSource, 4445 Willard Ave., Chevy Chase, MD 20815; (301) 841-2700; fax (301) 841-2340; www.capitalsource.com

CB Richard Ellis, 255 S. Grand Ave., Los Angeles, CA 90071; (213) 613-3333; fax (213) 613-3005; www.cbre.com

Centennial Mortgage Inc., 112 W. Jefferson Blvd., South Bend, IN 46601; (574) 233-6773; fax (574) 233-6855; www.centennialfhaloans.com

Charter Municipal Mortgage Acceptance Company, 625 Madison Ave., New York, NY 10022; (212) 421-5333; fax (212) 751-3550; www.CHARTERMAC.com

Collateral Mortgage Capital, LLC, 524 Lorna Sq., Birmingham, AL 35216; (205) 978-1840; fax (205) 978-1852; www.collateral.com

Column Financial Inc., 3414 Peachtree Rd., Atlanta, GA 30326; (404) 239-5300; fax (404) 239-0491; www.columnfinancial.com

Corus Bank N.A., 3959 N. Lincoln Ave., Chicago, IL 60613; (800) 890-8837; fax (773) 823-3540; www.corusbank.com

Country Bank, 200 E. 42nd St., New York, NY 10017; (212) 883-6480; fax (212) 883-6450; www.countrybankonline.com

CTL Capital, 300 Park Ave., New York, NY 10022; (212) 572-6205; fax (212) 572-6424; www.CTLcapital.com

CW Capital, 63 Kendrick St., Needham, MA 02494; (781) 707-9300; fax (781) 707-9303; www.cwcapital.com

Dominion Mortgage Corporation, 11355 W. Olympic Blvd., Los Angeles, CA 90064; (310) 477-3041; fax (310) 477-1601; www.dominfin.com

Equity Plus Financial, 9750 Miramar Rd., San Diego, CA 92126; (858) 566-3500; fax (858) 566-8785

FarmandRanchLending.com, 2450 Colorado Ave., Suite 4000 West, Santa Monica, CA 90404; (800) 705-9003, x1061; fax (310) 315-8646; www.farmandranchlending.com

Financial Federal Savings Bank, 6305 Humphreys Blvd., Memphis, TN 38120; (901) 756-2848; fax (901) 756-2155

First Blackhawk Financial Corporation, 3021 Citrus Circle, Walnut Creek, CA 94598; (925) 648-3067; fax (925) 648-3068

GE Real Estate, 292 Long Ridge Rd., Stamford, CT 06927; (800) GE-FIRST; fax (203) 357-4475; www.gecapitalrealestate.com

Glaser Financial Group Inc., 2177 Youngman Ave., St. Paul, MN 55116; (651) 644-7694; fax (651) 644-0923; www.glaser.com

Globe Mortgage Inc., 2 University Plaza, Hackensack, NJ 07601; (201) 996-6000; fax (201) 489-1865

Green Park Financial Limited Partnership, 7501 Wisconsin Ave., Bethesda, MD 20814; (301) 215-5500; fax (301) 634-2151; www.greenparkfinancial.com

Hall Financial Group, 6801 Gaylord Parkway, Frisco, TX 75034; (972) 377-1100; fax (972) 337-1170; www.hallfinancial.com

iCap Realty Advisors, 77 W. Wacker Dr., Chicago, IL 60601; (312) 673-4227; fax (312) 553-0767; www.iCapRealty.com

Imperial Capital Bank, 888 Prospect St., La Jolla, CA 92037; (858) 551-0511; fax (858) 551-0625; www.imperialcapitalbank.com

iStar Financial, 1114 Avenue of the Americas, New York, NY 10036; (212) 930-9400; fax (212) 930-9494; www.istarfinancial.com

Kennedy Funding Incorporated, 2 University Plaza, Hackensack, NJ 07601; (201) 342-8500; fax (201) 342-8373; www.kennedyfunding.com

Key Commercial Real Estate, 127 Public Sq., Cleveland, OH 44114; (888) KEY-2221; www.key.com/cre

Lend Lease Mortgage Capital, 700 N. Pearl St., Dallas, TX 75201; (214) 758-5800; fax (214) 953-8400; www.lendleasenei.com

Liberty Mortgage Acceptance Corporation, 4980 Hillsdale Circle, El Dorado Hills, CA 95762; (916) 568-0100; fax (916) 568-0110; www.libertymac.com

Lichtenstein Capital Markets, 5770 Palisades Ave., Riverdale, NY 10471; (800) 242-9888; fax (212) 255-5277; www.doctormortgage.com

M&T Bank, 350 Park Ave., New York, NY 10022; fax (212) 350-2065; www.mandtbank.com

Malone Mortgage Company, 8115 Preston Rd., Dallas, TX 75225; (214) 696-0386; fax (214) 696-5162; www.malonemortgage.com

Manulife Financial, 200 Bloor St. East, Toronto, Ontario M4W 1E5, Canada; (416) 926-0100; www.manulife.com

Mony Realty Capital Inc., 10475 Park Meadows Dr., Littleton, CO 80124; (303) 325-1050; fax (303) 325-1029; www.mony.com/realestate

Mortgage & Investment Corporation, 3001 Cambridge Place NW, Washington, DC 20007; (202) 944-3001; fax (202) 944-8002

Newman Financial Services, 1801 California St., Denver, CO 80202; (303) 293-8500; fax (303) 294-3280

NorthMarq Capital, 500 Newport Center Dr., Newport Beach, CA 92660; (949) 717-5200; fax (949) 729-4620; www.northmarq.com

Origen Financial LLC, 27777 Franklin Rd., Southfield, MI 48034; (972) 349-3200; fax (972) 349-3265; www.origenfinancial.com

Pacific Mortgage Funding Corporation, 11924 E. Firestone Blvd., Norwalk, CA 90650; (562) 864-4006; fax (562) 864-6125; www.pacificmortgage.com

PMC Capital Inc., 18111 Preston Rd., Dallas, TX 75252; (972) 349-3200; fax (972) 349-3265; www.pmccapital.com

Principal Real Estate Investors, 801 Grand Ave., Des Moines, IA 50392; (800) 533-1390; fax (515) 235-9700; www.principalglobal.com

Prudential Mortgage Capital Company, 100 Mulberry St., Newark, NJ 07102; (888) 263-6800; fax (873) 367-8210; www.prudential.com/prumortgage

PW Funding Inc., 200 Old Country Rd., Mineola, NY 11501; (800) 566-7933; fax (516) 873-0080; www.pwfunding.com

Quantum First Capital, 8235 Douglas Ave., Dallas, TX 75225; (214) 346-0200; fax (214) 436-0244; www.qfclp.com

Reilly Mortgage Group Inc., 2010 Corporate Ridge, McLean, VA 22102; (703) 760-4700; fax (703) 760-4056; www.reilly.com

Related Capital Company, 625 Madison Ave., New York, NY 10022; (212) 421-5333; fax (212) 751-3550; www.relatedcapital.com

Sterling Commercial Capital, 53 Unquowa Pl., Fairfield, CA 06824; (203) 256-9068; fax (203) 256-9564; www.sterlingcommercialcapital.com

Tremont Realty Capital, 125 Summer St., Boston, MA 02110; (617) 439-6700; fax (617) 951-1477; www.tremontcapital.com

USA Capital, 4484 S. Pecos Rd., Las Vegas, NV 89121; (702) 734-2400; fax (702) 734-0163; www.usacapitallender.com

WACHOVIA, 301 S. College St., Charlotte, NC 28228; (704) 383-6315; fax (704) 374-6345; www.wachovia.com

Webster Bank, 185 Asylum St., Hartford, CT 06103; (860) 692-1693; fax (860) 692-1624

Final warning: As I said earlier, lenders may change their policies and lending objectives. So please, please do *not* threaten me if some of these lenders have changed their business goals. If you do, I will refuse to assist you in any way whatsoever. And as proof of the accuracy of the listing, I have—in my own business corporation safe—the original of each ad from which the information was taken, along with the full details on the date and publication in which the ad appeared. You are free to inspect these at your convenience. Just let me know a few days in advance so the material can be removed from the safe and presented for your inspection.

MORE REAL ESTATE LENDERS FOR YOU

I'm a great believer in a number of business methods that have made me more than $6 million. These methods are:

- Work *fast,* grow *fast,* build *fast.*
- Do your own research—quickly.
- Buy and use good business books.
- Learn fast, act fast.
- Never give up—and you are *never* too old!
- Use your head at *all* times.
- Expand your know-how and fill your pockets.

Most of these methods are covered elsewhere in this book. And in chapter 15 I give you a list of the books that I call the keys to some 5,000 sources of ready real estate money. Using some of these books might help you find the real estate money you need.

GET YOUR REAL ESTATE MONEY NOW

Since real estate is a borrowed-money business, all you need to do is follow these seven magic steps:

1. Find the real estate you want.

2. Get a price from the seller.

3. Study your profit potential using the *income and expense statement* given to you free of charge by the seller of the property.

4. Make an offer based on your study.

5. Borrow the money you need.

6. Go on to great wealth success.

7. Expand your real estate holdings.

GET REAL ESTATE LOAN HELP ON THE INTERNET

If you use a computer at home or on your job, you can get information on real estate loans from the Internet. You still have to fill out a loan application and submit it to the lender. And your application must have a "live" signature: ink on paper.

Here are a number of Internet sites from which you can get data on real estate loans for income properties of various types and sizes:

Commercial mortgage finance: www.chase.com

Full range of finance capabilities: www.wachovia.com

Commercial and multifamily lending: www.pacificsecuritycapital.com

Commercial mortgages of many types: www.gmaccm.com

Commercial real estate lending: www.prudential.com

Construction/permanent financing: www.orix.com

Financing that meets your needs: www.LoopNet.com

Internet searches for real estate loan sources can be helpful. However, directories of the lenders in printed form—such as those listed in chapter 15—can often give a broader view of the lending world. As a real estate wealth builder, you can never have too many loan sources. Hence, lender directories in book form will be your mainstay in finding the borrowed money you need.

KNOW THE MAGIC OF REAL ESTATE

Many BWBs overlook the real magic of Other People's Money (OPM) when they use it to purchase real estate. To help you understand exactly how you can go from pennies to millions in real estate in three years, I've expanded the above seven magic steps into related steps in chapter 5 of this book. When you've finished reading that chapter I'm sure you'll be willing to say: "Real estate is the best business known to BWBs anywhere!"

But to motivate you more strongly, and convince you that you can get rich in real estate on borrowed money, I want to share with you two more letters from readers who're getting rich today:

> Hi—you bet your ideas work. In the last six months I've made several purchases of real estate. Three of these were with *no money* of my own but I finished with thousands of dollars in my pocket to make other purchases. And the income from these properties services [pays] the loans, plus taxes, insurance, and other expenses, with money left over for me. The secret is to use your suggestions, work days and some in the nights, while having fun and enjoying every minute of it!

A reader who's hit it bigger than many others—in what I call the Mega-Money Class (over $5 million personal worth)—writes:

> It has been a number of years since we last talked. [It was five years, actually.] I'll never forget the time you spent with me both over the phone and in your office in New York City.
>
> Your books were the beginning of a new direction in my life. In those years I was starting to venture out of a shell of captivity through your writings and personal conversations. The next year— as you said so many times it would—success hit.
>
> And, as you said, real estate is *the* best investment in good or bad times. How do I know? In the last five years I have turned $1,000 into several real estate corporations worth in excess of $12 million!

It's the Mega-Money Successes that made me change the numbers in the title of this book from one million to millions. Their letters just keep coming in. Who am I to argue with their success?

And—to further serve this Mega-Money Tide—I developed a new kit called *Mega Money Methods Success Kit* to serve the "big thinkers" who are looking for $5 million or more in real estate. It tells you the *how, why, where,* and *when* of raising $5 million to $999 million for real estate investments. (I stopped just below a billion because that number is just too big for me right now!) Priced at $100 from IWS Inc. (P.O. Box 186, Merrick, NY 11566), it's very popular with people seeking to build big real estate fortunes. And I want *you* to be one of my readers who *does* build a megafortune for yourself!

Just remember that I'm here to help you with advice, motivation, *and* financing, if you need any of these. Try me and see for yourself.

Points to Remember

- Real estate is a borrowed-money business.

- More people probably borrow more money for real estate than for any other business.

- Beginners in real estate can usually borrow money for their deals almost as easily as experienced people.

- It's often possible to get 100% financing of real estate (that is, taking over property without using any of your own money).

- With thousands of real estate lenders in business today, you can usually find the real estate financing you seek.

- Real estate is a great business for BWBs.

- I am here—ready to help you with advice, motivation, *and* financing, if you need any of these.

FOUR

HOW TO AVOID BEGINNERS' MISTAKES IN REAL ESTATE

If you could sit with me in my office during the day, or at home in the evening for three or four days or nights while I answer phone calls from readers, I think you'd learn something about beginners' mistakes in real estate—and how *you* can avoid them. But my office is too small to accommodate all who would want to listen, so I'll have to tell you about those calls in this book.

SIX MISTAKES BEGINNERS MAKE

After listening to thousands of real estate beginners' proposals, I think I've been able to isolate the six most common mistakes beginners make. Here they are, in summary form. After you read the list, we'll discuss each mistake and show you why you should avoid it.

1. Trying to buy—as the first property and with 100% financing—a nearly new income property costing $2 million or more.

2. Trying to buy—again as the first property and with 100% financing—a nearly new motel, hotel, or other type of short-term-residence facility.

3. Trying to buy raw land, which is non-income producing, without any cash available or cash to "carry" the land.

4. Mistaking a business such as hog raising, rabbit farming, or mink ranching for real estate.

5. Unwillingness to upgrade no-cash, easy-to-get property to raise its income and value while increasing your wealth.

6. Denial of the basic real estate fact of life: it takes time to make money in real estate.

Let's look at each of these mistakes. By telling you about them *now*, I hope to show you how to avoid these mistakes.

And by learning *now*, you will—I hope—be able to build your real estate riches faster and with fewer problems. So we're learning, in a positive way, how *not* to make real estate mistakes!

BUY RIGHT FOR YOU—NOW

The calls come to my office week after week, month after month, year after year. Though the words differ a bit from caller to caller, the message is much the same:

> Ty, I've found this great, great income building! They're asking $2 million for it, with $500,000 down. It has everything—pool, garage, security system. And the income is nearly half a million a year! I don't have any cash but I'd sure love to get this building now. How can I get this property? And another thing, Ty. Time is of the essence—if I don't get the cash in the next three days, I'll lose out on this deal! You *must* help me get this money for the down payment—now!

I've heard this plea over and over from one end of the world to another. Yet the calls keep coming, despite the fact that:

- The "debt service"—what you have to pay to pay off your loans—almost wipes out your profit on this type of building.

- Your chances of borrowing $500,000 with no cash in your pocket, no assets, sparse credit history, and little or no real business experience are practically nil!

- In real estate, when you start small, you have to build *reasonably* slowly. You can build from zero dollars to holdings of millions in three years. To start with a property costing $2 million or more, however, is difficult. I've seen it happen a few times, but not too often.

MOVE AHEAD SLOWLY WHEN YOU'RE STARTING

The real name of real estate is *time*. You must—when you have no cash to start with—build slowly. I have found that the way to go from zero cash to property worth millions in three years is:

- Start small with a building you can finance with 100% borrowed money.

- Improve the value of this property by having it repaired and painted if necessary.

- Raise the rents to increase your income.

- Show on your financial statement the results of your efforts by increasing the value of the first property you purchased. (The increase you show could range from a low of 5% to a high of 30%.)

So listen to me for a moment. You *might* be able to build holdings of $1 million in one year, or $5 million in three years, as some of my readers have. But the *usual* reader might raise his or her worth by about $1.5 million per year, starting with *no* cash.

Your best road to real estate wealth, starting with *no* cash, is the 36-month step sequence shown in chapter 14 of this book. While you can easily exceed this schedule, let me say this:

If you stick with me, I'll try to make you the proud owner of $5 million worth of real estate in three years, starting with no cash. Then—in your second three years—you can easily outpace my modest goals by $10, $20, or $30 million!

Yes, good friend, I *can* give *you* the lazy person's way to riches—if you're willing to put in three years of your *spare* time. And, while you're building your spare-time million-dollar fortune, you can:

- Hold another job

- Run another business

- Travel, vacation, work, or play

- Build an empire in another field

- Do anything *legal* that pleases, amuses, or delights you

Just remember this fact: the real name of real estate is *time*. If you buy real estate at the *right* time—when prices are low—you can sell soon when prices are higher. But if you buy when prices are high and you have *time,* you will still make money! So my conclusion is this:

There is probably no wrong time to buy well-located real estate— if you have time to wait for the price of the property to go up!

SMALL STARTS MAKE BIG FORTUNES

In my wide travels through the real estate world I've met more million-aires who started small and grew big than I have those who started big and grew bigger. Here are a few of the small starters.

Floyd C. works for an airline as a ground supervisor. At his West Coast–based airport, Floyd noticed that many of the young flight attendants didn't want to stay in the company-rented hotel rooms while off duty. Instead, they wanted to stay in a place of their own. This gave Floyd an idea.

Why not take over one or more older buildings, have each converted into two or more apartments, and rent them out to the attendants? Floyd did some research, asking the many flight attendants who passed through his office each day if they liked the idea. The response was an instant and delighted *yes*!

One other important point came out during Floyd's research. About half the attendants said: "Get a place near the beach!" So Floyd decided to get two places—one near the airport and the other near the beach. Flight attendants from either place could use the other for free.

So Floyd started looking for suitable houses to convert. He soon found that there were plenty of garden-apartment-type buildings priced at $1 million and up. But after calling me, Floyd wisely decided that this type of building was *not* for him at the start because:

1. He had little cash—$200 to be exact.

2. His chances of borrowing the needed down payment (about $300,000) were slim.

3. He'd be better off starting small and growing big.

So Floyd took over two repossessed four-family houses for no cash down. He then quickly borrowed $7,500 on each house to have improvements made. Six weeks after taking over each building, Floyd had rented out all eight apartments with five women in each at a monthly rental of $450 per apartment. Thus, Floyd's monthly income is 8 × $450 = $3,600.

Today, two years later, Floyd has 10 houses near the airport and eight near the beach. His monthly income is over $60,000, giving him a yearly gross of over $500,000.

"Soon," Floyd says, "I'll take over a garden-type apartment house with 40 to 50 units in it. But when I do, I'll:

- Know what the building will need in the form of down payment, mortgage payments, and so on

- Make a profit from the very first day

- Be sure to build my wealth faster"

Yes, you *can* make millions in real estate starting with *no* cash. But the best way that I know of is to start small and grow big—fast. So take my advice and start with the least cash possible. If you do, you'll probably find I'm right—while you're making your millions. I have nothing to sell you except your success!

TO AVOID FOOLISH MISTAKES, USE YOUR LOCAL PAPER FOR HELPFUL REAL ESTATE INFO

Many local newspapers, and almost all real estate newspapers, can be a treasure chest of valuable data for your real estate success. Typical data you can get from such newspapers include:

- Date of sale of each property

- Listed (asking) price of each property

- Selling price of each property

- Seller's name

- Buyer's name

- Annual real estate taxes

The only valuable bit of data that may be missing from such listings is the length of time the property was on the market before it sold. If the property was sold by the owner (FSBO = for sale by owner), it's almost impossible to learn how long it took for the property to sell. Why? Because owners become particularly uncommunicative after a sale! Their attitude is "I have my money; the details are none of anybody's business!"

When a real estate agent is part of the sale, you can usually find out how long the sale took. How? By simply calling and asking the real estate person how long the property was on the market before it sold.

Some newspapers do list the time the property was on the market and give both the listed (asking) price and the selling price. Thus, a large-city newspaper, in its Sunday real estate section might say, after describing the property in terms of its number of rooms, types of rooms, number of baths: *Listed at $379,000; sold at $375,000; 12 weeks on the market.*

How can you use this valuable free sales data available from various newspapers? Here are several ways to use this *business intelligence* in your real estate wealth building.

1. *Date of sale:* Compare the number of sales each month for a one-year period by counting the reported monthly individual sales. This info will tell you the best month for sales, the second best month, and so on. Thus, you can aim to put your property up for sale during the best selling months when you can ask for, and get, the highest price.

2. *Listed (asking) price of the property:* This number shows what the seller thought his or her property was worth before its sale. The greatest value of this number to you is when you compare it to the next number—namely the actual selling price. Studying the asking and selling prices for a number of deals will show you the approximate "discount" in operation in your area at the time you're selling. You might even wish to raise your asking price enough to offset the expected discount so you get the money you seek.

3. *Selling price:* Use what real estate appraisers call "comparables"—that is, comparable properties and the price they sell for. Comparables might show you've lowballed your price—that is, asked for too little for the excellent property you're offering for sale. Answer? Raise your price! You'll get more from the sale and feel better about it.

4. *Address of property:* Keep a careful watch on sales data and you'll soon know what areas are "hot"—that is, racking up lots of sales. If your property is in one of these areas, you can certainly ask for and get more money for the property you're selling.

5. *Number of weeks on market:* Average the selling time for a number of properties similar to yours and you'll know in advance the approximate number of weeks you'll have to wait to sell your property. You'll find that your selling time can vary from as little as one week to as long as 26 weeks, depending on your price, location, and state of the real estate market at the time you sell.

6. *Annual real estate taxes:* If the taxes on your property are lower than those reported for similar properties in your area, you can use this as a selling point. Having info on comparable taxes is a valuable selling tool.

So don't overlook local sources of real estate info. They can often put thousands in your pocket for an investment of just pennies!

STAY AWAY FROM MOTELS AND HOTELS

Motels, hotels, and other short-term-residence buildings are *businesses* that sit on real estate. Thus, many motels and hotels get more income from their restaurant, bar, and catering facilities than they do from their rooms. So unless you know the motel or hotel business well, stay away from both at the start. Why? Because motels and hotels:

- Are labor intensive—you need a big staff with high labor costs

- Many different skilled trades may be needed in a hotel—cook, maid, bartender, night clerk

- A good motel or hotel location often has a much higher land cost or rental cost than can be justified by the business income for a beginner

- Land values seldom rise as fast for motels and hotels as for other real estate

So unless you've had years of experience as a motel or hotel operator, stay away from these businesses as your first real estate investment.

Later, after you've made big money in conventional apartments or commercial property, you can take on a motel or hotel as a *business* deal. By that time your experience will guide you.

BE CAREFUL OF RAW LAND DEALS

Many people dream of hitting the big money in raw land. "Buy good land in the path of development and hang onto it," these folks say. "When land use catches up with your piece of Mother Earth, you'll make a bundle! All you need to do is sit tight and wait."

It's so true, I sigh. But there's an enormous *if* behind all raw land buys. This big *if* can be summarized thus:

- *If* you have the money to put down on the land
- *If* you have the money to pay the real estate taxes until you sell
- *If* you can wait for land use to catch up with you
- *If* you can sit on a no-income property for long enough

Land use moves outward from the central area of a city at the speed of about one mile per year, when the city is expanding. But:

- Not all cities are expanding.
- Land values go up by different amounts, depending on location.
- When you start with no cash, you need a cash *producer,* not a cash "eater."

Sure, raw land *can* make you big money! But the time to speculate in raw land is *after* you make your millions in income real estate. Then you can afford to:

- Wait until land values rise
- Pay real estate taxes from other income
- Have a cash eater instead of a cash grower

Income real estate gives you two big pluses that are lacking from raw land: (1) cash flow and (2) a tax shelter that allows you to keep more of your cash. And if you have other income from sources different from real estate you might be able to (1) reduce the overall cost of borrowing money for business and (2) shelter some of your other income from taxes. But all of these advantages assume that your real estate "pays its freight"—that is, has a cash *income*. Raw land seldom has a cash income. Later—after you're worth millions—you can get into all the raw-land deals that interest you!

DON'T CONFUSE REAL ESTATE AND BUSINESS

In real estate you profit two ways:

1. From rental of space to your tenants

2. From the growth in value of the property you own and rent out

In business you profit only *one* way—from the sale of the product or service that you are marketing. So real estate and business *are* different! This brings us to an important fact:

Unless the beginning wealth builder (BWB) sees the difference between real estate and business, he or she is likely to earn less money because most businesses allow you to earn money only one way.

Thus, hog farms, rabbit farms, and mink ranches are essentially businesses. True, the real estate they require may go up in value. But, like motels and hotels, you must be in a business before you make the big money in real estate.

Ted C. learned this important fact when he bought a mink ranch. In buying the ranch, Ted thought he was getting into real estate in a big way. But Ted soon found that the ranch needed more business skill and experience than he had.

"What can I do, Ty?" he wailed over the phone one night. "I can't meet the monthly payments on the ranch because the business isn't giving me the cash flow I expected."

"What do you *really* want to be in?" I asked him. "Real estate, not minks," he groaned. "Then get yourself a mink rancher, someone who understands the business, and let him run the ranch for you while you concentrate on real estate deals." "I'll try," Ted said, sounding defeated and beaten.

I didn't hear from Ted for three months. Then one night the phone rang and it was Ted. "Ty," he said excitedly, "your methods really do work. I didn't believe you when you told me to get a rancher to run the ranch. But I figured I had nothing to lose. So I got the guy and put my time in on the real estate. In three months I've sold off half the ranch for a profit of 60 grand. And it looks like I can get 90 or 100 grand for the other half! How does that grab you?"

"Great," I said, laughing. "You now see the difference between real estate and business." "I sure do. Thanks to you I'll make my millions—in real estate," Ted said with a tone of gratitude in his voice.

If you want to make *your* fortune in real estate, keep the basic differences in mind. Then you'll have a much better chance of getting richer, sooner!

Later in this book you'll learn how to combine real estate and a business successfully.

MAKE MONEY FROM LOW-COST PROPERTY

"Ty," people often say when they call me about real estate, "I'm only interested in top-quality, high-cash-flow properties in a good part of town. I won't touch anything else."

"Great," I reply. "How much cash do you have to put into your real estate?"

"Well, that's my problem," most of these BWBs say, rather lamely. "I don't have any cash at all. So I'll need 100% financing. In fact, if I could get 105% or 110% financing, I could really swing the deal."

When I hear such remarks from people who:

- Have never made a dime in real estate

- Don't have any cash of their own

- Refuse to start small and grow big, and

- Fail to learn the facts of this business,

I'm likely to explode. "Darn it," I say to them, "if you know so much about the place you want, why do you bother me?" And the usual answer is: "Because I don't know how to get the money I need. Won't you please help me, Ty?"

"Sure, I'll help you," I usually say. "But you'll have to do things *my* way. I'll bring you to the point where you're a multimillionaire in three years. After that, you're on your own."

"Okay," the caller usually replies. "How do I start?"

"You start," I say, "by going where the money is—namely to no- or low-down-payment buildings that can grow your riches in just a few months."

"But what about the neighborhood?" the caller asks.

"Friend," I reply, "a dollar of income from a no-down-payment house is the same as a dollar of income from a high-cost house. And what's more, the income dollar from low-cost property will probably be a much more profitable dollar to you because less of it will go for paying various expenses. By this I mean that you'll be able to spend, on yourself, 20¢ to 30¢ of the dollar you get from low-cost income property. But you'll be able to spend only 3¢ to 6¢ of the dollar you get from high-cost, newer housing."

So don't be afraid to start building your first million in the less attractive parts of town. Why? Because:

- You get more income for your money.

- Properties can be taken over faster.

- Many zero-cash deals are possible.

- One-hundred percent—and better—financing is common.

- Your spendable income is much higher.

- Tenants are often more loyal.

- Labor is easier to get.

- Repairs and improvements will cost you less.

Sure, there are problems with low-cost real estate. But you'll also have problems with high-cost real estate. So unless you have a bundle of money you inherited from a rich relative, or won at the races, steer clear of high-cost income property at the start of your career. You'll make your first million much faster—if you take my advice!

A recent detailed letter shows what you can accomplish with no-down-payment, low-cost property. In this deal—as in many others you might work—the reader walked away with Money in Fist (MIF I call it). Others call it *mortgaging out*—that is, getting money for taking over a property that gives you a positive cash flow without putting up a dime from your own pocket. Here's what the reader says:

I'm taking this time to thank you for helping me get started in real estate investing.

We negotiated for a three-family house for the purpose of rehabilitating it and selling two units while holding onto the third. During this period I read your book *How to Borrow Your Way to Real Estate Riches* and became very excited.

We had no collateral and very little cash at the time. We applied to many conventional banks, private lenders, and mortgage firms, using the info in chapter 7 of your book as a guideline for a loan package. We received many compliments on the professional appearance of our package.

The purchase price was $140,000; fix-up costs $80,000; total, $220,000. The seller took a $40,000 second mortgage subordinate to the construction money and we put down $5,000 (which we borrowed from our credit-card line of credit). So we needed $175,000 ($220,000 – $45,000), made up of $80,000 fix-up money and $95,000 to close. Further, we wanted to finance the monthly expenses until we sold the property. Based on the market value after fix-up, the property would be worth $330,000. So we applied for $195,000 (59% of market value), which was $20,000 more than we needed.

I knew that if we applied to enough lenders we would get the loan. After getting as many as 20 rejections, we finally got a commitment for the $195,000, two days before closing!

In summary, we put $1,000 of our own money into the deal, own a piece of property worth $330,000 with $90,000 equity, and have $20,000 cash left to help with the expenses. One further point: I was a part-time newspaper driver; now I'm a full-time investor!

This letter tells it all. That is, the reader:

- Used creative financing by working with the seller. (*You* can easily do the same on many deals!)

- Borrowed the down payment using his credit card line of credit. (*You* can do the same, using your own credit card or a partner's card.)

- Mortgaged out with money in fist. (Though this reader says he put $1,000 of his own money into the deal, he got that back in the $20,000 extra that he borrowed using the property as collateral.)

Be sure to note that this reader "had *no* collateral and very little cash at the time." If this reader can go from *no* collateral and *very little* cash to the ownership of a property worth $330,000, *you* can do the same! Why? Because:

- *You* have me here to advise you.

- *You* have me here to help with the financing.

- *You* have a ready friend to help you every way he can.

TIME IS REAL ESTATE

If you want to make a million dollars in six months or less, don't get into real estate. Instead, go into a mass-market item like computers, software, Internet services, hula hoops, license-plate holders, or washing-machine soaps.

With a mass-market product you can either: (a) hit the big money fast or (b) go broke in a few weeks. By contrast, in real estate, you can: (a) make millions in three years, with great certainty, and (b) seldom lose your money if you pick reasonably well-located income properties and wait for your rewards!

So you *must* be patient in real estate—there is just *no* substitute for time that:

- Pushes the value of your properties up

- Gives you rental income

- Helps reduce what you owe

- Provides you with experience

- Develops your judgment

- Gives you a tax shelter

If you're in a big hurry for riches, don't go into real estate. Instead, go into another business. You'll be much happier—and you may make big money faster. Then again, you may not!

LEARN NOW FROM OTHERS' MISTAKES

You now know the six common mistakes that real estate beginners make. Don't you make any of these mistakes! Why? Because, by using the advice in this book, you can:

- Build a multimillion-dollar real estate fortune in three years or less

- Go on to greater wealth

- Branch out to other businesses if you wish

While there are other mistakes beginners make in real estate, the above six are probably the most common mistakes that I've seen. So avoid them whenever you can!

Points to Remember

- Mistakes can hurt you in real estate, just as in any other business.

- Try to avoid buying nearly new property with 100% financing at the start of your real estate career.

- Recognize the difference between real estate and other businesses.

- Don't let non-income-producing raw land run you into heavy debt.

- Never be afraid to upgrade zero-cash property.

- Never confuse a *business* (hotel, farms, etc.) with *real estate*.

- Remember, always, that the secret of real estate wealth success is *time*!

- And never forget that you have a friend in me—to answer questions, guide you, and help you with real estate financing you may need.

FIVE

SEVEN LUCKY STEPS TO BECOMING A REAL ESTATE MILLIONAIRE

Since some of my readers have made millions in real estate in three years or less, I'm positive I can show you how you might do the same. And in this chapter I'd like to give you the seven lucky steps that I think will make *you* a real estate multimillionaire in 36 months or sooner. Here are these seven lucky steps written especially for you:

1. Get started with the *right* view of your future real estate wealth.

2. Pick the way *you* want to make your real estate wealth.

3. Find the financing sources you need, using the hints in this book.

4. Look for the type of real estate that you've decided will make your fortune.

5. Take over the real estate you want.

6. Build the income and value of your property.

7. Continue expanding your real estate empire until you reach your money goal.

Now let's look at each of these seven lucky steps from *your* view. You'll soon see how you can make a real estate fortune in three years, starting with *no* cash.

GET STARTED WITH THE RIGHT VIEW

Chapter 4 told you how to avoid beginners' mistakes in real estate. Read that chapter again and again because it will help you keep the right view of real estate at all times. The information is condensed into these nine key ideas:

1. Real estate is a business. You buy property for only one reason—to make money from it.

2. You must *not* look at property as though you were going to live in it or use it—you must look at a property for its income potential.

3. Real estate is a borrowed-money business, so you must seek to put the least money into *every* property.

4. You must know in advance the exact profit each property will pay you, based on your careful study of the income and expense statements of the properties you're considering.

5. Once you take over a property, the next step is to raise its income because this gives you a bigger cash flow and a larger value for your property.

6. Get started in your real estate fortune building with a plan that points you toward the amount of wealth you seek—$1 million, $10 million, $100 million.

7. Learn now, and repeat it here, that real estate is forever tied to time—without time real estate won't make you the big money you seek.

8. Put yourself into your real estate, making your holdings *you* and you alone so your tenants recommend you and your properties to others. Do this by being available day and night, 7 days a week.

9. Save the money you make from your real estate and put it into more property until you reach your wealth goal.

To summarize these nine key ideas about your real estate future, you can say:

Real estate is a borrowed-money business in which fast income from property held for a number of years can easily make you a multimillionaire.

Get started right in your real estate wealth-building career and I guarantee you that great wealth will soon be yours. Remember, I have nothing to sell you but your success! Here are two examples of how people got started right and hit the big money.

One of my East Coast readers, a young person with a growing family, took over 400 rental units in less than three years, using borrowed money. With an average rental of $600 a month, his yearly income, before expenses, is $2.8 million! Thus, he used the *borrowed-money* aspect of real estate to the hilt. The borrowed money is repaid from the cash flow his rental units generate. And a Western reader writes: "We, my wife and I, have been using the zero-cash approach to real estate for several years. Today we have 72 units and we are constantly looking for more. Our income is more than $100,000 a year." This, again, is an example of using the *borrowed-money* way to wealth in real estate!

PICK THE WAY TO YOUR FORTUNE

In my opinion, there's just *one* fast, easy, sure way to *your* first real estate fortune—and that is through income property. Now I'm *not* saying that you must be in any special type of income property. But I am saying that:

Income property can make you a multimillionaire. Non-income-producing property can break you.

The income property you pick can be of many types, such as:

- Apartment houses
- Town houses
- Factories, warehouses
- Parking lots, auto wrecking yards
- Tennis courts, swimming pools

- Stores, shopping centers

- Hospitals, health clinics

- Office buildings

But no matter what type of property *you* pick, your cash income from the property *must* be greater than your expenses related to this same property. Always apply the acid test for real estate success invented by your author, Ty Hicks, namely:

To decide if real estate property will be profitable to you, ask yourself the question: How much cash income from this property can I spend each month on items other than the property?

The larger the amount of cash you have left each month, the better, in general, the property will be for you. When you look at the income summaries of various properties, you will often see numbers such as these:

Gross income:	$82,000
Total expenses:	84,000
Income or (loss):	(2,000)
Amortization:	10,000
Net profit:	8,000

At first glance it seems that this project is giving you $8,000 a year in income. But it isn't! Instead, the "income" property is *costing* you $2,000 a year in money that you'll have to put into the building to keep it going. Keep this important fact in mind at *all* times:

You cannot spend amortization.* So you must be able to "walk away" with real cash at the end of each month.

---

*Amortization is the amount you reduce (pay down) the principal (the dollar amount you owe) of the mortgage each year. The amortization is money paid from the income you receive from the property. True, you have more *equity* (ownership) in the property after you make each mortgage payment. But none of the amortization dollars go into your pocket today. You recover these dollars *only* when you sell or trade the property.

To provide cash income, these figures should look like this:

Gross income:	$82,000
Total expenses, including amortization:	68,000
Net profit:	14,000

So choose your projects carefully. Go into whatever type of real estate interests you. Just be certain that the cash flow is high enough to cover your vacancies. The usual vacancy rate used in figuring an apartment-house income is 5%. This means that a property that is figured to yield $100,000 income per year when fully rented will, for your planning purposes, be figured to give you only 95% of this, or $95,000 income per year.

Your Cash Flow Must Be Positive!

As you look around for properties, you'll run into some sellers who'll tell you:

> Sure, there's a negative cash flow on this building. But in a couple of years after the neighborhood "turns around," you'll have a positive cash flow. It's such a good situation that I'd keep this building forever. But my wife wants to move to a warmer climate—that's why I'm letting it go cheaply!

With a negative cash flow you have to lay out money from other income just to keep the building from going under. This is *not* the way to get rich in real estate! Insist—for *every* property you take over—that you get income *now*—today! Not next year, or the year after. But *today*!

People call me on my toll-free number after they subscribe to my newsletter *International Wealth Success* and say:

> I've been looking for income property for three days and I can't find any with a positive cash flow. I've decided to pick up a few that have a negative cash flow and wait for them to go up in value.

This type of call just makes me laugh. Why? Because it takes more than three days to find a property with a positive cash flow! Further, most of these callers have little (in some cases, *no*) extra income. So how can the person expect to "carry" a negative cash flow property?

Take it from me, good friend:

- There *are* positive cash-flow properties available in every area today.

- You *can* find such properties, but you *must* look for them for longer than three days!

You will meet many "experts" during your real estate career. Most of these so-called (by themselves) "experts":

- Have *never* owned a piece of real estate in their lives

- Have held a "secure" job at no risk to themselves

- Rarely—or never—take a financial risk

- Are basically very poor because they're wage slaves

Yet they'll tell you all about real estate—a subject they really know nothing about! Don't listen to them. Listen to what I tell you, which comes from my own experience and that of thousands of my millions of readers. Like these two who write about *positive cash flow*—the *only* way to go in real estate at any time in history:

I thank you. After reading one of your real estate books I went out and bought my first four-plex. It has made me money every day since.

And,

Each of my properties [this reader has six] has provided a positive cash flow from day one.

In the loan group of which I'm a director—where we lend money to beginning wealth builders (BWBs) to buy income properties—we *must* be certain that *every* property has a positive cash flow. Why? Well, if a property has a negative cash flow:

- We won't have our loan repaid from the income

- Meaning that we'd show a loss on the loan

Yet in 30-plus years (at this writing) of making loans to BWBs all over this great world of ours:

- Almost every borrower has repaid in full his or her loan.

- Some borrowers have had as many as four loans with us.

- A high percentage of loans have been repaid—happily I might say!

Now lets see how other BWBs make money picking the kind of real estate that interests them. Here are two real-life incidents I've heard of.

Recreational Real Estate Pays Off

Bert K. is a tennis "nut." He plays tennis day and night. I've even seen Bert "playing tennis" in his office while talking on the telephone. The way he does this is to bounce a ball off one wall in his office, using his tennis racquet, all the while talking on the phone. The horizontal dividing line between the lower paneling and the plaster upper portion of the walls forms his "net."

So Bert's natural desire, you might guess, is to own a tennis court. The only trouble is that Bert is a young (32-year-old) family man with big responsibilities. So when he asked the seller for the price of a new indoor tennis building with four courts, he was almost floored by the figure given him—$450,000, with $150,000 down. "There must be another way," Bert said to himself. (This "must-be-another or better way" is an attitude of most BWBs I meet.)

So Bert decided to see what other kinds of tennis courts he might buy, starting with no cash. He quickly found another kind—the inflatable building that is kept up by low-pressure air being fed into it by a small air compressor. And though they might look flimsy, records show that these inflated buildings are seldom blown down and are almost never blown away in storms. Better yet, Bert found that he could rent a building and compressor, with *no* cash down. Now all he needed was land.

Searching his local newspapers, Bert found two acres of land advertised for rent on the outskirts of town. But the land wasn't improved—that is, it did not have electrical, sewer, or water service. Fortunately, by using his head, Bert was able to work out a way of renting a portable generator, a water tank, and two chemical restrooms. To protect himself, Bert had an option-to-buy clause written into each rental lease. This clause allowed him to buy the building and equipment during the first year, getting full credit toward the purchase price for the rent he had paid.

To get some operating cash, Bert formed a tennis club and sold 20 memberships in his tennis club for $1,000 each. With this money he had the land flattened and clay courts installed. Soon, other people joined the club, but their membership fees were $1,500 each because the club was about to open.

Four months after opening his club, Bert was taking in $3,500 a month in court rental fees. Six months later Bert bought the land, building, and equipment. Today Bert has six such tennis buildings in various locations. And already he has sold the land for five of his buildings and leased it back from the buyer. By doing this, Bert was able to convert his "land-heavy" position into a "cash-heavy" position, improving his financial condition. For, as Aristotle said, "Even happiness requires some external prosperity."

Strings of Income Properties Pay Off

Kathy L. works as an executive secretary in a large firm. While this title may sound great, "the job is nothing more than a glorified secretary's spot," Kathy says. "The pay is low, the hours are long, and the chances for moving ahead are nil. So why do I stay?" Kathy asks. "For just two reasons—my time is my own and I can come and go as I please. This allows me to spend time on my spare-time business during the day. And having a job that gives me an important-sounding title enables me to borrow money for my business. This is very important to me."

But getting money for her business wasn't always easy for Kathy. When she started in real estate, Kathy dreamed of a brand-new, spotlessly clean, 100-unit rental property on which she could borrow the down payment. Kathy soon got a rude shock when she learned that: (1) Some banks avoid lending money to women, thinking they are less reliable than men. (This is a narrow-minded view of half of our population!) (2) Borrowing a 100% down payment for a new, recently completed building is often difficult and expensive.

But Kathy didn't give up. "There must be some way around the discrimination and cost problems," she said to me on the phone one night. "There sure is," I replied. "Do the bankers a favor and take over some of their repossessed properties. They'll forget your gender and will even pay your closing costs!"

So Kathy "lowered her sights," as she said, and decided to do the possible, instead of not doing the impossible. By visiting banks during early or late morning hours, when bankers were less busy, Kathy found them both interested in, and willing to listen to, her requests.

In just six months, Kathy took over a number of older buildings having a total of 300 rental units, with an average "talking" rental* of $300 per month. Kathy's cash flow from nonjob sources went from zero to $90,000 per month. Once she achieved this level, Kathy sat back for a while to survey her business and rearrange her financing.

Another six months passed. During this time Kathy made many improvements in her buildings and was able to raise her cash flow to $135,000 per month. With such a cash flow and an impressive list of real estate holdings, Kathy easily borrowed the 100% down payment for the original building she wanted. Today her realty income holdings exceed $5 million.

What Kathy's experience shows is: (1) You *must* not give up—you have to keep trying, and 2) you *must* begin with the possible and go on from there to the "impossible." Why? Because when you start with *no* cash, it is difficult to "write your own ticket." Later, when you have the income *and* the assets, you can do what you want to do!

So you see, you *can* do what you want to do in real estate. But you *must* pick a way to your real estate fortune that:

- Is possible for you

- Gives you instant income

- Fits in with your capital

- Can build your fortune fast

So, please, listen to me until you earn your first million in real estate! After that you can do as you wish. You can even tell me how you'll make your second million!

FIND THE FINANCING YOU NEED

Real estate is a borrowed-money business. By this I mean that most real estate deals are worked out with OPM—other people's money. This means that you can get started on zero cash if you want to avoid putting

---

*An average monthly rent in the area.

any of your own cash into a deal. You can, if you wish, borrow real estate money from many sources, including:

- Commercial banks
- Savings and loan associations
- Insurance companies
- Mortgage lenders
- Savings banks
- Government sources
- State sources
- Second-mortgage lenders

If you want to learn some of the quickest ways to finance your real estate, I suggest that you do two things:

1. Continue reading this chapter carefully.
2. Study the real estate financing courses mentioned on page 266.

Now let's look at *fast* financing methods for real estate. Why do I put emphasis on *fast* methods of financing? Because:

Fast financing of real estate is both possible and practical and allows you to build great riches sooner and with less delay.

SEVEN METHODS FOR FAST FINANCING OF REAL ESTATE

Since many old-time real estate people are geared to a slow pace in their business activities, I've spent much time devising *fast* methods for you to get the real estate money you need. These fast methods are just as good as (or maybe even better than) the slow methods. Further:

Fast financing helps BWBs in the area they usually find the most difficult—namely money. And these methods help quickly.

Since most BWBs who come to me are in a hurry, they welcome my fast financing methods. And even those BWBs who aren't in a hurry seem to welcome fast financing of their real estate fortune. Let's look at seven of these fast-financing techniques that you can use quickly:

1. *One hundred percent financing* by taking over repossessions from banks, insurance companies, and savings and loan associations is quick, easy, and painless. If you have a good credit rating you can in some cases be collecting income from your property in just three days. And your legal fees, real estate taxes, and escrow account will often be paid in full, in advance, when you take over the building. This saves you a bundle of cash.

2. *Second-mortgage advance financing* can cut weeks off the time needed to take over a property. In this approach you arrange with a second-mortgage lender a tentative financing for a type of income property that you choose in step 2, page 77. Thus, you might tell a second-mortgage lender that you'll probably need a $75,000 to $100,000 second-mortgage loan when you take over a property generating, let's say, $100,000 a year in income. You supply the facts about yourself that he needs and he gives his tentative approval of your loan application. Then, when you get the information on the property you want to buy, your loan can be approved quickly (in a day or two) if the property meets the requirements of your lender.

3. *Setting up a "blind card" limited partnership* (LP) or real estate investment trust (REIT) before you find the *income* property you seek can give you the money you need the *same* day you find the property! Actually, you can have your money long *before* you find the property you want because in a "blind card" LP or REIT, you do not tell your investors exactly what types of properties you'll invest in until *after* you've invested their funds.

4. *Sell stock* in your own real estate corporation before you take over any property. As an officer of the corporation (such as the president or vice president), you are usually allowed to sell shares of stock without being a registered representative. This means you can build a nice balance in your corporation, ready for investment in property when you find it.

5. *Borrow from private or specialty lenders* you search out using your own ingenuity or the help of a publication such as *International Wealth Success,* my monthly newsletter of borrowing and wealth opportunities for both beginning and experienced wealth builders. This publication has thousands of real estate lenders available. They are listed in the various books and kits published by IWS that are described in chapter 15.

6. *Become a financial broker-finder-business broker* and find the money *you* need while being paid to look for and find money for *other* people. An excellent course, called *Financial Broker-Finder-Business Broker-Consultant Success Kit*, showing you how to get started in this exciting profession is available for $99.50 from IWS.

7. *Borrow or rent collateral,* such as stocks, bonds, letters of credit, and leases, for the money you need *before* you need it. To use this method, just estimate, *in advance,* how much money you'll need for your future real estate deals. Then rent the collateral you'll need. (Your banker will tell you how much collateral you will need for a loan of a given amount—say $200,000 or $400,000.) Firms renting collateral are sometimes listed in the *IWS* newsletter. Thus, in one recent issue an advertiser offered to rent high-grade municipal bonds (acceptable by almost any lender as collateral) for 3.5% a year. Thus, to rent $10,000 bond would cost you $350 per year. This is a relatively low cost compared to the power you can get from fast financing of real estate using OPM backed by rental collateral!

There is a great potential for you as a financial broker in the real estate field. Thus, a reader recently wrote: "Thank you for IWS! Inside of the last three weeks I got a deal closed concerning construction financing . . . for a contractor. I made somewhat over $2 million. Needless to say, I am still very happy over that accomplishment! Just thought that you would personally like to know this as this package came as a direct result of a connection made through IWS! . . . It is you that I have to thank most of all, due to the above-mentioned circumstance . . . Go! Go! Go! Never give up! Thank you sincerely, sir."

Yes, you *can* find quick, zero-cash financing for the real estate you want. And you can often get this financing even though you have *no* cash to start with. Here are two living, breathing BWBs who did just that:

Get Your Money First

Doug T. wanted to buy a 150-unit income apartment house but he had *no* cash. He went to his banker anyway and told him he'd like to buy the property that was fully rented and on the outskirts of town.

"How much are you going to pay for the property?" the banker asked Doug. "I don't know yet," Doug replied. "Why don't you have it appraised and tell me what you'll lend me."

The bank appraised the building as worth $1.3 million. Doug figured this was 80% of what the bank thought the building was really worth, or $1.62 million. Also, he knew the bank would lend 80% of the appraised value, or $1.04 million. Knowing what the property was worth, in the bank's opinion (that is, the appraised value), and how much the bank would lend him on the property, Doug offered the owner of the property $800,000 cash as the total price of the building. The owner screamed, stamped his feet, threatened to cry—and sold out to Doug for $900,000, about 10% higher than Doug's offer.

Doug got his $1.04 million loan from the bank, paid the owner $900,000 cash, and had $140,000 of *tax-free* cash left over. He had *mortgaged out* and had obtained about 115% financing, starting with *no cash*. Yes, good friend, it *can* be done, *is* being done, and *you can* do it now, today, here!

Cut Your Cash Needs

BWBs who visit with me during lunch in midtown New York City, and those who read my many money books and my column in *International Wealth Success,* know that I'm a strong believer in quick education to increase your moneymaking ability. Now I'm not talking about four years of college. Instead, I'm talking about the many short, quick courses that cost little and might put millions into your pocket.

This is the kind of course I told Laura C. she should take when she told me she thought she could sell real estate in her spare time. Like most BWBs to whom I make suggestions, Laura resisted my idea that she take a short course and become a licensed real estate salesperson in her state. (Most BWBs I meet reject my ideas at first because the ideas are so simple and easy to use. Later on they use the ideas and are amazed that they work.) That's what Laura did—she bought a good book, studied it carefully, took the exam, and received her license.

Laura didn't use her license for several years. But having the license never hurt her. And the annual fee was only a few dollars. (Do I hear you saying: "See, the BWB *was* right; you had a bad idea"? If so, please read on.)

The first chance Laura got to use her license was on a building she bought for herself. A small office building came on the market, priced at $100,000 with $29,000 down. Laura had *no* cash at the time but she really wanted the building because it would clearly be a profitable takeover for her.

Laura asked the seller if she could act as the broker for the sale. He agreed and they signed a broker's agreement giving Laura a 6% commission, or $6,000 on the sale. This meant that if Laura bought the building she would need only $23,000 cash because the $6,000 commission could be deducted from the $29,000 cash down the owner was asking for the building.

Next, Laura had the building appraised by a bank and a mortgage company. The bank offered a $75,000 mortgage on its appraised value of $100,000. This meant that the bank would lend at 75% of its appraisal. But the mortgage company offered to lend 90% of the same $100,000 appraised value, for a loan of $90,000. Since the building would cost Laura only $94,000, that is, $100,000 less her $6,000 broker's fee, Laura had to come up with only $4,000 cash if she took the loan from the mortgage company.

Laura closed the deal shortly thereafter, taking over the building with *no* cash down. So once again, fast learning paid off for a BWB. Today, Laura's income from this building is over $12,000 a year. And, as she says, the building "runs itself."

For an excellent course on making big money from income property and vacant land of all kinds, you might want to order the *Real Estate Riches Success Kit* from IWS Inc. for $99.50. A companion course that concentrates solely on real estate financing and loans is *Fast Financing of Your Real Estate Fortune Success Kit*. It is also priced at $99.50, from IWS Inc. A third course, *Low Cost Real Estate Loan Getters Kit,* priced at $100 from IWS Inc., focuses on getting quick real estate loans of various types. See chapter 15 for ordering information.

LOOK FOR YOUR REAL ESTATE

There are a number of ways of finding the real estate that will make you a millionaire. These include:

1. Large-city and local newspaper ads

2. Real estate magazine ads

3. Bulletins from local and national real estate brokers

4. Word-of-mouth ads from friends and associates

During your first few months of real estate wealth building, I suggest that you use *all* these methods of getting to know what's available and where it's located. Why? Because by using a number of different means to find what property is up for sale, you:

- Quickly get info on what's available

- Build a fast price know-how

- Detect "lemons" that are being "shopped around"

- Find out typical cash-down needs

- Get to know people in the business

By looking for, and at, typical properties on the market, you will get a faster education than you ever thought possible. But in getting this education, you must keep an important fact in mind at all times:

There are high-cost properties and there are low-cost properties. If you look only at high-cost properties, you will be overlooking many gems among the low-cost ones.

Put another way, a dollar you invest in a low-cost property will often bring you much more income than the same dollar put into high-cost property. And the cash down payment you need for low-cost property is usually much less. This means:

By starting with low-cost property, you can usually: (a) take over more property, (b) with less cash down, (c) while earning a higher income from the money you invest.

So start the right way to build your real estate fortune! Get lots of rental units to bring in lots of profit dollars. And you can help yourself get started quickly by looking in real estate sources under the headings:

- Rental Property for Sale

- Apartment Houses for Sale

- Industrial Property for Sale

- Houses for Sale

Just remember to start off with something smaller than the Empire State Building, The Sears Tower, or Madison Square Garden! Then you may wind up owning it some day! But whatever you do, *keep looking until you find the right property for yourself!*

TAKE OVER THE REAL ESTATE YOU WANT

I've taken over or bought plenty of real estate in my business career. And I've worked with—and still work with—hundreds of BWBs taking over real estate today. The advice I give both myself and my BWBs is always:

Have an attorney represent you in every real estate deal. Don't try to save pennies and wind up wasting dollars!

To take over real estate that can make *you* a profit:

1. Find the property, as described above.

2. Decide what the property is worth to you.

3. Make an offer *less* than the asking price using a suitable "pack" factor from Table 1, page 91.

4. Settle on a price.

5. Reduce the down payment to zero, if possible.

6. Get your attorney in on the deal.

7. If you need cash, borrow it as shown elsewhere in this book.

8. Have your attorney write a contract to buy the property.

9. Meet with the owner and get the contract signed (have your attorney with you).

10. Finalize the financing, working with your attorney.

11. Close on the property (your attorney *must* be with you at the closing).

12. Begin collecting *your* income.

TABLE I

TYPICAL "PACK" PERCENTAGES FOR REAL ESTATE*

Price of Property Land and Buildings(s)	Typical "Pack" Percentage
$20,000	9%
35,000	8
50,000	7
80,000	6
100,000	5
150,000	5
200,000	4
400,000	3
500,000	2

*The percentage shown can vary from one area to another. But in an area where the table applies, you should offer no more than $95,000 for a $100,000 asking-price property. You get this from the 5% "pack" factor in the table. Or 0.05 × $100,000 = $5,000 "pack" in the seller's price—this is the amount he or she added to the price, figuring the buyer would negotiate the price downward. *Never pay the asking price for real estate!*

If you use the zero-cash methods I've told you about in this book, you can get the property you want without putting up any money of your own. And that, after all, is a good way to start. As I tell many BWBs, "Turn adversity into prosperity!"

GRAB AN ASSUMABLE MORTGAGE IF THE NUMBERS WORK

An *assumable mortgage* for income real estate you want to buy can offer you many advantages. Some of these may include:

• No credit check to get your mortgage

• Quick approval by the seller of the property

- Much less paperwork than for a conventional mortgage

- Faster acquiring of income properties for yourself

So how do you know a property has an "assumable"? Most sellers will say, in their ad for the property, "Assumable mortgage." Or, if you deal with a broker, that person will point out the assumable feature. To make an assumable work, you must:

1. "Work the numbers" of the property *before* you make an offer. You *must* figure your potential profit.

2. Start with the asking *price,* get the *down payment asked,* and *annual income* and the *annual expenses.*

3. Using your numbers, figure your income after paying all *expenses* except your *assumable* and any *other loans* (down payment, etc.) you take out.

4. Figure your *monthly mortgage payments.* You *must* have a positive cash flow (PCF) after making *all* payments, including *all* mortgages!

Here's an example of a typical property. Your author has rounded off the numbers *upward* to make them easier to follow. But the rounding does *not* change the deal! If anything, the rounding makes the deal less attractive! For this 20-unit residential property:

Asking price = $800,000; assumable mortgage = $640,000 at 7%; down payment = $160,000; annual expenses = $71,000; annual income = $158,000 per year *before* expenses.

Income before mortgages = $158,000 − $71,000 = $87,000. Assumable mortgage monthly payment on 30-year loan = $4,300 or $51,600 per year; second mortgage down payment loan on $160,000 at 8% for 10 years = $2,000 per month, or $24,000 per year; total mortgage payments = $75,600 per year, leaving you an income of $87,000 − $75,600 = $11,400 per year, for your positive cash flow.

Note: Your author will work the numbers for you, one property at a time, if you're a subscriber to one of his newsletters.

So what's your whole key to this deal? It is: *Getting the $160,000* *down-payment second mortgage for at least 10 years and at a suitable interest rate, namely less than 10%! Keep looking and a deal like this may become yours!*

BUILD PROPERTY INCOME AND VALUE

The purpose of your real estate is to build a steady income for yourself that's at least $100,000 a year. Sure, it's nice to stand in front of one of your properties and say: "I own that—it's all mine."

But if the property doesn't pay you the income you seek, then you may be less than proud. So aim at income—money is what will build your wealth faster than anything else!

To speed your income and wealth building, think in $500 or $800 units, depending on the going rent level in your area. Thus, you can quickly figure your monthly and yearly income before expenses by making up a short table like this, assuming 100% occupancy:

MY REAL ESTATE INCOME

Number of Rental Units	Monthly Income $500/month	Monthly Income $800/month	Yearly Income Before Expenses $500/month	Yearly Income Before Expenses $800/month
10	$5,000	$8,000	$60,000	$96,000
20	10,000	16,000	120,000	192,000
30	15,000	24,000	180,000	288,000
40	20,000	32,000	240,000	384,000
50	25,000	40,000	300,000	480,000
60	30,000	48,000	360,000	576,000
80	40,000	64,000	480,000	768,000
100	50,000	80,000	600,000	960,000

So you see, when you get 100 or more income units, your dollar flow can get interesting—and lucrative! Here's a good example of that.

Make a Million Helping Others

Jim T. always wanted to be rich. When we first talked, I told Jim: "Become a professional moneymaker in your own thinking first. Then pick a business in which you help others. Think of yourself as a professional and you won't go wrong!"

Jim had always wanted to own real estate. So—thinking of himself as
a professional moneymaker—he took over a 50-unit building with *no*
cash down because this gives a beginner the biggest leverage possible in
local real estate. Since the property was a repossession in a depressed
area, Jim knew he'd be helping people. And using a $300 unit as his base,
Jim knew his income would be $15,000 a month, or $180,000 a year,
before expenses and debt payoff.

Not having any cash on hand to fix up the building, Jim offered one
month's free rent to each tenant who would fix up his or her own apartment. Most tenants agreed quickly to this fix-up plan. Within two months
the value of the property skyrocketed and Jim was able to get a $30,000
building-improvement loan to fix up the exterior. He also raised the rent
of new incoming tenants to $350 a month.

Today, using this zero-cash approach to increasing the income and
value of property, while helping people in depressed areas, Jim owns
3,000 apartment units, giving him a monthly income of $900,000, and
a yearly income of $10.8 million! And he did this on zero cash, using the
methods I suggest. You, too, can do the same—if you try!

CONTINUE EXPANDING YOUR HOLDINGS

Set yourself a yearly money goal, such as a profit of $100,000 a year.
Then set out to reach your goal in a year or less.

Next, set a total worth goal—say $5 million. Choose a target date for
reaching this goal, such as three years from today. Then work at applying
the methods I give you in this book. You, too, may become a real estate
millionaire in three years, starting with *no* cash! Now here is one more
method you can use—my million-dollar real estate secret.

MILLION-DOLLAR REAL ESTATE SECRET

Many real estate BWBs ask me how they can get started in real estate on
zero cash. One little-known secret way that I tell BWBs to explore is:

> Visit or call your local apartment owners association and tell the
> person there that you're interested in taking over or buying some
> income property. Leave your name and address for use either on
> the bulletin board or in the association's publication.

Now here's what will often happen.

Older apartment owners may be seeking to sell their buildings. But they frequently can't find a suitable buyer. So when you walk in seeking to buy, you are welcomed with open arms. And if you are a reliable and dependable person, you can often swing deals such as many other BWBs I know have, namely:

- Zero-cash down takeovers of valuable income properties

- One hundred percent financing by private mortgage from the owner

- Valuable mortgage windfalls giving you cash in hand for buying a profitable property

- Free financing without credit check, employment investigations, or long applications

- A continuous supply of valuable leads on good properties for sale

- Friendships with people in the know in your local area

Build Riches through Friendships

In my travels about the world for business seminars, conferences, meetings, and various profitable deals, I've often noticed that many people are lonely. Tim K. found the same in his own "backyard" when he joined his local apartment owners association. Older members of the association whom Tim thought should be active, happy, and busy because they had 100 units ($50,000-per-month, and $600,000-per-year income) were not. Instead, they were lonely, bitter, unhappy.

Tim, who was 32 years old at the time, decided to make friends with as many of these lonely people as he could. He talked to many members of the association whenever he attended a meeting. To his delight, he found the lonely members ready and willing to talk. And as they talked, Tim could see some of the bitterness leave their faces. But what was more important, these people told Tim about their buildings and the problems they were having with them. So Tim found he was helping others while helping himself learn about properties!

Tim told several people about this situation. He was young, strong, ambitious, and anxious to own 50 or more income units. But he had no cash, collateral, credit, or cosigners. To Tim's delight, his new friends at the association became very sympathetic and wanted to either "mother" or "father" him, depending on the person to whom Tim was talking. In less than two weeks Tim had three offers to take over income units for no money down. He took over all three. Since the sellers gave him 100% financing, Tim put *no* money down, had *no* credit check, filled out *no* loan application! In 11 months Tim doubled his goal by taking over 100 units, giving him an income of $50,000 a month, before expenses. Today Tim is rapidly on his way toward becoming a real estate tycoon on zero cash!

You can put this million-dollar secret to work today. How? Just get in touch with your local real estate group and go on from there to join the property owners association. Then—with a little time, dedication, and work—you're on your way to your first $5 million in real estate—and probably in less than three years!

To find the address and telephone number of a nearby apartment owners association, look in your phone book. You can also do the same for the real estate association. Or ask a local real estate broker for this information.

Points to Remember

- Start fast with the *right* view of real estate.

- Before you start, pick the way you want to make big money in real estate.

- Use ingenuity and reliable data to find the financing you need.

- Form the habit of regularly reading the real estate ads for the type of property you seek.

- Try to take over your income property for *no* cash down.

- Build the income and value of your property.

- Continue expanding your real estate holdings until you reach your wealth goal.

SIX

TAKE THE RAW LAND
ROUTE TO WEALTH

Raw land is usually *unimproved land,* that is, it does *not* have:

- Sewers
- Streets
- Lighting
- Curbs
- Water supply

or other improvements. Because nothing has been done to it, raw land is usually:

- Cheap
- Readily available
- Easy to buy
- Full of profit potential

But this is not all a song of plenty. Why? Because raw land:

- Pays you *no* income
- Can be a big tax burden

- May take years to develop

- Can be a drain on your income

"If all these drawbacks are true, why bother me with raw land?" you ask. Because, good friend, raw land—which you carefully select—can put you into the chips quickly and effortlessly. Let's see how.

WHY RAW LAND IS VALUABLE

The major reason why land is valuable to people is:

Land is a limited-availability commodity because there is only a certain amount of land available and there is a growing demand for land almost everywhere.

Whenever you have a situation in which there is only a limited amount of a commodity available, and a growing demand for this commodity (such as land), the price of that commodity will rise. And the longer such a commodity is held, the higher (in general) its price will rise. So you can't lose on raw-land investments if you:

- Pick your land carefully, after you

- Analyze the direction of development,

- Study the speed of development, and

- Wheel and deal for the lowest price.

ANALYZE THE DIRECTION OF DEVELOPMENT

Towns and cities usually grow in population as time passes. This growing population needs space—that is, land. To satisfy the demand for more space, almost all communities expand horizontally. To expand horizontally, or on the flat, land must be developed, that is, subdivided into:

- Lots, with

- Access roads and

- Side streets, having

- Sewers, and

- Water supply, and
- Electricity.

If you can predict the probable direction of horizontal expansion of a town or city, you can make big profits by:

- Buying raw land in the path of the community growth
- Holding the land until the growth reaches you
- Selling out to developers at a suitable price

Or you can, if you wish:

- Hold onto the land, instead of selling it
- Develop the land yourself
- Sell the developed raw land to builders
- Go into the construction business and build houses or other structures on your developed land

Thus, you can see that your potential is almost unlimited—*if you buy in the direction of growth.*

To analyze the direction of growth in an area you're considering, try the approach used by Saul C. to build a fortune in raw land. For each area you're considering:

1. Draw a map, such as Figure 1, of the town or city and surrounding land, including the land you're considering. (Or you can use an Army Corps of Engineers survey map or a road map of the area.)

2. Read all the local papers, paying close attention to:
   - Housing-development ads
   - Shopping-center ads
   - Industrial-plant construction information
   - Any other item showing that people, or firms, are investing money in the area

3. Using a suitable symbol, plot each important item on your map.

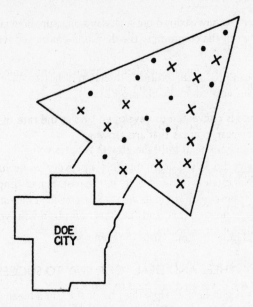

Figure 1 Mark the location of new stores, shopping centers, and housing developments to learn expansion direction.

4. Continue plotting these points until you think you see a direction of growth emerging, such as that shown in Figure 1.

5. As soon as you see a direction of growth, buy land in the way of this growth. Buy the land at a distance from the community center that agrees with your analysis of the speed of development.

FIND THE SPEED OF DEVELOPMENT

Saul C. kept a record of the speed of development on his map. You can do the same and learn an enormous amount about your area and ways you can make money from it. Here's how:

1. Pick some measure of development—such as the purchase of land for a shopping center.

2. Enter on your map the date this event occurs.

3. Keep adding dates to your map as you learn of each new event, such as the breaking of ground for a new factory.

4. After you have six or more such dates, measure how far *out* from the center of the community the development moved with each date.

Saul C. did this for the raw land in Figure 1 and came up with what he thought was a great discovery, namely that:

Raw land is converted to developed land at the rate of about one mile per year in areas that are growing.

Only later did Saul C. learn that this "discovery" of his had been made by other real estate wheeler-dealers in the past. Stated simply: *A growing city or town moves outward in its direction of growth at the rate of about one mile a year.* Knowing this, and the direction of growth, you're ready to wheel and deal for your land.

WHEEL AND DEAL YOUR WAY TO SUCCESS

What's a wheeler-dealer? How does he or she run a business? Why be a wheeler-dealer? Here are the answers to these basic questions. These answers could put a million dollars into your pocket in just a short time.

A *wheeler-dealer* is a businessperson who:

- Never pays the asking price

- Keeps his or her cash payments low

- Tries many alternate schemes

- Works business deals fast

- Develops unusual financing plans

The wheeler-dealer runs his or her business so that its costs are minimal and profits are the highest.

Many wheeler-dealers almost run their business out of their hat—that is, they have no office, secretary, files, or big investment.

You should consider becoming a wheeler-dealer because you'll:

- Live more creatively

- Earn higher profits

- Get richer faster

- Have fewer worries

- Run your business from your home

LOW COSTS CAN MEAN BIG PROFITS
FOR WHEELER-DEALERS

Here's an example of how a beginning wealth builder (BWB) is using speed and good cost control to build a fast fortune as a wheeler-
dealer.

In an issue of *International Wealth Success,* the newsletter for which I
write a monthly column, I recently wrote on how big a business one person could run. Here's what one reader who successfully invests in raw
land wrote in response to that column:

> Several months ago I read your book on building a business using
> *other people's* money.* I put some of the ideas to work and now
> have a very profitable business going.
>
> This morning I received your March issue of *IWS* and I read
> your page with interest as to how big a business one person can
> run. Let me tell you my experience.
>
> I devote about 75% of my time to this business and have a part-
> time office assistant. In the four months I've been in this business,
> my volume is already over $400,000. The only thing that is holding
> me back from doing $1 million per month is the money to work
> with . . . Thanks for the inspiration.

HOW TO WHEEL AND DEAL IN RAW LAND

To wheel and deal in raw land you must:

1. Decide that you *will* be a wheeler-dealer.

2. Use the methods of the wheeler-dealer, that is:

   - Never pay the asking price

   - Keep cash payments low

   - Scheme your way to great success

**How to Borrow Your Way to a Great Fortune*

- Work fast

- Be creative about financing

3. Keep thinking of new deals, new ways, new approaches at all times.

Now I'd like to give you an example of a creative raw land wheeler-dealer. I've chosen him to tell you about because he used all the above approaches.

Cary D. wanted to invest in raw land in his area. But Cary had problems, namely:

- Very little cash—only $150

- No access to cheap land

- A miserable credit rating

- No source of loans

When Cary analyzed his situation and came to realize how badly off he was, he almost cried. But hope springs eternal in the heart of every BWB and Cary was no different from the others. "If I could only be more creative," he said to himself. So Cary decided to be more creative, by using a method called the psychology of the possible. It is based on the belief that *anything you can conceive you can achieve*.

LIST YOUR MONEY NEEDS

Cary sat down and listed his money needs. If he were to wheel and deal in raw land real estate, he'd need:

- Cheap land

- A source of money

- An income

Cary thought the land in his area was overpriced. This meant he'd have to go outside his area. The realization that he'd have to go elsewhere was Cary's first step toward great wealth, but he didn't realize this at the time.

Looking around for somewhere to go, Cary glanced out of his window.

To the east he saw some low hills about 20 miles away. These hills were once the home of several mining towns. But the ore petered out and people left the towns for better digs elsewhere. As Cary stared at the hills, his eyes suddenly widened. There lay the answer to his raw land dreams. Here's what Cary did.

GIVE YOURSELF A MILLION-DOLLAR GIFT

Cary jumped into his car and raced to the hills. The first deserted town he came to had a weed-cluttered main street, a crumbling church, a dusty saloon, and a rotting mine-shaft housing. Cary dug around the old buildings until he found the name of the town.

Moving farther into the hills, Cary did the same in three other towns. When he had all the information he could conveniently gather, Cary returned home.

The next day he visited his local library and did a quick research job on each of the four towns. To his amazement and delight, two of the deserted mining digs were classified as cities. Now here's what Cary did within the next few weeks:

1. Asked his state government (by letter) for permission to restore one city.

2. Named himself mayor of that city.

3. Prepared a circular offering municipal bonds for sale for restoration of the city, its land, and its buildings.

All Cary's steps were successful and he was able to restore the city as a tourist attraction. Further, he received a good salary as mayor from the proceeds of part of the bond sale. With this money he was able to take over some of the surrounding land. As the tourist business increased, Cary sold off part of his raw land at an excellent profit. He developed the remaining land to the point where it paid him an income. Today, three years later, Cary is a multimillionaire. Truly, he gave himself a million-dollar gift!

BE MORE CREATIVE IN YOUR RAW LAND DEALS

Cary used great creativity in the land deal you just read about. You, too, can be creative in *your* raw land deals. Here are a few ways to be more creative:

1. Search for the unusual deal—such as the estate sale, land auctions, the unusable pieces of property.

2. Move farther away from the city center but stay in the path of population expansion.

3. Be alert to industrial land buying by large firms—such buys almost always signal an upsurge in surrounding land values.

4. Jump onto the rocketing land values induced by huge theme parks such as Walt Disney World and Six Flags Over Texas.

5. Keep tuned to government land offers—you can, at times, take over land for as little as $1 an acre.

6. Go foreign—to Canada, Nova Scotia, South America, Central America, the Caribbean, Europe, Africa. Land is land and if you get it cheap, it usually can do nothing but rise in value. Use a local firm to hold the land.

7. Check out wetlands (land underwater). Bargains today can become "money machines" tomorrow. But you must be aware of, and ready to comply with, rules governing wetlands.

8. Search out raw land with a good location—such as spectacular views, waterfront areas, and lake sites. Location *always* pays off—if it's good!

9. Explore the possibilities of "non-land" raw land, such as air rights over existing developed land, like railroad tracks, drainage tunnels, marinas, rivers, etc.

10. Watch for the growth of new town, multiple-family housing developments, and similar projects in raw land areas. They signal big profits for holders of raw land farther out.

11. List ways *you* can make *your* raw land more profitable. Consider any of these techniques—subdividing, developing to the point of streets and sewers, or actual construction of buildings.

A recent letter from a reader gives one BWB's plan for making money from land. The reader writes:

I would like to thank you for showing me how to buy improved lots at a good price on my own terms with no money down, after banks and private parties were not interested in helping me. I

have 40 lots in one section and 22 in another. I'm going to build modular housing on these lots.

SPECULATE IN RAW LAND

When you speculate in raw land, you will usually:

1. Take over land with the least cash

2. Hold the land for as short a time as possible

3. Sell the land for the highest price

4. Accept a long-term payoff for the balance

Let's take a look at how a speculator can make *big* profits with just a few dollars to start.

Sell Before You Buy

To act as a real estate broker, you must be licensed in most states. But you don't need a license to sell raw land on which you have an *option* to buy. Freddie L. uses the option technique to take over raw land with little cash down. And since raw land is cheap to start with, Freddie gets by on pennies. Let's see how.

Based on a study of the *direction* and *speed* of land development, Freddie takes a one-, two-, or three-year option to buy selected raw land. To get the option he pays the owner 0.5%, 1%, or 1.5% of the asking price of the land. Thus, on a $10,000 raw-land property, Freddie would pay $50, $100, or $150, depending on how long he thought he'd have to hold the property before he could sell it. These sums are so nominal that most BWBs can raise them quickly.

Once Freddie has an option to buy a piece of raw land, he has control of it until he either sells the land or his option time expires. When his option expires without his having sold the land, Freddie either renews his options or loses his option payment.

While loss of the option payment might annoy some BWBs, Freddie believes that the loss is small compared to the profit opportunity he has while he's holding the land, ready for sale. To sell "his" land, Freddie:

1. Makes a list of its good features

2. Lists the potential uses for the land

3. Figures the type of customer (builder, developer, industry, etc.) for which the land is best suited

4. Prepares a mailing piece describing the land, the features, price, etc.

5. Mails the piece to potential buyers

6. Lists the land for sale on the Internet

Using this technique Freddie is able to sell over 95% of the raw land on which he takes options. And he *always* prices "his" raw land at twice its cost to him. Once he finds a buyer, all Freddie has to do is close the option deal, turn around, and sell the land to his buyer. So, by combining raw land and mail/Internet selling, Freddie has made himself $1.5 million in his spare time in five years—selling before he buys!

Sell Lots for Future Homes

Tom Q. makes more than $100,000 a year selling raw land lots for future homes. But instead of selling to the retiree on Social Security, Tom sells to:

- High-income executives

- Second-home enthusiasts

- Horse, cattle, and sheep grazers

- Housing developers

These people have the money to pay for well-located land that can:

- Go up in value

- Be developed

- Be used for grazing or other purposes.

So Tom doesn't have to spend a lot of time trying to convince his prospects that well-located land has real potential. Instead, Tom aims at volume turnover to skyrocket his income and automatically build great wealth. How? Here's his technique.

Tom forms limited partnerships to take over thousands of acres of good land at a time. These limited partnerships are set up to produce the capital required for each block of land—the amount of money obtained from the limited partners can range from as little as $50,000 to as much as $1 million. "I got much of the information I needed on limited partnerships from the IWS *Starting Millionaire Program,*" Tom says. "This great course even includes the forms you need to set up such a partnership, using the guidance of your attorney."

Tom doesn't put up any money himself. Instead, he runs the partnership and gets a piece of the action—varying from a high of 20% on a $50,000 deal to a low of 5% on a $1 million deal. Now here's the procedure followed by Tom and his associates:

1. Locate suitable land.

2. Draw up the limited partnership.

3. Collect funds from sale of partnership units (similar to shares of stock).

4. Advertise the land after listing its features.

5. Sell the land at a profit.

6. Pay off the partners, or invest in other properties, depending on their wishes.

Using this technique, Tom has built a neat fortune for himself in just a few years. Real estate is the basis of almost every fortune and it certainly is for Tom.

Note that the limited partnerships I recommend to you are *money-making* groups! They are *not* tax-shelter deals designed to lose money. The only real estate deals you should ever consider are those that make money! And if you ask me to take part in a deal designed to lose money, I'll tell you to "get lost"!

There's only *one* reason to put your time and energy into real estate. To make money! And *every* deal should make money for *you*!

DON'T LOSE MONEY ON RAW LAND

Raw land isn't all gold—you can get trapped into losing deals if you're not careful. Why is this possible? Because raw land:

• Pays you *no* income

• May have high taxes on it

- Can go down in value

- Sometimes is slow to rise in value

Now there are ways to get around most of these problems. The main problem, of course, is the lack of income from raw land, combined with the real estate taxes you might have to pay. To take care of the taxes, convert your raw land to a *taxpayer*—that is, property rented for business purposes temporarily to pay all, or most, of the real estate taxes on the property. Typical taxpayers you might consider renting your raw land for include:

- Parking lots

- Carnivals, fairs, flea markets

- Tennis courts

- Aboveground swimming pools

- Athletic fields

- Temporary storage of large items

MAKE TAXPAYERS PAY OFF FOR YOU

Two friends of mine own some waterfront raw land. This land is so far from nearby towns that it has been slow in developing. So taxes were a heavy burden on these wealth builders.

Craig, one of these friends, said to his partner, Bill: "We just have to get some money out of this land, Bill. If we don't, the taxes will kill us." Bill agreed, but he didn't have any creative ideas.

When Craig came to me, I told him to analyze his land and then come up with a moneymaking idea. "Break down your investment into its elements, Craig," I said. "This will often help you decide what will make money for you."

Craig did as I advised and quickly found that his waterfront land offered:

- Space—acres of it

- Flat terrain

- Millions of gallons of water in the bay on which the land bordered
- Easy access by a wide road
- Electric power outlets

Considering these facts, Craig decided that a tenant needing space on level land adjoining water was his best prospect. With this "service" in mind, Craig made a list of prospective tax-paying tenants, such as:

- Boat storage for builders, marinas
- Heavy machinery storage
- Truck storage

As he wrote the last two words in his list, "lightning" struck. Just a mile from his land was a large fire engine factory. This factory tested its finished fire engines in its rear yard by spraying streams of water into the air. Nearby residents were constantly complaining about the noise of the engines and the wind-carried spray from the nozzles. Craig's land would, he thought, make an ideal test area for the fire engines.

MOVE FAST ON LAND IDEAS

Craig called the president of the fire engine factory immediately and told him about the land, stressing its level layout, easy access, and unlimited water supply. The company president promised to visit the land the next day.

Craig and Bill were on hand when the president arrived to inspect the land. Within minutes Craig explained his idea to the company president. Together with Bill, he pointed out the good features of the land for fire engine testing. There was:

- Easy drive-in access
- Plenty of flat parking surface
- Unlimited water
- No nearby complaining neighbors

The fire engine firm president agreed to lease the land at twice the annual payments Craig and Bill were making for taxes, interest, and mortgage. Today these two land speculators are sitting pretty as they collect a sizable income from their formerly "useless" land.

USE THE POSITIVE FORCES OF RAW LAND

Many beginning wealth builders overlook the great advantages that raw land offers them, including:

- *Time factor*—time works *with* you in raw land, instead of against you, as in many other investments. For instance, many raw land parcels will double in value in five years.

- *Population demands*—with a rising population in certain areas, greater demands for raw land are being made every year.

- *More leisure time*—with the shorter work week, more people are seeking second homes, vacation retreats, and snug hideaways. Raw land is the main satisfier of these drives.

- *Limited supply*—"Our maker ain't makin' no more land for us," a poor farmer once said to me. "That's why I'm holdin' onto the back forty—may make some dough from them acres, someday." And sure enough, a year later he sold out for $200,000—more money than he'd earned in the last 10 years.

- *Enormous creative possibilites*—for making big money from the land while you wait for its value to rise. For instance, by converting the raw land to farming use, you can collect *big* subsidies—often as much as $200,000 a year for either:

  1. Growing certain crops, or

  2. *Not* growing certain crops

  Thus, you win whether you grow them or don't grow them!

- *Chances for big leases to large firms*—such as leasing corner highway properties to oil companies for gas stations. (The biggest leasing deal in history is that for the United States embassy in London, England. The owner leased the land on which the embassy is built to the U.S. for 999 years! Top that deal, if you can.)

- *Exploration for natural resources*—can help reduce your income taxes on income from other activities. Thus, raw land may contain oil, gold, copper, uranium, silver, mercury, etc. You can take a *depletion allowance* when your land produces certain of these minerals or petroleum. This depletion allowance helps you shelter some of the profits from your land's resources.

- *Temporary hobby use*—such as horseback riding, model-airplane flying, tennis, baseball, jogging, etc.—can turn a "loss-leader" property into a real winner. Your land pays you income while it generally doubles in value every seven years, or less.

GIVE YOURSELF A MILLION-DOLLAR FORTUNE

Raw land can be *your* key to:

- Greater wealth

- A happier life

- Fewer problems

- More spending money

- Fast growth of your money

This chapter gives you ideas that can get you started in raw land, here and now. Throughout the rest of this book we'll point out other ideas you can use to make raw land or million-dollar money machine. So keep alert because there's gold waiting for you in raw land—if you're willing to go after it. As a final example to prove my point in this chapter, I'd like to show you how you can get the cheapest land on earth for no more than a few gallons of gasoline, a stimulating summer vacation, and a minimum charge.

HOW, AND WHERE, TO GET RAW LAND
FOR UNDER $30 AN ACRE

Many people criticize the U.S. government. But to me, our government is the greatest in the world! And, friend, I've been all over this world of ours.

For instance, the federal government holds more than 750 *million* acres of land in the western states. To claim some of this land, all you need to do is load up your car with some two-by-four stakes, drive to a piece of federal land you think contains minerals, and hammer in the stakes at the boundaries of the piece you want. Then you register your claim in a local state office and, essentially, the land is yours!

Should you want full title to the land, you:

1. Apply for a *patent*.

2. Prove there are some minerals on the land.

3. Pay a nominal fee for the land.

When you get your patent from the government, you don't have to develop the minerals. You own the land and you can sell it, develop it, hold it, or do anything else legal on the land. At a price that can be as low as $2.50 an acre, you're getting raw land at the cost of only about .005¢ a square foot, or you get about 200 square feet of land for 1¢! Can you beat that deal in any other business? I don't think you can! (See the books on raw land in chapter 15 for additional ideas on making money from vacant land.) In the next chapter, we will look at another profitable aspect of real estate—residential properties.

Points to Remember

- Raw land is valuable because its supply is limited.

- To make money from raw land, buy in the direction of growth.

- City areas often grow from their center at a rate of about one mile per year.

- You can wheel and deal in raw land and make a fortune.

- Being creative pays off in raw land deals.

- Be careful to make *all* raw land pay for itself.

- Some of the biggest bargains around today are in raw land.

SEVEN

MAKE RESIDENTIAL PROPERTIES YOUR WEALTH SOURCE

Every human being in this world has two basic needs: food and shelter. Without food, we can't exist. But once we have food, the next greatest need is a roof over our heads. Supplying this roof for a number of people may make you richer than you ever thought possible in just a few years. Let's see how.

WHERE THE MONEY IS IN RENTAL PROPERTY

Good, well-located rental property is always in demand by:

1. Young marrieds

2. Singles

3. Older, childless couples (often called "empty nesters")

4. Non-homeowners

True, the demand for apartments may change from year to year. But, as a rental property owner of long standing, my income records and experience show that:

- Rental properties are safe investments

- Little management time is needed for them

- Your income is a steady cash flow

- There are plenty of zero cash, 100% financing deals around

- Income property is ideal for most beginning wealth builders (BWBs)

In rental property you can own a variety of types of buildings such as:

- Luxury apartment houses

- Older, middle-class buildings

- Single-family houses

Now most BWBs think that shiny new apartment houses are the answer to getting rich fast in real estate. Could be. But plenty of rich BWBs wouldn't agree with this. Talk to them and they'll tell you that:

The biggest real estate fortunes built by beginners are in older, lower-down-payment buildings that stay fully rented at moderate to high rents.

Further, you can often take over old buildings with *no cash down,* provided you are willing to assume—that is, make—the mortgage payments. Remember this fact about older buildings:

No lender wants to foreclose (take back) a building, because his or her business is the lending of money—not the operation of buildings.

So you can find no-down-payment buildings that will produce good, spendable income for you. We'll soon show you exactly how to build your real estate riches—starting with either some capital (money), or *no* money.

Readers write to tell me how they're getting good properties for zero cash down. Like these readers who write:

In three days I'm closing on an 11-unit apartment building. We obtained a first mortgage [this is a long-term loan for up to 40 years] and the balance we have secured with a purchase-money mortgage. So there is no cash!

And

> Within the last year I bought two eight-unit apartment buildings at a time when I had no money. I used 100% borrowed money. Both apartment buildings are in my own home town, population 1,300.

And

> Ty, thanks for writing your real estate books. I have bought several homes over the years. Last Friday I closed on a 12-unit apartment complex for no money down. A $225,000 value for $185,000. I assumed first and second mortgages; owner gave a third, interest only. Ty, I'm on my way!

HOW TO GET STARTED IN INCOME PROPERTIES

To get your *fast* start as a real estate empire builder, take these seven profitable steps:

1. Decide what type of property you'd like to own.

2. Calculate how much money you can invest.

3. Look for property of the type you want.

4. Wheel and deal for your property.

5. Close the deal.

6. Start operating your property.

7. Expand your property holdings.

Now let's take a quick look at each step and learn how you can make real estate millions yours in the shortest time possible.

DECIDE WHAT TYPE OF PROPERTY YOU WANT

In residential income property you can choose from among:

- New single-family houses
- Old single-family houses

- New multiple-family buildings
- Old multiple-family buildings

We'll take a look at each type to see which is best suited for your fortune building. Perhaps you'd be best off with a combination of units.

Single-Family Houses Build Wealth

Single-family houses have strong advantages and disadvantages for your wealth building. The advantages are:

- Many single-family houses are available for *no cash down*
- Lower maintenance costs
- Fewer tenant problems
- Smaller building cost
- *No* heating bills
- Lower land taxes

Against these advantages you have to balance the disadvantages of single-family houses, namely:

- You're either fully rented (one family) or fully vacant
- When fully vacant, you have to make house payments out of your other income
- Tenants may not stay so long in single-family buildings as in multiple-family properties

Is there a way of avoiding the disadvantages of single-family rental housing? Yes, there is! "What's the way?" you ask, sensing that I may have your answer to building a fortune in real estate in three years. Here's the answer.

To make big money in single-family houses, take over a "string" of them—say 10—with no cash down. Then operate them as a "horizontal" apartment house.

Tim K. did just this, taking over 12 single-family houses in four months with *no cash down*. Here's what his profit-and-loss statement looks like:

Monthly rental income = 12 houses × $350 per month each	=	$4,200
Annual rental income = 12 months × $4,200 per month	=	$50,400
Annual mortgage interest, and tax payments = 12 houses × $2,500	=	$30,000
Annual gross profit	=	$20,400
Annual maintenance cost @ $200 per house × 12 houses	=	$2,400
Annual net profit	=	$18,000
Tax shelter from interest, depreciation, and repairs	=	$16,800
Taxable income	=	$1,200
Annual equity (or ownership) buildup	=	$3,600

Tim saved the $18,000 income he received during his first year of owning these houses and used it as a reserve fund to cover unexpected vacancies, emergency repairs, and similar expenses. At the same time he took over 24 more single-family houses, giving him a total net income of a little over $55,000 a year—without having invested a cent of his own!

In any of the heavily populated areas of the United States, you can easily take over 36 such homes a year, giving you a total income potential of $162,000 a year at the start of the fourth year! And if you use the collateral provided by the houses and land, you can:

- Get tax-free second mortgage home-equity loans

- Take over other types of property

- Raise your income *each* month

- Use home-improvement loans to improve your property

HOW TO TAKE OVER SINGLE-FAMILY UNITS

To make millions in real estate in three years starting with no cash by investing in single-family units:

1. Look for *resales* or *repossessions* in the real estate ads of your newspapers.

2. Check out the cash needed—some of the ads will say *no cash down*.

3. Try to find the FHA, VA, and bank resales and repossessions—many have *no* legal fees, either.

Once you locate one or more such houses, inspect them. Look for major defects, such as:

- Leaky roof
- Cracked foundation
- Flooded basement
- Broken beams
- Defective heating system

Don't worry about minor defects—you can get your tenants to:

- Repair broken windows
- Paint the inside or outside of the house
- Fix minor leaks
- Trim the grass, hedges, etc.

Now here's a valuable tip you can keep in mind whenever you are working out a deal for a no-down-payment house:

Buy the materials and supplies (lumber, paint, etc.) for your tenants and they'll do most of the minor repairs the house needs while paying off the house for you and giving you a profit in the form of income and tax savings!

For best results, *always* have an attorney on hand when you take over *any* real estate. In some repossessions, the attorney may be furnished you free of charge by the:

- Bank

- Mortgage firm

- Government agency

- Seller

If you're short of cash and have to pay the attorney (which you often *won't* have to do), get the attorney to agree to allow you to pay him or her out of the rent you receive. This will delay your payment and save you from having to put up any cash.

When taking over a property from a bank you'll deal with their *REO Department*. Don't let the initials frighten you. They mean *Real Estate Owned*—a situation all banks hate. What they want is to get a monthly mortgage payment from a happy owner. I want *you* to be that happy owner!

Yes, you *can* make *big* money from single-family houses. Just be sure to:

- Take over with no cash down

- Aim for *volume* income

- Get your tenants to do work on the house

- Have an attorney at your side

If you'd like to learn of other ways to earn money from single-family homes (SFH), get copies of the M-3 and M-4, listed in chapter 15. Just $12.50 each, they are complete business plans prepared by SFH BWBs earning money from nonrental activities. You will get a different perspective on getting rich from SFH in your area.

BUILD A FORTUNE IN MULTIPLE DWELLINGS

A *multiple dwelling* is any building having two or more families. Two-family units are also called duplexes; three-family, triplexes, etc. But when real estate people talk about multiple-family buildings, they're usually talking about 20-, 30-, 50-, or even 300-unit buildings.

Let me show you the arithmetic of multiple units. Suppose that you have 1,000 rental units in 20 buildings. (This is easy because all you need is 20 buildings each having 50 apartments. This gives you a total of 20 buildings × 50 apartments = 1,000 apartments.)

Now if the *average* rent per apartment is $400 a month (which is a *low* rent today), your monthly gross income will be $400 per apartment × 1,000 apartments = $400,000. In a year you'll take in $400,000 per month × 12 months = $4.8 million. And, friend, it's easy to take over buildings having 1,000, or more, apartments—if you're willing to work hard at your real estate business! (One real estate fortune builder I know of has 7,000 such apartments!)

The real beauty of the multiple-family building can be summed up for you thus:

- You can start with zero cash

- Competition is modest

- Pressures are few

- Cash comes in *every* month

- You have big tax advantages

- Inflation improves your investment and income

- You don't have to work eight-hour days—four hours a week is enough

- You have an unlimited world for expansion—if you want to take on a large number of buildings

- You get rich while you sleep because your properties earn money every minute of the day and night

HOW TO MAKE A FORTUNE WITH ZERO INVESTMENTS

Each year I talk to hundreds of BWBs. While they differ in age, race, gender, religion, education, and ability, almost every one of these BWBs has the same basic problem, namely:

Almost all BWBs lack start-up money. Ideas, energy, get up and go, they have. But money to start a business is almost nonexistent.

This is why I want to show you every possible way I know of to make millions in real estate starting with zero capital.

You can get good, solid, profitable rental multiple-dwelling buildings in large cities anywhere if you look for properties that are:

- In changing neighborhoods
- Abandoned by owners
- Being "carried" by the city or state
- Being "carried" by banks
- Being "carried" by mortgage lenders

You can get any number of good buildings from such sources just by making a phone call or a short visit. Once you take over the building, with *no* cash down, you are on your way to your first million dollars in real estate.

"But why will they let me take over a good building with no cash down?" you ask. "Good question," I reply.

Learn this fact of real estate life here and now:

No bank, mortgage lender, city, or state wants to be in the business of operating a building if its major purpose in life is something else—as it usually is.

So when a bank, mortgage lender, city, or state is "given" a building because the owner can't pay for it, the first step the organization takes is to look for someone to take the building off their hands. That someone could be *you*!

To make a fortune in real estate with *zero* investment, take these tried and proven steps:

1. Locate one or more suitable buildings by using your local large-city newspaper, the monthly newsletter *International Wealth Success*, or other suitable publications—such as those listed in the IWS *Starting Millionaire Program*.

2. Inspect the building; study the income and expense statement that the seller must provide to you free of charge.

3. Offer to take over the building if it appears to be sound and rentable.

4. Once you have possession of the building, take steps to find any additional tenants needed.

5. Collect a suitable rent security—one to three months' rent from each tenant if the former owner had no rent security.

6. Take over the rent security from the present tenants in the building if the security is held by the seller.

7. Arrange for all future rents to be paid to you by mail, or by credit card through your own merchant account.

8. Have any needed repairs made to the building.

9. Scout around for the next building to take over.

RIDE THE TRANSITIONAL NEIGHBORHOOD CHANGE WAVE

More and more depressed areas around the world are becoming *transitional neighborhoods*. That is, they're rising above crime, drugs, and vandalism to become desirable areas in which to live. And the motivating force behind such changes is often one that's easy to spot.

Thus, in one Chicago neighborhood the construction of a shopping mall resurrected the entire area. Why? Because:

- Local shopping facilities save residents the long trips they formerly made to downtown shopping malls.

- Bright, clean, safe stores give a new zest for local living, causing residents to repair their homes and spruce up parks, schools, train stations, and athletic fields.

- New job openings for entry-level and experienced help inject more money into the local economy, raising the living standard of most residents.

You can often take over run-down properties in such neighborhoods before, or shortly after, the change starts. Such properties can be in foreclosure and you get them for zero down. Or a bank or desperate seller will allow you to take over the property for a nominal good-faith down payment—say $100.

Then, all you need to do is:

1. Wait for the transition in the neighborhood to start before you make any large investments in rehabbing.

2. Use local skilled laborers to do your rehab work. They'll work for less and they'll often give you leads on dependable buyers or renters.

3. Stick with the area's traditions when rehabbing. Don't put a mansion in an area of brownstone duplexes and triplexes! Retain the brownstone exterior while improving kitchens, baths, heating, and air-conditioning (AC).

4. Feature low-cost tenant attractions. For example, put in a roof garden with comfortable seating when your property has good, or even nearly good, views of the local area.

5. Install energy-efficient heating and AC units. Make your building "green"—environmentally friendly. Try to have each tenant pay his or her heating, water, and AC bills. You'll save bundles on expenses and your profits will soar.

6. Look for easy city or state funding. There are many local programs that will lend you rehab money at extremely low rates. Some even offer 0% interest when your properties serve low-income families.

7. Expect a fast sale if or when you sell your rehabbed property. In today's hot real estate market, brokers report that many properties are selling in one-third the time it took just a year or so ago!

8. Remember that condos are selling at breakneck speed and sky-rocketing prices these days. So be prepared for fast action. This means that you'll be better off pricing your condo property (if that's what you're dealing in) at overmarket levels and then reducing—if needed. Don't underprice because you may regret for years "giving away" a hot property that could have sold for thousands more! Never let yourself be a victim of bottom-fishers who go around making lowball offers in the hope that in ill-informed person will accept their woefully low price!

Transitional neighborhoods can be *your* future source of real estate wealth. So keep an attentive eye on any opportunities that may develop in your area. Wise choices can put you in the millionaire class sooner than you think!

TO GET STARTED FASTER IN MULTIFAMILY UNITS, WITH LESS FEAR, USE SECTION 8 OPPORTUNITIES

Many readers call me saying, "I'd love to get started in multifamily income real estate but I'm scared. What can I do to overcome my fears?" The answer is simple:

1. Contact your local housing authority and ask if they need Section 8 housing (so named after a government program that provides government-subsidized low-income housing) in your area. They probably will. (You'll find the housing authority listed in the "Government" section of your telephone book.)

2. Buy low-cost multifamily income property in areas in which you can afford the purchase and for which Section 8 housing is needed. Be sure the property meets the basic requirements for this type of housing with respect to room areas, number of bathrooms, bedrooms, and other standards.

3. Offer your property to Section 8 tenants. In many areas there are long waiting lists of tenants seeking this type of housing. So your rental problems will be solved quickly and easily. Further, there are other important advantages for you, as shown below.

Section 8 Tenants Will Give You Steady Rental Income

Section 8 of the federal government housing program pays you a portion, or all, of the rent for homeless or low-income families renting apartments as homes. In the New York City area, for example, the Emergency Assistance Rehousing Program (EARP) not only pays you the Section 8 rent for homeless families, it also pays you a one-time rent bonus as the property owner after the family moves in. This bonus, at the time of this writing, is:

FAMILY SIZE

Number of People	One-time Bonus
2	$2,000
3	3,000
4	4,500
5	6,000

Number of People	One-time Bonus
6	7,000
7	9,000
8	10,000

$1,000 for each additional family member

To make the program more attractive to you as a building owner, the city has added Section 8 subsidies, permitting rent payments up to the fair-market rates. Maximum rental fees at the time of this writing were:

FAIR-MARKET RENTS

Studio	$845
1 bedroom	940
2 bedrooms	1,069
3 bedrooms	1,348
4 bedrooms	1,515
5 bedrooms	1,753
6 bedrooms	1,992

Since rents rarely decline, you can expect these subsidies to rise as time passes. Thus, you have a bright future with Section 8 housing.

Other features of Section 8 rent subsidies are:

- The rent subsidy does not include the gas and electric for the apartment. The tenant pays these charges.

- Your bonus is paid in a single payment once the tenant is approved and signs a lease with you, the building owner.

- Many areas have waiting lists of Section 8 tenants. So you can rent your apartment as soon as it becomes available.

- You choose the tenant from a pool of eligible homeless families approved for Section 8 vouchers. You are *not* forced to accept a tenant you disapprove having in your building.

- Inner-city areas, where buildings may be cheaper, are often popular for Section 8 tenants. Hence, you have the double advantage of lower priced properties and the availability of Section 8 tenants.

COLLECT CASH FROM THIN AIR

Mel T. had a common BWB problem—no cash. He tried all sorts of lenders but his poor credit history prevented him from getting the loan he needed. Reading his local large-city newspaper, he saw several ads for no-cash-down buildings. Since one of the buildings was in his neighborhood, Mel decided to check it out. To his amazement, this sturdy, if old, building:

- Was 100% rented
- Contained 150 apartments
- Had $45,000 in rent security on deposit
- Was available for *no cash*
- Could be had by just signing a few papers
- Did *not* require a credit check

After checking out the building, Mel went home almost reeling with joy. Here was a gold mine of cash (the rent security account would put $45,000 into *his* bank in his security-account name—more money than he ever had in his life before). Yet he felt full of fear. Questions ran through his mind:

- What if something went wrong with the building?
- Suppose all the tenants moved out?
- Would the taxes go up?
- Could the tenants stop paying rent?

STOP WORRYING AND START ACTING

Mel called me at my office, full of joy and fear. The rent security, which would become his as soon as he took over the building, attracted him like a magnet. But the imagined problems repelled him. "Ty, I don't know what to do," Mel moaned over the phone. "I'm so scared I think I'll pass out."

"Mel," I said, "stop worrying and start acting! Worrying won't get you anywhere—taking action will put *big* money into your empty pockets!"

Then I analyzed the building and outlined the choices open to him. Here's what I told Mel:

1. With 150 apartments at an average rental of $400 per month, the monthly income would be $60,000; the annual income $720,000.

2. The $45,000 rent security could—in some states—be used as a compensating balance for a loan of five times that amount, or $225,000, provided Mel paid his tenants interest on their rent security (a legal requirement in some states). And—if he was lucky—Mel might be able to borrow as much as 10 times $45,000 from a "hungry" bank!

3. He could get a $720,000-per-year income and $45,000 cash without a credit investigation. And, stretching a point a bit, I told Mel that this was probably the *only* way he could get the money without having his credit checked.

Now, regarding Mel's worry about the building, this is what I told him—and these facts apply to most multiple-family residential buildings:

1. Every building has something "wrong" with it. But in older buildings the "wrongness" was usually corrected long ago. So really very, very little can go wrong with such a building!

2. Few buildings are ever vacated 100% by their tenants if the buildings are well kept, warmly heated, safe, and repaired when necessary. It is usually easy to maintain the 80% occupancy that is needed to break even (that is, pay all expenses in such a building).

3. Real estate taxes almost always go up. To take care of this, you just put a clause in each lease, allowing you to raise the rents when the taxes go up a certain amount.

4. Tenants *can* stop paying rent. But they won't—if you keep a clean, neat, warm, safe building, no matter how old the building may be.

I must have convinced Mel (and I hope you) because the next day he called a lawyer and took the action he should have taken—namely, the signing of the agreement to buy the building.

Within a month Mel had full title to the building and—for the first time in his life—$45,000 in his bank account. Using this as a base of his real estate empire, Mel soon expanded to a million-dollar real estate empire. You can do the same, provided you:

- Are willing to work hard
- Are ready to search out no-cash deals
- Get good legal advice
- Keep expanding your ownership
- Raise the rents when necessary
- Take good care of your buildings
- Forget your fear of the unknown

USE OPM TO TAKE OVER PROPERTY

You may not like the kinds of buildings you can get on zero cash. Or there may not be any buildings available in your area. So, if you still want to go into rental property, you'll have to put up some cash to take over one or more buildings. And if you don't have this cash, you'll have to use OPM—other people's money.

In rental real estate OPM can take several forms, such as:

1. A purchase-money (PM) mortgage from the property seller.

2. A personal loan or credit-card advance for the down payment.

3. A business loan for the down payment.

4. Mortgaging out with 100%, or better, financing—also called a windfall.

Let's take a look at each form of OPM to see how you can use it to build your real estate empire.

GET THE SELLER TO HELP YOU BUY

Many sellers of real estate are anxious to sell their property. Why? For hundreds of reasons, including:

- They're fed up with tenant complaints

- They don't want to run property they inherited from a deceased relative

- They're too old to stay in real estate

- They want to move south, west, north, east, up, down

- They want to get out of real estate and go into the stock market, the hotel business, or some other business

When you find a seller who wants out, you're in an ideal position to get the seller to *help you* buy his or her property. How?

By having the seller give you a purchase-money (PM) mortgage— that is, the seller lends you the cash you need to buy the property.

Let's see how you can use this method right in your own city or town.

Build Wealth with No Cash

Let's say you find a 10-year-old 50-family building that's for sale for $750,000, with a $150,000 cash down payment. The seller is the estate of the former owner of the building. After seeing an ad for the building in the newspaper, you call the attorney representing the estate. You tell him of your interest in the building and he takes you on a tour of it.

You like what you see and ask for the figures on the building. Here's what they show:

Annual income		$170,000
Annual expenses	30,000	
First mortgage payments	50,000	
($600,000 for 30 years)		
Real estate taxes, fees, etc.	28,000	
Total annual expenses		108,000
Annual cash flow		62,000

"I don't have $150,000 cash," you tell the attorney. "But I'd be glad to take the building off your hands if you'll give me a five-year PM mortgage."

"We wouldn't let this building go for no cash," he snorts. "It's too valuable a piece of property."

"It's valuable," you reply. "But here's my business card, just in case you change your mind. I hope to hear from you soon."

Now here's what you're figuring. The building statement shows an annual cash flow of $62,000—say $60,000 for talking purposes. You plan to pay off the $150,000 PM mortgage in five years and will offer the seller 10% interest. This means your PM mortgage payment will run about $39,000 per year, leaving you $23,000 positive cash flow per year for taking over a beautiful piece of income property.

Nothing happens for five weeks and you start to feel depressed. Then, late one evening, the phone rings. It's the attorney. "We're ready to talk about a no-cash deal—if you're still interested," he says.

Your heart jumps because you know that you have him where you want him. "I'm busy the rest of the week," you tell him. "I'll call you next week to make an appointment." (You need the time to contact your attorney and to make plans for working out the shrewdest deal possible.)

A month later you own the building—without putting up a dime. You had to pay a slightly higher interest rate—11%—than you expected. But you're still doing well. And since you expect to raise the rents soon, your cash flow will increase to a level where it is more than your higher interest cost.

MAKE MILLIONS IN THREE YEARS ON ZERO CASH

Assuming that you're willing to wheel and deal the way we just described, here's how *you* can make millions in real estate in three years, starting with zero cash. I'll give you this well-proven, nearly foolproof method in eight easy steps.

1. Pick the area in which you want to operate (large cities are usually best).

2. Locate your first building, as previously detailed.

3. Buy the building using zero cash.

4. Give yourself two months to get the building in good working order.

5. Locate a second suitable no-cash building.

6. Use your first building as an asset, which, in your opinion, reflects the increase in value of the building resulting from your present and planned improvement of the condition and income of the

building, and the effect of inflation. Thus, the value of your building could, in your opinion, rise 5% to 10% in three months.

7. Take over the second building with no cash down.

8. Repeat this process until you have made your millions.

Now what's the key secret to this Million-Dollar Method (MDM)? The
key secret is this:

**Using MDM, you raise your assets from a small amount to a large
amount without putting up any money of your own.**

THE MDM AT WORK FOR YOU

Let's see how the MDM might work for you, starting with the building
you considered earlier. You'll recall that you "paid" $750,000 for the
building. You "pay" the following amount for the apartment buildings
you buy over a three-year period:

Building Number	Price You "Pay"
1	$750,000
2	500,000
3	360,000
4	825,000
5	435,000
6	200,000
7	908,000
8	452,000
9	155,000
10	875,000
Total investment	$5,460,000

Thus, in three years you buy 10 buildings, "paying" almost $5.5 mil-
lion for them. Yet, if you pick the buildings right, you won't have to put
a penny down on these buildings. Now let's see what happened to your
net worth in this time:

Your real estate net worth at start	=	$0 (we've assumed this)
Investment in holdings at end	=	5,460,000

Appreciated value of holdings	=	6,000,000
Equity increase of holdings—what you paid off on mortgages	=	400,000
Spendable income from holdings during three years	=	300,000

So, your net worth rose as follows during the three years:

Spendable income	=	$300,000
Equity increase	=	400,000
Property value increase	=	540,000
Total net worth increase	=	$1,240,000

You have thus made yourself $1.2 million in three years and own property worth $6 million—all on borrowed money! Let's take a closer look at each part of your new fortune.

KNOW WHAT MAKES YOUR FORTUNE

You are now about to learn the inside facts on making your fortune in real estate without putting up a penny of your own. Please read the following words carefully—for *your* sake—not mine. Your Million-Dollar Method made you a multimillionaire in three years by giving you:

- *Spendable income* of $300,000 from the rents you collected from tenants. This spendable income is money in fist (MIF) because it is what you have left after you pay all bills—such as repairs, taxes, light, heat, and mortgages.

- *Equity increase* is the amount of the mortgages you have paid off during the three years. Were you to turn around and sell all the buildings at exactly the *same* price as you "paid" for them, you would walk away with $400,000 cash in hand. And this equity increase has *all* been paid for by the loyal tenants of your buildings in their monthly rent payments to you!

- *Property value increases* of $540,000 result from steady appreciation of property prices throughout the world. The property value increase is the amount of profit you would earn if you sold your buildings at the end of three years of holding them.

So you see, you *can* make millions using borrowed money. All you need to do is put the MDM into action today!

BEWARE OF WEALTH-BUILDING PROBLEMS

When you use the MDM, however, you are almost certain to run into problems. Why? Because when you get income-producing property with no money down, you are usually dealing with buildings that:

- Are in changing areas

- Have tenants who often move

- May have serious maintenance needs

So don't say I didn't tell you! But let me also say this about the MDM:

Everyone who has ever built a million-dollar fortune in real estate says that the results are worth all the effort and problems!

So resolve *today* that you *will* consider using the MDM to build your real estate fortune. If you do take the big leap, I'm sure you'll be happy. And even if you don't take the leap, you'll still be happy because you've learned something. But I can also tell you this:

Not taking the leap will probably make you less happy than taking it!

HOW TO GIVE OLDER RENTAL UNITS
A QUICK NEW LIFE

You can often take over older multifamily residential units (also called apartment houses, garden apartments, two-, three-, fourplexes, etc.) for little or zero cash down. But what do you do with these older units today to make them rentable?

One good answer is *wire them*! "And what do you mean by wiring them?" you ask. The answer is simple. You install wires for today's infor-mation age for:

- Cable television

- Fax machines

- Satellite television

- High-speed Internet access

- Telephones of various types

- Computers—both desktop and portable

- Entertainment systems

- High-speed data transmission

- Digital telecommunication services

We live in a wired world today. Hardly any older buildings can handle the new technologies that many tenants want. Provide the wiring for easy access and your building will fill up faster than you'd ever imagine. And the higher rents you can charge will quickly pay for the cost of the additional wiring.

Conceal the new wiring behind baseboards, attractive wiring enclosures, ceiling moldings, or in mail chutes, elevator shafts, trash tunnels and shafts, or any other unused space and your information-hungry tenants will love you! Why? Because they can say good-bye to a tangle of wires giving the spaghetti-like existence common in many information-unready apartments today.

With more people working at home today, you can get quicker rentals if you provide:

- Fiber-optic lines for faster communications

- Coaxial cables for TV access

- High-speed copper wiring for a variety of devices

- Internet access at high speed via coaxial cables

- Digital telecommunications services

- Wireless Internet service

How can you pay for installing such information-ready wiring? You can take these easy steps:

1. Contact communications companies.

2. Offer your roof area to firms needing it.

3. Provide space for satellite dishes, microwave antennas, and other communication devices used by these firms.

4. Work out an annual rental fee with each firm, requiring three months' advance rental. Some rental fees run $18,000 a year and up!

5. Use the funds from your roof rental to pay for the internal wiring in your building. Or work a swap deal to have the communications firm install the wiring in place of paying rent for several months for your roof area they use.

6. Figure your costs for data transmission, video and voice wiring as running between $2,000 and $7,000 per apartment, depending on how the wires have to be run, how many outlets you install in each apartment, and what method you use to conceal the wiring. All work will normally be done by outside contractors.

7. Plan your wiring so it provides the services your tenants seek and need. Be certain your wiring is reliable, that the outlets you furnish are easily reached in each apartment, that you provide lots of bandwidth, and that new developments in information services can be easily handled.

Using these methods, you can easily convert older, run-down properties to desirable state-of-the-art rentals. You'll have a tenant waiting list for your buildings in no time at all! Try it and see for yourself.

BUILD YOUR REAL ESTATE RICHES IN CANADA, TOO

People call again and again saying, "I'm a Canadian and I want to earn money in Canadian real estate. Do your methods really work in Canada?"

And my answer is always "They sure do!" For example, here's a real-life Canadian multifamily building income and expense statement sent to me by a Canadian reader. All the numbers are in Canadian dollars. Look them over and see how you can prosper in real estate—in Canada! (I've rounded the numbers to make the deal look less favorable.)

INCOME AND EXPENSE STATEMENT FOR CANADIAN MULTIFAMILY PROPERTY

16-Unit Apartment Building

Asking price	=	C$179,000
Annual income	=	C$72,000
Annual expenses	=	C$34,000
Net annual income = annual income − annual expenses	=	C$38,000
Down payment	=	C$36,000
First mortgage @ 6% for 30 years on $143,000	=	C$858/mo. or C$10,300 per year
Second mortgage for down payment @ 10% for 5 years on $36,000	=	C$765/mo. or C$9,180 per year
Total annual mortgage payments	=	C$10,300 + C$9,180 = C$19,480
Annual positive cash flow	=	C$38,000 − C$19,480 = C$18,520

Thus, you'll have a monthly income of over C$1,500 while this 16-unit building pays for itself. Your only major challenge, after finding such a property, is to find the down-payment money. Other chapters in this book show you how to do that.

After you pay off your second mortgage loan your income will jump by $9,180 per year! So the answer to the often-asked question is: *Yes, these methods do work in Canada!*

Points to Remember

- Income residential property can easily make you a millionaire.

- The biggest fortunes made by beginners in real estate are in older income buildings.

- There are seven easy, profitable steps to getting started in income property.

- You can build a fortune in both single- and multifamily income units.

- Zero-investment fortune building is easier in income property than in many others.

- OPM—other people's money—works for you in income property.

- Grow rich using the MDM—million-dollar method—in income property.

- The methods given in this chapter also work for BWBs who buy and operate Canadian real estate.

EIGHT

CAPTURE RICHES IN COMMERCIAL AND INDUSTRIAL PROPERTY

The first seven chapters showed you some of the riches you can build in residential real estate and raw land. Now you're ready to see how you can capture riches in commercial and industrial property.

KNOW WHAT COMMERCIAL PROPERTY IS

Commercial property is real estate that is rented, leased, built, or sold for use in commercial or business activities. Commercial property includes:

- Stores
- Factories
- Mobile home parks
- Garages
- Parking lots
- Shopping centers
- Office buildings
- Any other property for business use

Property rented out for factories and manufacturing plants of various types is often called *industrial real estate*. Property that is rented out for stores, theaters, and the like is usually called *commercial real estate*. But in this book we will use the term *commercial* for both types because it is easier to understand.

You can make a big fortune from commercial property—if you know how to acquire and rent this type of property. But you can also lose every penny you have (or borrowed) if you carelessly select and rent commercial property. Let's see how you can make your real estate fortune in profitable commercial rental property.

LEARN THE UNIVERSAL RULE OF RENTALS

Most of the steady income in commercial property is earned from rentals. By steadily buying or building commercial or industrial rental units, you can gradually increase your clear cash money in fist (MIF) rental income from zero to $25,000, or more, per month. Plenty of commercial real estate operators earn an income in this range. But those who do this well know universal rule of commercial real estate:

As an owner of commercial or industrial rental real estate, you are part of your tenant's business. Should his or her business fail, your real estate investment could be in serious trouble.

Knowing this rule, you can keep out of money problems in commercial and industrial real estate. Here's how.

HOW TO MAKE BIG MONEY IN REAL ESTATE

To make big money in commercial and industrial rental real estate, use these seven powerful tips:

1. Pick your tenants with care.

2. Check the credit rating of each prospective tenant.

3. Insist on a three-month security deposit from each tenant.

4. Use a two-year, or longer, lease for each tenant.

5. Don't pay for improvements for the rented quarters—have the tenant pay for all improvements.

6. Refuse to pay for special electric or other power needs of your tenant—this can break you faster than you think.

7. Try to arrange to receive a percentage of the gross income of your tenants when you rent shopping-center and similar commercial property.

Knowing these methods, you are ready to start building your wealth. To start in commercial real estate, you might want to use my Real Estate Riches Method. It has worked well for others and I have high hopes that it will work for you.

PROFITABLE REAL ESTATE RICHES METHODS

To hit it big in commercial real estate:

1. Find zero-cash property.

2. Take over the property.

3. Rent or lease all or part of the property to one or more suitable tenants.

These three steps sound simple. And they are simple—if you know what you're doing. Let's see how you can do things right from the first day you start to build your fortune in commercial real estate.

FIND ZERO-CASH PROPERTY

There are a number of excellent real estate books available that I suggest you study after you finish this book. I've read many of these fine books and learned much from them. But the one drawback I found to all these books is that they assume you have money to start building your real estate empire!

My experience with beginning wealth builders (BWBs) in many countries shows that most BWBs have very little money to start building their real estate empire. That's why I concentrate on zero-cash real estate in this book. Further, you can use the methods I suggest whether you have money, or not!

You *can* find zero-cash real estate. It just:

• Takes you a little longer

• Requires more looking

• Needs more negotiating

While these needs may seem like hard work (and they are), I find that having to work harder:

- Gives you more fun in life
- Makes you more creative
- Improves your wealth-building skills
- Brings you riches sooner

So don't give up before you begin! At least listen to me to learn what kinds of money you can earn from zero-cash commercial real estate. To find zero-cash commercial real estate:

1. Read the real estate ads in several large local newspapers every day and on Sunday.

2. Read the monthly newsletter *International Wealth Success* every month of the year. It lists both zero-cash real estate and capital sources for property that you can buy using OPM, giving you, in effect, zero-cash real estate.

3. List yourself with several real estate brokers who handle the type of commercial property that interests you. Have them call you when a suitable commercial property becomes available.

4. Send for the *free* government, city, and state notices that list auctions of zero-cash and very low cash real estate. An IWS list of these sources is available free to subscribers to *International Wealth Success*.

5. Look for For Sale signs on property in your area. You can often work zero-cash deals with anxious owners who want to get out of their property responsibilities.

6. Watch for notices in your local newspaper of:

- Sheriff's auctions
- Bank disposals of property
- Tax lien sales
- Other low-priced sales

You can often buy such property using borrowed OPM, giving you, in effect, zero-cash property.

7. Get the word around to all your friends and business associates that you're in the market for zero-cash property. Advertise in your local paper, in *IWS,* and similar publications. You may soon have more offers than you can handle.

UPGRADE YOUR ZERO-CASH PROPERTY

Zero-cash commercial real estate will often need repairs, new tenants, and other improvements. Once you start to make such changes, you can raise the rents you charge, thereby improving your income from the property. And since rent controls may not apply to commercial property, you don't have to worry about this aspect of government regulation.

To get the most profit from the improvements to your property that you make or authorize:

1. Try to get your tenants to pay for the improvements. This helps you operate on larger amounts of OPM than just your mortgage.

2. Work with a contractor to have the tenants' work done. Collect a percentage fee on his or her work as your commission for giving the job to him or her. (Be sure your tenant knows of, and approves of, this fee, if your attorney so advises you.)

3. Raise the rent of each tenant for whom you: (a) pay for improvements, (b) supervise or plan the improvements, or (c) work with the contractor on the improvements on a fee or any other basis.

4. Once you have rent increases in effect for one group of tenants, raise the rents for the remaining tenants in the building.

5. Ask for—and get—a percentage of the *gross* income earned by your tenants in the improved quarters, if you don't have such an arrangement now. If you do, then increase the percentage of the gross that you are to receive.

6. Build a reputation as a money-hungry landlord who treats tenants well but expects, and gets, top rents.

GET IN ON THE BIG-MONEY ACTION

I have grossed over $7 million from my various business ventures, so I know what I'm talking about when I suggest that you get in on the big-money action. To do this, you:

> Arrange to take a percentage of the business income of firms or people you serve—that is, get others to work for you while you invest nothing more than the time needed to sign a piece of paper—an agreement that the firms or people pay you part of their gross income.

The sharing in the gross income of a business that rents your building, land, or other real estate is a common practice. The typical percentage you can charge is 2% to 5% of the gross income your tenant earns in the premises he or she rents from you. Let's look at an example of how this might work for you.

Your tenant rents a store from you in a shopping center you own. The tenant pays you $2,000 a month in rent. Your lease agreement with the tenant states that you will receive 3% of the gross sales in *this* store. So, besides the $2,000-a-month rent, you'll receive one of the following amounts each month, depending on how much gross business the tenant does:

Monthly Gross Business (dollars)	Your Share (dollars)
$1,000	$30
5,000	150
10,000	300
25,000	750
50,000	1,500
100,000	3,000
150,000	4,500
200,000	6,000
250,000	7,500

The beauty of this setup for you and your fortune-building work is that:

The harder your tenant works and the larger his or her gross income becomes, the higher the rent payment you receive.

And with your lease agreement based on the tenant's *gross* sales, your income is assured, whether the tenant makes a profit or not! So be sure to have your agreement written by your attorney in the way that I recommend. Why? Because your success is tied in with that of your tenant!

You *can* get a business-share clause in every commercial lease you write—if you offer tenants a good location and adequate facilities. Your commercial property will have these fortune-building features if you follow the profit-laden ideas offered throughout this book. Let's now take a close and careful look at each of the types of commercial properties listed at the start of this chapter.

USE STORES TO BUILD A FAST FORTUNE

Stores can be large or small, grouped or single, one story or multistory. Important aspects to keep in mind are:

- *Profit potentials*: Get a percentage of the gross *plus* a profitable monthly rental for each store. Try to get store complexes—that is, two or more stores per location (sometimes called shopping strips). Use long leases—5, 10, 20 or more years—where you have a tenant with a long history of profitable business. Limit new firms to short leases—1, 2, or 3 years at the most. Make your tenants pay for all improvements; collect commissions on these whenever you can.

- *Risk factors:* Never rent to new, untried businesses if you can get experienced tenants. Be careful of single stores—you can go broke fast when a single store is vacant. Try to get yourself a shopping center sooner than later—if stores are your way of building great wealth fast. When you're low on cash, use the syndicate method (covered in chapter 11) to raise money to buy, build, or improve a shopping center.

TRY FACTORIES FOR A STEADY INCOME

Factories and industrial plants can give you steady rental income. And when you get tired of a steady income (as some people do), you can almost always arrange to sell your factory to the company that is renting it from you, or to another firm needing industrial space!

- *Profit potentials:* Try to rent only to proven firms; demand the right to see and evaluate the financial statements for the three years before the year the firm applies for space in your premises. Whenever possible, get a lease that gives you a percentage of the gross plus a fixed monthly or annual rental. Sign a short lease (one or two years) the first time with a new tenant; sign a longer lease *after* he or she proves his or her reliability.

- *Risk factors:* Watch for signs of business troubles, such as slow payment of rent, checks that bounce, or bad debts with other firms. Be tough and firm in all rent problems. Move in fast when you spot signs of money troubles. Charge your tenants for every improvement request. Have your tenants pay for the water, electricity, gas, oil, heat, and other utilities they use.

GET IN ON THE AUTO BOOM

One of the differences between capitalistic and socialistic countries is the automobile. (We have multimillions; the socialists have only multi-thousands.) Though you may hate the auto (I love my Caddie), the car, truck, and motorbike can make you a fortune. How? By the rent their owners pay you for the garages you own.

Your garages can be of two main types: active or inactive. In an *active* garage, you have a staff to:

- Pick up and deliver cars

- Wash and polish cars

- Do routine auto maintenance

- Store cars for extended periods

- Sell gas, oil, parts, and accessories

Thus, in an active garage you get income from two sources: storage and service.

In an *inactive* garage you obtain income from only one source: storage. You may have a small staff to park and fetch cars, but that's all. The inactive garage can be a real money machine if it's located downtown in a large city—New York, Chicago, Detroit, Dallas, Los Angeles, San Francisco. But the downtown garages are more expensive to buy than suburban garages on the outskirts of a city.

Suburban garages tend to have a steady, predictable income because people keep their cars in them for years. Your downtown garage, in contrast, can have a highly cyclical income. Thus, you'll make a bundle on theater matinee days if you're in the theater district. The same will be true for you on big shopping days.

One of the huge payoffs in garages can come 10, 20, or 30 years after you buy the garage. Land values can zoom in your area and the land on which your garage sits can be worth many times what you paid for the garage. You sell out for a huge gain—after having had years of profitable income from your garage.

- *Profit potentials:* Charge high rent for your garage space. Demand payment in advance for monthly and weekly rentals. Give *good* service to your customers. Know what your competition is charging and reduce your rates below those of your competitors when you begin to lose tenants. Keep good income and expense records.

- *Risk factors:* Set up fire safety standards for your garages so you don't have any claims that can skyrocket your insurance payments. Be careful to prohibit storage of fuel, oily rags, and other flammable materials in any containers other than those approved by fire underwriters and local fire regulations. When your garage personnel deliver and pick up cars as part of your service, be certain that your drivers are properly licensed, insured, and bonded.

BUILD A PATCH OF LAND INTO WEALTH

Parking lots are seldom more than a patch of land in a place where people want to park their cars. Add a little blacktop and a security guard's shack and you're in business. In some areas where land is really scarce—such as downtown Washington, D.C.—you may want to install simple, low-cost hydraulic lifts so you can park two cars in the space usually occupied by one. This allows you to double your income from the same patch of land.

To me, the parking lot is the simplest of all businesses. Your only fixed expenses are:

- Land taxes

- Attendant's salary

- Electricity (in some cases)

And if you want to cut out the attendant's salary, you can install parking meters in your lot. Then you can have a part-time checker who looks into your lot once or twice a day. He or she can also empty the parking meters once every third day. Your part-timer's salary will be much lower than that of a full-time attendant.

- *Profit potentials:* Parking lot profits come from parking *activity*—and the more cars you park, the higher your profits because your land doesn't cost you any more when it has 100 cars on it than when it has one car on it. Treat parked cars with care and you'll have plenty of repeat business. Use smart rates—high hourly charges for busy times, lower charges for slack periods and for overnight parking.

- *Risk factors:* Since your parking lot is a *cash* business, take steps to carefully control the renting of space and the collection of money for the rental. Be certain that your attendants (if you use them) are safe drivers—damaged cars can waste your time and money. Try to buy parking lot land that will have future "higher" use—such as for a building site. Then you can have the potential of a high capital gain on the sale of your land, after you've made good parking lot profits for years.

GET IN ON THE OFFICE BUILDING BOOM

Businesses everywhere—including your own business—need more and more office space. And you can get in on this booming demand for office space if you know how.

To build or buy your first office building using your own money is almost unheard of these days. Instead, you use OPM. You can get OPM for commercial real estate in various ways, such as:

- Borrowing from banks

- Forming a real estate syndicate

- Using a limited partnership

- Making a public stock offering

- Forming a REIT—real estate investment trust

You can get full information on each of these methods from IWS Inc., P.O. Box 186, Merrick, NY 11566, as follows:

Borrowing: Business Capital Sources, book, $15; also *2,500 Active Real Estate Lenders*, book, $25.

Real estate syndicates: Real Estate Fortune Builders Success Kit, course, $99.50.

Limited partnerships: Starting Millionaire Success Kit, course, $99.50.

Public stock offering: Financial Broker-Finder-Business Broker-Consultant Success Kit, course, $99.50.

Forming a REIT: How to Build Your Real Estate Fortune Today in a Real Estate Investment Trust Kit, course, $100.00.

Unusual financing methods: Fast Financing of Your Real Estate Fortune Success Kit, course, $99.50, and the *Low Cost Real Estate Loan Getters Success Kit*, course, $100.

Using any of the above methods, you can more easily get the money you need for a new or existing office building. And the beauty of an office building is that with carefully selected tenants, you:

- Are paid your rents on time

- Have few tenant complaints

- Can fax or e-mail your monthly rent bill to them, saving postage

- Can sign long-term leases

- Are able to operate with absentee-management

- Get good tax deductions

Lenders in general like to make loans on well-built office buildings because:

- Their income is dependable

- There are few loan defaults

- The interest rate provides a good profit

- *Profit potentials:* Charge high rents for your office space. Keep your building in top-notch condition (regular cleaning, group replacement of lighting bulbs) at all times. Have your tenants pay for all improvements (such as adding walls, cubicles, dividers) they make in their space. Insist on liberal rent security payments. Invest these payments to your own advantage, using all the legal avenues open to you.

- *Risk factors:* Avoid long leases (more than a year) with new firms. Never pay for improvements after a tenant has signed a lease, unless you agreed to make such improvements to induce the tenant to sign the lease.

USE A PURCHASE MONEY MORTGAGE TO BUY REAL ESTATE

A *purchase money mortgage* is a loan a seller makes to you to help you buy a commercial property with little or no money down. Thus, a seller wants $300,000 for a commercial property with 20% (or $60,000) down. But being anxious to get rid of the property, the seller might accept a promissory note from you for $60,000 over five years, allowing you to buy the commercial property for zero down. Your promissory note then becomes the purchase money mortgage. For more details on how this can work, let's look at a real-life example.

A BWB wants to buy a 10-unit commercial office building property. But this BWB has poor credit (a FICO score of 450), has a low-paying job which started two months ago, and no previous real estate experience. But, this BWB has a burning desire to own income property and:

- Has learned as much as he can about commercial real estate by studying good books and courses

- Spoke to the seller telling her how much he wants to get started in commercial income real estate

- Prepared a short two-page statement for the seller showing how he'll take care of the property once he owns it

- Suspects the seller is "motivated"—wants to sell quickly

- Is frank about his financial condition, telling the seller he has little cash but lots of drive and ambition

- Suggests to the seller that he give her a purchase money mortgage for the down payment, and that he be allowed to assume the first mortgage

- "Works all numbers" of the property: price: $300,000; income = $62,000 per year; expenses = $18,000 per year; down payment = $60,000 (20%); existing mortgage on the property = $240,000. Buyer will take a $60,000 purchase money mortgage for five years at 12% interest, meaning that purchase money payments will be $1,335 per month or $16,020 per year. His first mortgage payments on the $240,000, 8%, 25-year first will be $1,853 per month, or $22,234 per year

- Figures his profit. Annual expenses = $18,000 + $16,020 PM + $22,234 first mortgage = $56,254. Profit = $62,000 − $56,254 = $5,746 per year/$478.83 per month

While $478.83 per month profit may not seem like much, remember that you're starting out in commercial real estate with essentially no cash investment of your own. And the asset you're buying—the multiunit office building—is paying for itself while giving you a positive cash flow. To get the purchase money you want or need:

1. Prepare a typed proposal showing a seller how he or she will benefit from selling to you using a PM. Include tax savings!

2. Feature (a) good care of the building; (b) freedom from future mortgage payments; (c) monthly income at a high interest rate (12%) from the PM; rent increases over time.

3. Give your personal guarantee that you will pay off the PM exactly on time and in full because you seek success.

4. Be convincing and sell strongly! *It will pay off!*

CAPITALIZE YOUR WAY TO
COMMERCIAL-PROPERTY WEALTH

You *can* get richer quicker in commercial real estate. But to build your wealth faster, you have to use your head and your ingenuity. Here are a few things you can use right now:

1. Locate OPM sources you can tap when you find the right deal. Use the books *Business Capital Sources* and *2,500 Active Real Estate Lenders* and the *Low Cost Real Estate Loan Getters Success Kit* mentioned earlier.

2. Look for, and advertise for, commercial property of the type you seek. You can advertise free of charge in the monthly newsletter *International Wealth Success*, if you are a one-year, or longer, subscriber.

3. Choose the property you want to buy, after you look at several. Note that you may not need a large down payment for your commercial property—some of these properties are turned over for as little as $1 down payment!

4. Borrow the money you need for the down payment. Use the IWS *Low Cost Real Estate Loan Getters Success Kit* as a source of borrowing ideas.

5. Take over the property. On the usual office building you will earn a return of 8% to 9% on your investment—if you operate the building in the conventional, conservative way. But if you really swing in your management, as we've already discussed, you can earn as much as 20% on your investment. Since you're investing borrowed money, your return is really much higher. (Shopping centers typically earn 6% to 8% on the investment.)

One of the fastest ways to capitalize your way to commercial property wealth is by using the *inflation factor* in your property appraisals. Here's how.

BUILD THE WORTH OF YOUR HOLDINGS

Let's say you take over a $200,000 office building for $20,000 down. You borrow the down payment by taking out a $25,000 36-month second-mortgage property loan. Three days after you apply for your loan, you have $25,000 in the form of a $25,000 check. You use the extra $5,000 above the down payment for paying the closing costs on the building.

Now you call this first office building "Building A." Two months after you buy Building A, you discover a second attractive and profitable office structure, Building B. The price of this building is $215,000. You buy Building B, but you get this second building easier and faster. Here's how.

You go out in front of Building A for which you "paid" $200,000 and study its appearance. "Gee," you say to yourself, "in the last two months the value of this building has risen, in *my* opinion, from $200,000 to $225,000—particularly when you consider the major impact of inflation on real estate values, and the improvements I've made and plan to make." So when you apply for the loan you need for the down payment, you list the value of Building A as:

Estimated replacement price	**$225,000**
Owed (price – down payment)	**180,000**
Your "equity"	**$45,000**

So your net worth has risen by $45,000, based on your own appraisal of the building. With such a net worth it is easy for you to borrow the $25,000 down payment you need for Building B.

Now let me make one very important point about building the worth of your holdings:

It is perfectly legal for you to use *your* own estimated valuation of your property on your financial statement because this valuation is your opinion. And—in this world—a man or woman is still entitled to his or her opinion.

The inflation factor approach takes into consideration two items in your real estate life:

1. Inflation is constantly increasing the value of your real estate.

2. Inflation is constantly increasing the value of the improvements you make in your real estate.

Note that you can make all kinds of improvements in your real estate. Some of these improvements will cost you cold, hard cash. Other improvements will be what I call the "ghost" type, such as:

- Raising the rent of the tenants
- Reducing maintenance expenses
- Getting a better grade of tenants

These, and similar, improvements cost you little or no money. Yet by making these improvements, you increase the income from your property. And whenever you raise the income of a piece of real estate, you automatically raise its value. The higher the value of a property, the greater *your* borrowing power on the property!

CONTINUE BUILDING YOUR PROPERTY VALUES

Using the estimated—or appraised-value—approach for your improved commercial properties, you can quickly build your real estate holdings. Thus, Chris T. took over $1.2 million worth of buildings in 11 months. Yet he started with zero cash! But he worked hard to improve the condition and income of each of his commercial properties so that his borrowing power rose every time he took over a building. A score sheet Chris prepared for his small low-cost buildings looked like this:

Building	Month Acquired	Price	Borrowed Down Payment
A	1	$175,000	$20,000
B	3	325,000	35,000
C	6	260,000	22,000
D	8	140,000	15,000
E	11	300,000	32,000
	Total	$1,200,000	$124,000

Of the $124,000 down payment, Chris didn't put up a dime! He borrowed the first $25,000 using a bank loan. From there on, Chris used each of the buildings as either part, or complete, collateral for the loans, giving him the down payment on the next building.

This method of building wealth is called *capitalizing, leveraging,* or *zero-cash takeovers.* Why? Because you use:

- Borrowed money to start
- Appreciated (increased) values as collateral

- More borrowed money based on your appreciated collateral

- Continuation of the capitalization or leverage using borrowed money (zero cash) and increased property values

SEE THE REAL WORTH OF COMMERCIAL PROPERTY

Let's say that you're interested in shopping centers as a source of real estate income. You and a group of friends build a $20-million center, using borrowed money to pay for the land, construction, and all other expenses, including you and your friends' salaries.

Do you know what your shopping center is worth the day you finish it—and before you have one tenant? Your $20-million shopping center is now a product, just like a bar of soap, a refrigerator, a car, or a computer. Instead, you want to hold onto it and collect nice fat rent checks every month. So what do you do? You go out and get 100%, or better, long-term—20, 30, or 40 years—financing. Let's see how this works.

GET 100% FINANCING FOR YOUR COMMERCIAL DEALS

Your shopping center (or any other commercial development) cost you—we'll say—$20 million to put up. You have it appraised on completion and the value put on it is $30 million.

Depending on money conditions at the time you apply for your long-term mortgage, you can get 80% of the appraised value, or $24 million, in a tight-money market, or 90%, or $27 million in a loose—or easy-money—market.

Figuring 10% for closing fees, points, and other costs, you walk away with either $2 million or $5 million for your "trouble" in building the shopping center. Since you'll probably have other people in on the deal with you, your personal take will be somewhat lower.

And by keeping title to the shopping center, you will probably be able to net about 9% on your investment from the center. This should give you a cash income of at least $100,000 a year. And for the first ten years or so, your cash income will probably be completely—or nearly completely—tax free because of the depreciation tax shelter you get on the buildings. So you see, it is possible to get full 100% financing of your commercial real estate deals.

In this deal, if you received a $24-million long-term mortgage, you'd be operating with 120% financing. With a $27-million long-term mortgage, you'd have 135% financing. And note this:

Any money you get above what you need for long-term financing may be completely tax free to you because it is a loan, and the proceeds of a loan are usually tax free.

For a full discussion of a variety of 100% financing methods, be sure to see my book *How to Borrow Your Way to Real Estate Riches*.

WHY COMMERCIAL REAL ESTATE RISES IN VALUE

If you're wondering why a shopping center costing you $20 million to build is worth $30 million, or more, on completion, just glance at the following facts:

> *Building material costs* increase an average of 1% per month
> *Land costs* may increase an average of 15% a year
> *Labor costs* may increase an average of 10% a year

So while you're building your shopping center, its value is rising because the prices of the items you bought for the center (materials, land, labor) are rising! This is true of nearly all real estate.

CAPTURE COMMERCIAL-PROPERTY RICHES

There are billions to be made from commercial and rental property deals of all kinds. Here are a few examples of how other people, just like yourself, made *big* money in commercial property, starting with little or no cash and operating on borrowed money.

Fourplexes Build Wealth

Mary T. borrowed $200 from her uncle to take over a four-store minimall (which had been taken over by the city for nonpayment of taxes) in a depressed neighborhood for no cash down. Within three months she owned *every* fourplex store on both sides of the street—a total of 10. Yet she didn't have to put a cent of her own down for one building. Sticking to fourplexes because she likes their easy renting and care, Mary T. now has a total of 80, giving her 320 store rental units. At an average monthly rental of $100, Mary T.'s income is $32,000 per month, or $384,000 a year, before expenses. Since her expenses are low, Mary is making a fast bundle without having put up a penny.

Garages Are Moneymakers

Tim K. is an auto mechanic who tired of working for hourly wages while his boss grew rich from Tim's labors. So Tim decided to become a boss himself. But after looking at the risks and rewards in running a gas station and repair shop, Tim decided he wanted something different. "What I wanted—and still want—is a steady, stable, predictable income," Tim says.

Checking around, he decided that auto garages would give him the kind of income he sought and needed. But Tim's problem was—like that of so many other beginning wealth builders (BWBs)—how to get the money to buy his first garage. When Tim called me about his money problems, I told him that he should go about raising the money he needed in two ways:

1. Seek out lenders everywhere.

2. Try to get one or two zero-cash garages.

Now why did I recommend these *two* approaches? Because they would give Tim maximum leverage in finding, and taking over, the garages he needed. Tim also studied current issues of *Business Capital Sources, International Wealth Success,* and *Money Watch Bulletin,* all of which give the names of hundreds of lenders. And, as a trial, Tim applied for a $10,000 loan from several lenders. *All* approved his application in a day!

But the day Tim's loan applications were approved, a better event occurred. Tim was offered a zero-cash garage. Here's how this happened.

Tim had spread the word that he was looking for a zero-cash garage. When the owner of an old, but moneymaking, garage passed away, the family immediately contacted Tim. The family knew Tim to be honest and dependable. Knowing that he didn't have much money, the family offered Tim the garage:

- For *no cash down*

- With a 20-year payoff time

- In an *as-is* condition

Tim jumped at the chance. In three months he had the garage looking like new and fully rented to its 200-car capacity.

Next Tim invited several local bankers in to see his garage. While showing them through the garage, Tim told the bankers of his interest in buying a string of good garages. "That's a great idea," said one of the bankers. "If you need any help, just give us a ring. We'll be glad to study your deal."

Tim did call this banker when he found the next profitable garage. The banker liked the deal and Tim got a loan for $50,000 for the down payment on the garage. Today Tim has 10 well-maintained garages that give him an income of more than $100,000 a year. "Not bad for an ex-auto mechanic," Tim says proudly as he shows you around his neat garages.

GO WHERE THE MONEY IS

There's big, big money in commercial real estate. And you can easily make some of this big money yours! All it takes is:

- A desire to be rich
- Drive to find what you want
- Careful deals with an eye on profits
- Constant expansion until you reach your income goal

To prove to yourself that you *can* hit commercial real estate big money, just put some of my tips into action. I guarantee you that you won't be sorry you did! Get started today—*now*.

Points to Remember

- As an owner of commercial property, you are part of your tenants' business.
- Pick your commercial tenants with extreme care.
- Insist on rent security deposits from commercial tenants.
- Try to get a share of the gross income from every commercial tenant you have.
- Look for—and find—zero-cash commercial property.
- Use the increased value of your property as collateral for additional loans to buy more commercial real estate.

NINE

HOW TO WHEEL AND DEAL WITH LEVERAGE IN PROPERTIES

A real estate wheeler-dealer is a person who buys, sells, or deals in real estate properties of all kinds. As a wheeler-dealer your main goal is to make money quickly by buying low and selling high. And one nice feature of being a wheeler-dealer is that you *don't* need any type of:

- License
- Permit
- Registration
- Certificate
- Diploma
- College (or even high school) education

Let's see how we can make *you* a highly successful real estate wheeler-dealer in a short time.

WHAT YOU'LL DO AS A WHEELER-DEALER

A wheeler-dealer will do anything *honest* to make money. But in the real estate field, you may, as a wheeler-dealer:

- Buy cheap; sell high
- Operate on 100% to 150% financing

- Never really *own* anything
- Run your office from your head
- Spend more time *not* working than working
- Get rich in a hurry

Let's put you into the easiest money you've ever earned by making you a wheeler-dealer in real estate properties of various kinds.

BUY CHEAPLY, SELL HIGHER

Let's say that you work a deal just like one young wheeler-dealer, Lennie S., worked recently. Here's what he did, and what *you* might also do.

Step 1: Buy 75 acres of raw land for $1 down per acre. (The total cost of the land is $7,500.)

Step 2: Go to your local zoning board and have the land-use category changed from industrial to commercial-residential.

Step 3: Contact a builder and suggest that he consider putting up a combined office-apartment house tower on the land.

Step 4: Send news releases to your local papers telling them about the plans and suggestions.

Step 5: "Talk up" your idea and project wherever you go in your local area.

Step 6: Publicize the availability of your land on the Internet.

If you obtain the same results as Lennie did, you'll sell 50 acres of the land to the builder for $4,000 per acre, for a profit of $192,500. You find your gross profit by subtracting your land cost, $7,500 here, from your land selling price, or $200,000 here. And since you sold only 50 of the 75 acres, you still have 25 acres left. It is hoped that you can also sell these acres at a big profit some time in the future.

When you sell the remaining 25 acres, your profit = selling price − sales costs (which are usually small) − land cost (which is zero because you've already paid in fully for the land). When you sell the remaining land, your profit may be even higher than from the first sale. Why? Because land values will probably have increased and the new construction on the first portion of your property will make the second section more valuable!

KNOW THE BASICS OF WHEELING AND DEALING

As a wheeler-dealer you will repeatedly use several basic concepts:

- Profitable ideas
- Unique approaches
- Carefully planned publicity
- Belief in your ideas
- Patience to wait for the big deal
- Charging high prices for your ideas
- Getting wide publicity on the Internet, if you want to use this method

In the deal previously described, you used a profitable idea (buying the raw land), followed a unique approach (having the zoning changed), carefully planned publicity (news releases to newspapers, personal contact), and believed in your ideas to net yourself a big bundle of profit.

You will, of course, use other approaches and methods when you're wheeling and dealing. But you'll develop these as you gain experience with people in various businesses around the country. You'll find that while your basic activity is real estate, your deals will vary when you work with people and firms having different uses for the land or building you are handling.

BE WELCOME WHEREVER YOU GO

Let's say you are working at a fairly interesting and moderately well paying job. But you want to wheel and deal—particularly in real estate. Suddenly you're given a four-week "vacation" (without pay) from your job. "I really don't know what to do with the time," you say to me during a telephone conversation about your future. "I'd sure like to turn it into some extra income."

"Why don't you come with me on my next business trip for two weeks and I'll show you how to make some extra money as a wheeler-dealer," I reply.

You agree to come along. "I'll show you how to be welcome *wherever* you go," I promise with a laugh. "You'll learn the one specialty that all wheeler-dealers push."

"That's exactly what I've always wanted to know," you say happily.

Wheeler-dealers throughout the world have one specialty that they *all* plug when they're looking for new business. That specialty is: *Finding the money a business or individual needs to complete a specific deal.*

Yes, that's right, as a successful wheeler-dealer you'll be welcome everywhere in this world if you can:

- Find money for businesses or individuals needing money

- Arrange financing for a deal

- Negotiate a loan

- Place a mortgage with a lender

- Pick lenders for a deal

- Process loan applications for a client

Now don't let this list frighten you. You're about to learn how you can have 99% of this work done for you by others at a very low cost and hardly any investment of *your* time or money. Knowing how to have others do most of your work for you will make you a big success because:

The wheeler-dealer who can bring money to a deal is welcome everywhere in this world because every business needs money at some time during its history.

My own personal observation—with which you may or may not agree—is that:

Every small business I've ever been close to can always use some extra cash!

So if you can come up with the needed cash in the form of a loan that you obtain, you'll be doubly welcome by almost *every* business, everywhere! And let me tell you this, good friend: It's a lot easier to do business when you're welcome than when you have to spend a lot of your time and energy selling people your ideas!

KNOW WHERE THE MONEY IS

As a real estate wheeler-dealer, you'll run across deals where you'll want to find money for:

- Property down payments

- Mortgages—first, second, third

- Building and property improvements

- Construction of buildings of all kinds

- Standby-purpose mortgages

- Takeout mortgages

- Wraparound mortgages

Knowing how and where to get this money can get you in on deals you might otherwise lose.

How can you get the knowledge you need to set up loan deals for the clients you get? The best way that I know of is to study and use the IWS *Financial Broker-Finder-Business Broker-Consultant Program*. This hard-hitting program contains eight easy-to-use speed-read books that show you *exactly* how to:

- Set up your own financial-broker business

- Arrange financing deals

- Get the money you need

- Find lenders (thousands of names and addresses are given to you in the program)

- Take a company public to get money that does *not* have to be repaid

This big, but easy-to-understand program should have you wheeling and dealing within a few days after you receive it. The big-money book, *Business Capital Sources for Financial Brokers,* which lists more than 2,000 money sources, is included in the program.

WHO SAYS "ZERO DOWN" FOR
REAL ESTATE DOESN'T WORK?

The ultimate in wheeling and dealing is the zero-down deal. Why?
Because:

> People sometimes say zero down is tough to do—if you can do it
> at all.

Yet we continue to get letters and faxes saying people *are* doing zero-
down real estate deals. Here's a fax that came in not long ago:

> We spoke on the phone recently and I told you your methods
> work! I bought my first property a month ago with an $8 out-of-
> pocket expense. That's right, $8! The $8 was a bank fee for the
> cashier's check for the down payment. When I went to closing
> the owner (seller) wrote me a check that paid me back all I had
> put down, except the $8 cashier's check.
>
> I have just purchased my second property essentially the same
> way. By this time next month I will have closed on four more prop-
> erties where the owner (seller) is holding a second mortgage for
> the down payment. These properties will pay me approximately
> $600 to $800 a month after all expenses. My goal is to own 30
> properties five years from now. But who knows? If I can do one a
> month, I'll have more than 60!

This letter gives you several important tips about zero-down real estate deals, namely:

1. Have the seller take back a second mortgage for your down payment. While the buyer above did have to pay $8 for the cashier's
   check, the charge is so small compared to the price of the property that you could call it a near zero-down deal!

2. Be certain you'll have a positive cash flow from the property after
   you buy it! You don't want a zero-down deal on property you
   can't rent after you own it. So do your checking *before* you buy!

3. Seek as high as possible positive cash flow (PCF) from the property. Thus, the $600 to $800 per month this reader expects will
   bring him either $216,000 per year with $600 per month PCF

and 30 properties, or $288,000 per year with $800 per month PCF and 30 properties. Most folks we know can "get by" on either annual income!

4. Set up goals for yourself for your real estate investing. Have these goals guide you to fulfilling your dreams of building wealth in your own real estate business! Then go out and make your goals your reality—starting *now*!

OPERATE ON 100% FINANCING

Plenty of real estate wheeler-dealers never put up a cent of their own money. Instead, they operate entirely on borrowed money, or 100% financing. To run your business on other people's money, you have to:

- Line up some lenders

- Find one or more good deals

- Take action on a deal

- Bring the money and deal together

Let's see how you might use 100% OPM to put a few deals together.

USE THE REFINANCE ROUTE TO TAKE CASH OUT OF YOUR PROPERTIES

Some of your income property purchases when you're wheeling and dealing may involve complicated negotiations because you have either no cash or very little cash. "Not to worry," as the British say. You can get around these difficulties!

How? You take these simple steps:

1. Get control of the property you want to buy. You must have title to a property before you can use it to build future wealth for yourself via refinancing.

2. Own the property for at least six months; upgrade it and make plans for future improvements you'll make to the property as time goes by. Put all your plans in writing. Arrange them neatly and be certain they're typewritten or printed out from a computer. Show the rent increases you plan to make, based on upgrades to the property.

3. After six months of ownership, prepare a new appraisal of your property. Thus, if you paid $300,000 for the property, you might estimate that its value—after your upgrade and rent increases— might be $380,000.

4. Visit a local lender with your plan and new appraisal in hand. Tell the lender you'd like to refinance the property based on your appraisal of its current value. Ask for the largest loan they're willing to give you on the property.

5. With smart refinancing, you can probably walk away with anywhere from $25,000 to $50,000 cash in hand from this property. Other properties can give you more cash, if they are priced higher. And, if interest rates declined between the time you bought the property and the time you refinance it, your monthly payment may be even smaller than at the start! There's no guarantee of this. But it can happen—and I hope it happens to you!

MAKE OPM WORK FOR YOU

In almost every wheeling and dealing real estate deal you'll ever swing, the biggest part of it is defined by a five-letter word: *money*. Sure, you may have a few temporary problems with items like the title search, escrow account, and utilities approval. But these problems are minor if you have the money needed for the deal.

For instance, let's say that you, like another BWB named Ken T., spot an ad for a factory building for sale in your area. You check out the building and find that it:

- Is available for $25,000 cash down

- Has three good tenants; one unreliable tenant

- Is of sturdy construction

- Might be sold at a profit, or could be held and run at a profit

You have your lenders lined up and ready to advance you the money you need. (You lined up your lenders in advance by using the methods in the IWS *Financial Broker Program*. Briefly, you called on local prospective lenders, told them of your plans to invest in real estate, and asked them if they'd be willing to lend you the money on the *right* deal. Several said yes; a few said no.)

Wheeling and dealing, you offer $18,000 down for the factory. In making this offer you are using Hicks's first rule of wheeling and dealing, namely:

Rule 1

Never offer to pay any asking price for anything. Always try to negotiate a reduced price.

For instance, say that the seller finds your $18,000 offer on the above factory unacceptable. The most he can do is say: "No, I won't sell at that price." If you still want the factory (or any other property for that matter), you can raise your offer.

You do raise your offer for this property—to $20,000. This is still not attractive to the seller. So you go to $22,000. He accepts. You've thus saved yourself $3,000, or more than 10% of the asking down payment.

Contacting your lender friends, you describe the deal to them. They ask for more information in an organized arrangement and give you some forms to fill out. The forms are really a comprehensive loan application that you fill out and have typed up. Three days later *two* lenders call. Both say: "Your application has been approved! Come on over and pick up your money." You decide which lender you'd like to work with, and get your check.

PUT ACTION INTO YOUR PLANS

Three weeks after your loan application is approved, you take over the factory. As you analyzed it earlier, you may be able to either sell the factory quickly, or rent it at a good profit.

To find buyers you publicize the future availability of the factory— starting the day your loan is approved. You get free publicity through your friends, local business and trade associations, the *IWS* newsletter, the Internet, and similar outlets. While you do not receive any firm offers before you take over the factory, you get several interesting "nibbles." One of these, you hope, will pay off in the future. Thus, you've *actionized* your plans.

FOLLOW THROUGH ON YOUR PLANS

You continue to try to sell the factory. Meanwhile you take other actions, namely, you:

- Improve parts of the building

- Raise rents for all tenants

- Try to find the tenant another factory he can rent

So far your wheeling and dealing has been typical of what any other ambitious beginner might do. But suddenly you have an unusual chance. Let's see how you react. Here's what happens.

Your unreliable tenant—a small electronics company—stops paying its rent. You wait two months to see what will happen. Nothing does happen, as far as being paid the rent owed to you. But the owner of the electronics company does tell you that he'd like to sell out his business—cheap. Your ears perk up as soon as you hear the word *cheap* because that's how most wheeler-dealers try to get the items they take over.

You think—for a few hours—about the possibility of taking over the electronics company. While you know almost *nothing* about electronics, you decide that now—today—is the time to start learning the facts of life about electronics. Why? Because you're a wheeler-dealer and you have a feeling that you're on to something that could make you rich!

So you call the owner of the electronics company and tell him: "I'll take the company off your hands for no cash down. Besides the company, I'll take all your debts, including the back rent. This means that you can walk away tomorrow—free and clear!"

"Sounds good," the owner replies. "But I need some 'reserve' money until I find a job or start another company."

"How much do you need?" you ask. "Three to five thousand dollars," he replies. "I'll give you twenty-five hundred, and that's it," you say, again using rule 1. "You have a deal," he says happily.

You hang up and wonder: "Did I do the right thing?" "Yes," you say to yourself, "I did." So you contact your lender friend immediately and tell him about your new deal. "Twenty-five hundred isn't any problem. In fact, you can pick it up right after lunch," he tells you.

KEEP WHEELING AND DEALING

You visit your lender, get your money, and go home to think things over. "I really want to wheel and deal in real estate," you say to yourself. "Electronics isn't my bag." But you're using Hicks's second rule of wheeling and dealing, namely:

Rule 2

Never turn down a good chance outside your main field of interest—if you can make money.

Sure, you want to specialize in real estate. But if you can make money in another field, go right to it.

So you take over the electronics company, using rule 2 and borrowed money. But no sooner do you take over the firm than you learn that the main product is *not* a piece of electronic equipment and computers, or a part of them. Instead, the main product is a book on electronics! And these books are sold mainly overseas—not in the United States.

You take a deep breath and sigh—"Life isn't always as simple as you think it is." But wait, all is *not* lost. You *can* make money with *any* product, if you keep wheeling and dealing.

EXPLORE NEW MARKETS

The wheeler-dealer never gives up. If he or she fails today, he or she shrugs his or her shoulders, gets a good night's sleep, and starts trying all over again tomorrow. Since you're a confirmed wheeler-dealer, even though you're just starting, you decide to find out *why* this electronics firm you bought was going broke.

Two days' work shows you that the former owner:

- Made poor choices of ad outlets

- Delivered his products late

- Didn't send out bills on time

- Never built up a mailing list

- Knew little about product warehousing

Being an ambitious wheeler-dealer, you decide to correct these conditions. But to do so, you have to learn something about export-import! And to think you started out to be a real estate tycoon! You grit your teeth and resolve to learn export-import. In making this resolution you are using the Hicks's third rule of wheeling and dealing, namely:

Rule 3

Never let a lack of know-how stand in your way of making money. Get the know-how you need as fast as you can!

FEED YOUR BRAIN TO FILL YOUR POCKETS

Your decision to be a go-go wheeler-dealer gives you the zip and drive to find good deals and make money from them. This same zip and drive can help you build your know-how to solve practical business problems anywhere.

To learn export-import you buy a set of the IWS *Import-Export Program* for $99.50 and a copy of their big book *How to Prepare and Process Export-Import Documents: A Completely Illustrated Guide,* $25.

With the program and book in your home, you quickly learn how to handle the export of your new products. What's more, you also learn how to:

- Have an overseas business address without paying one cent in rent, by using a mail receiving service

- Sell overseas without having to register your company with any local government

- Store your products in a bonded warehouse overseas at *no* cost to you

- Get overseas loans for your customers so they pay you sooner

- Run ads in overseas publications

- Make mailings at lower cost using the many options open to mailers

- Have money that is mailed to your overseas address sent to you at home for deposit in your bank

- Make money on foreign exchange

- Take many other profit-laden business steps at no expense other than the investment of a little time

While I'd like to tell you how to take all these wheeler-dealer steps, we don't have enough space. Besides, this is a book on real estate, not export-import.

BUILD SALES TO SELL AT A PROFIT

There are really only two kinds of wheeler-dealers in this world today—those who:

1. Take over an ongoing business, improve the income, and then sell the business

2. Start a new business, build it to a profitable level, and then sell the business

You can make *big, big* money either way. But to do so you must keep Hicks's rule 4 in mind at all times, namely:

Rule 4

Know why you're wheeling and dealing in every business deal. Then there's little chance of making a serious mistake. Keep your goal in mind at all times.

When you're acting as a wheeler-dealer who's looking to sell an on-going business you took over, you know that for best results you must:

- Have the business show good profits

- Appeal to the prospective buyer's desire for instant income

- Show a potential for some future growth

To achieve these goals for your newly acquired business, you take several sensible steps:

- Advertise your products

- Get the account books in order (plenty aren't)

- See that all taxes have been paid

- Actively look for new business

- Build up a good work force

- Run the business profitably

- Advertise the business for sale

SELL OUT WHEN YOU'RE READY

You take these steps with your acquired business. Within a few days you're flooded with calls wanting to know more about the business you have for sale. During one of your discussions, a prospect asks: "Do I have to keep the business in the factory?"

Like a flash you realize that you have a profitable deal in your hands. "Yes," you say, "for at least two years." You answer this way because you've decided that any person or firm that you allow to buy your business *must* have a good credit rating, because you'll insist on this being so. This means they'll be reliable tenants. Also, you can keep an eye on the business. You are using the Hicks's fifth rule of wheeling and dealing, namely:

Rule 5

When you sell a business, arrange the deal so you have maximum control over the buyer for as long as possible—or until you get full payment.

Two weeks after you advertise the business for sale (and three months after you "bought" it for zero cash), you sell the business for $325,000. Of this total price you receive $50,000 in cash and promissory notes for $275,000, payable over three years. Thus, in just a few months, you:

- Bought and sold a business

- Received $50,000 in cash with zero investment of your own money

- Have been given notes that will pay you nearly $100,000 a year for three years

- Found a new, reliable tenant

- Have the chance to get your business back if the buyer can't pay off the notes

- Can sell the notes at a discount for fast cash

Two weeks after you sell the business, you receive a $500,000 offer for the factory and the land it sits on. You agree to sell at this price, if the buyer will put $100,000 cash down. But he tries to wheel and deal with you, using his version of rule 1. You combat the buyer with the Hicks's sixth rule, namely:

Rule 6

Never sell real estate, or any other valuable item, for a cash price less than what you seek. As a seller you have what a buyer wants; make him or her pay your price. When you're buying, wheel and deal for the lowest price.

You stick to your guns and eventually the buyer comes up with $100,000 cash. Being a person of your word, you sell to him at the price of $500,000, with $100,000 cash down. You now have the following from the two businesses you've sold, less your cost:

Cash: $150,000 – $22,000 = $128,000
Notes: $675,000 in money owed to you that will be paid off over a period of years

Yet you did all this on OPM—other people's money! Sound impossible? It isn't! The deals worked here are made every day of the week somewhere in this great world of ours. And perhaps *you* can do the same, if you use the rules and tips you've learned thus far in the chapter.

12 SIMPLE TIPS FOR WHEELER-DEALERS

1. Make speedy deal completion your goal in all transactions.

2. Remember that a fast deal can be just as profitable (and often more profitable) than a slow, dragged-out deal.

3. Get good legal and accounting help.

4. Study carefully the tax laws for your business.

5. Find out if, and how, you can shelter any of your income from high taxes.

6. Get yourself some useful and profitable specialized know-how—such as being the *Financial Broker-Finder-Business Broker-Consultant Success Kit* offered by IWS.

7. Use the six rules given in this chapter as guides to faster, easier, and higher profits as a wheeler-dealer.

8. Promote yourself and your business, using free ads whenever you can.

9. Be tough and aggressive in your business—your profits will soar if you demand, and get, your own way.

10. Try to create a *new* profit idea every day of the week. In wheeling and dealing, good ideas often pay your biggest profits.

11. Keep records of your deals. Try to use one notebook instead of many scraps of paper. One book will help you find your ideas at a later date and will clear up your thinking.

12. Push ahead continuously—regardless of how rough things may seem. Though your luck may appear to have run out, it will often improve if you just push ahead one more foot, one more hour, one more day!

THE BEST INVESTMENT ON EARTH

People have gone to the moon—and will eventually go to other planets. Yet, as a sage once said: "The best investment on earth *is* earth." Since I firmly believe this to be so—and have put my money where my computer word processor is (in my own real estate ventures)—I want to convince *you* of this fact.

If you wheel and deal according to the rules in this chapter, you will not go wrong. Why? Because if you're careful in your buying of real estate, the:

• Basic value of the property will usually rise

• Property values will seldom go down much

• Constant inflation pushes land values up

• Reduced amounts of land push prices up

So get yourself a piece of earth using wheeling-and-dealing tactics. You may profit way beyond your wildest dreams in fields you never thought you'd enter.

GET YOUR MONEY THE RIGHT WAY

Since I want you to wheel and deal with *no* money of your own, I'm a great believer in zero-cash 100%-financed deals. To get the money for such deals, you should try to get your loan application approved in 24 hours or less. Here are nine easy steps to 24-hour loan approval:

1. *Go to the right type of lender!* For a real estate mortgage, go to a mortgage lender. For a construction loan, go to a construction lender. Sounds very basic, right? But as a lender myself I *know* how many people come to us for types of loans we don't make! Go to the *right* type of lender—always!

2. *Use the lender's own loan application.* While a "general" application might get you the loan, delays may occur. So use the lender's application. To get a copy, just call, fax, e-mail, or write the lender.

3. *Type the loan application!* Handwritten loan applications are *out* in commercial real estate deals. If you can't type, or don't want to, hire someone. The cost is small—the rewards, enormous!

4. *Ask for a loan within the lender's limits.* For example, the lending organization I'm associated with goes up to $1 million on first mortgages. While we can go higher, the $1 million is our current limit. If you come to us with an $8-million application, we'll probably suggest that you go to another lender. How do you find a lender's limits? Just ask! Note that plenty of lenders go to $500 million; some go to $999 million for real estate. So, as I tell people, "We're just 'small potatoes' back East here. But we've helped thousands of people over the years, with loans exceeding $140 million since we started."

5. *Talk to, or write to, the lender* before *sending the loan application.* A little time spent talking to the lender (or getting answers to questions in writing) can save hours—even days—when your application arrives. Why? Because the lender "knows" you, knows your deal. So the lender is ready to act faster!

6. *Send the application to the person who sent it to you.* When you request an application by phone or mail, get the name of the person sending the application. Then send the filled-out application to that person. Why? Because you have either a spoken or a

written connection with that person. So your application finds a "home" quickly and easily—and a faster answer!

7. *Write a short cover letter for your application.* Tell how much money is needed, for what purpose, for how long, how you propose to repay the loan with details on the source of the repayment funds, and what information is included besides the loan application. Tell where and when you can be reached to answer any questions that may arise.

8. *Include a loan summary in the letter* showing the loan amount, purpose, and any interest restrictions the borrower might have placed on the amount of interest he or she is willing to pay. A summary might look like this:

Amount of loan sought: $4 million

Purpose of loan: First mortgage on garden apartments

Duration of loan: 30 years

Maximum interest acceptable: 12% simple

9. *Never set up any time requirements on your lender.* Never tell the lender: "Time is of the essence." It *always* is! Never say you must have an answer in X hours. You're just asking for a delay!

Points to Remember

- You can wheel and deal in real estate properties.

- No formal education, license, or other training is needed by wheelers and dealers.

- To make big money wheeling and dealing, look for profitable ideas and unique approaches.

- You can often operate on 100% financing when you wheel and deal.

- Make action, speed, and new ideas the key forces in your wheeling and dealing work.

- If you can't find another real estate lender, become a two-year subscriber to my newsletter and try me. We may be able to help you find a willing lender from among our lists of thousands of real estate lenders.

TEN

USE UNUSUAL REAL ESTATE WEALTH TECHNIQUES

Just as there are millions of ways to make a million in business, so, too, are there millions of ways to make a million, or more, in real estate. In this chapter I'd like to give you a number of *unusual* ways to amass great wealth in your real estate deals. I hope that at least one of these ways makes you the bundle of money you seek.

PROFIT FROM A PROPERTY'S LOCATION

As a boy, working in the engine rooms of oceangoing tankers, freighters, and passenger ships, I often thought about the run-down buildings behind the docks and oil terminals in the ports we visited. Many of the buildings were deserted, abandoned by their owners.

To a ship lover and a romantic like myself, these neglected buildings were a sinful waste of beautiful views of the harbor and all its waterborne commerce. Little did I know that years later I would be a real estate operator financing the rehabbing of many such buildings, turning them into luxurious and expensive homes and condos.

Today waterfront sites are prize moneymakers for real estate wealth builders. For instance, on the Hudson River in New Jersey, opposite New York City, condo townhouses—built on land formerly occupied by docks used by oceangoing freighters and passenger ships—sell for $300,000 to $1.2 million and up!

Yet just a few months ago the property was occupied by dilapidated and unused deserted buildings and docks. New condo town houses sell so fast that builders can't keep up with the demand.

Why? Because many people love a water view, especially when it's backed up by glowing city lights at night. "It's just spectacular—a never-ending light show," people gush when they see a city at night from across a river or lake.

A further incentive for builders is that rents for a typical 1,000-square-foot apartment in such areas are in the $2,500 per month range in larger cities. Yet a moderate-priced condo townhouse with a 30-year mortgage loan has a monthly payment of about the same amount—$2,500.

Thus, many renters opt to buy because with each monthly mortgage payment, their equity (ownership) of the property increases. This means their net worth rises, instead of staying constant, as it does when they make rent payments.

To profit from any property's location, take these easy steps:

1. Look for properties with desirable locations, such as those with water, golf-course, or mountain views.

2. Visit each property to see if it has any structures on it. Existing structures might have to be torn down. Or, with some creative re-habbing, they might be retained.

3. Estimate the cost of removing or rehabbing existing structures. Or call in an engineer to make such a cost estimate for you.

4. Compute the income you could earn from rehabbed or new structures you might build on the property. Do this by getting data on local rentals and sales prices for similar properties. Real estate brokers will supply this to you free.

5. Ask the seller what price he or she wants for the property in an as-is condition, and what type of financing currently exists on the property, if any.

6. Work the numbers to see if you can make money buying, fixing up, and either selling or renting out the property. If you plan to develop the property by building new homes on it, compute your potential earnings from such work.

7. Make an offer on the property, if the numbers show you can make a profit from the selling, renting, or developing of the property. Base your offering price on your profit projections.

8. Buy the property if your offer is accepted. Do the needed work and sell, rent, or develop the property as you planned to earn your targeted profit from the property's location!

Now let's look at several more unusual real estate techniques you can use in your wealth building—starting right now!

ISOLATE THE UNUSUAL

Every geographic area, every type of land, every place under the sun has an unusual way that you can make money from it. Here are unusual ways you might consider using in your area. Each way has made money for a beginning wealth builder (BWB) somewhere.

Unusual Real Estate Wealth Techniques

1. Specialize in islands.

2. Handle only view-type properties.

3. Concentrate on distressed-property, or foreclosure, sales.

4. Fix up run-down properties for profits.

5. Run motels with absentee management.

6. Rent post offices to the postal service.

Let's take a look at each of these techniques and see how *you* might use it to build a fast, easy-money fortune in your real estate deals. Or, if you don't like the method we give you, let's see how *you* can change it to suit *your* local conditions.

SPECIALIZE IN ISLANDS

"No man is an island," yet every man and woman has a dreamy, soft spot in his or her heart for an island "away from it all." To check this out, watch the expression on a person's face when you casually mention: "I'm thinking of buying an island."

The *second home,* or vacation home, is *big* business around the world today. And a second home (or even a first home) on an island is always a saleable item. By specializing in islands—with or without homes on them—you can possibly build yourself a big real estate fortune quickly and easily.

Where can you find desirable islands? The best ones are those off populated mainland coasts, such as:

- Maine

- Oregon

- North Carolina

- Florida

- California

- Texas

- New York

- Connecticut

- Canada

- Mexico

- South America

- Europe

- Africa

- The Caribbean

As a general guide, you can say that:

The closer an island is to the mainland, the higher—in general—its value to you and others.

For this reason I recommend that at the start you specialize in islands no more than five miles off the mainland. And you'll find that islands within one mile off the mainland are usually the most popular.

Why are close-in islands more sought after than those farther out? Because on an island your travel time to and from the mainland becomes a factor, particularly in bad weather. Since you almost always need a boat to get to and from an island (unless you can fly in and out, or use a bridge), the farther the distance from the mainland, the longer the boat trip.

HOW TO MAKE MONEY FROM ISLANDS

To make money from islands, take these steps:

1. Decide where you will concentrate your buying and selling by studying the areas you like.

2. Pick the size of the islands you'll work on—the smaller the better at the start.

3. Begin looking for suitable islands by scanning the ads in local newspapers, talking to people in the area you selected, and exploring by boat.

4. Once you find a few suitable islands, make offers to the owners. As a guide, use the tips on wheeling and dealing given in chapter 9.

5. Sometimes your best approach is to put down only a *binder* (a small amount that shows you're serious about the deal) to hold the island for 90, 120, or 180 days. The binder will cost you a lot less and—since you'll lose your binder if you don't buy the island or sell it to someone else—will act as a strong motivating force to make you a buyer. Your binder may also be called an *option* to buy. Either way, the effect is the same—*you* control the island for the stated period of the option. For a quick review of profitable ways to use options in all types of real estate, order a copy of the IWS *Options Wealth Opportunities,* described in chapter 15.

PROMOTE YOUR ISLANDS IN UNUSUAL PLACES

Once you've picked a few islands to sell, you'll want to sell them fast. You can get the action you seek if you promote and advertise in unusual places, such as:

- Boating magazines

- Camping publications

- Outdoors clubs

- Rifle associations

- Hunting clubs

- Bird-watchers' clubs

Note these facts about making money from island property:

1. You can't make money on islands in the middle of an ocean because people don't want to get *that* far away from it all.

2. Island buyers are usually also boaters, hunters, or outdoors people of some kind. Promote your islands to them and you'll sell
   your "products" (land surrounded by water) faster.

HOW ISLANDS CAN MAKE YOU MONEY

Here are a few typical examples of how beginning wealth builders just
like yourself have made *big* money wheeling and dealing in islands.

Maine "Island" for Farmers

Chris T. heard of a Maine "island" for sale cheap—just $2,000. Hav-
ing an area of three acres, this "island" was really only an island at high
tide! At low tide you could walk from the island to the mainland, using
a rocky reef connecting the two.

Chris put a binder of $100 down on the island with the understand-
ing that he could hold it for 120 days. With the binder (which he borrowed from a local bank) paid, Chris set out to find a buyer for his
island. But instead of searching for a real island buff, Chris reasoned,
he'd look for a couple.

Chris found the couple he wanted with a simple ad carrying the head-
line: WHEN IS AN ISLAND NOT AN ISLAND? The ad went on to describe how an
island-seeking couple could have a three-acre island at high tide and a
three-acre country estate at low tide. Chris ran his ad in a bird-watchers'
magazine. One month later he sold the island for $10,500—a neat profit
on a $100 investment!

Sell the Beach, Not the Island

Elmer Wheeler is famous for his remark "Sell the sizzle—not the
steak." Ken P. knew of Elmer when a beautiful 10-acre island came on
the market in his area of Connecticut. Ken studied the island and
decided—since the island had no buildings on it—that he'd have to sell
something else: the sizzle.

Though the island had no houses, it did have a beautiful half-moon-
shaped sandy beach. It was this beach that became Ken's sizzle. But who

would want an island without a house? Ken prepared a list of possible buyers:

- Yacht club

- Rifle club

- Bird-watchers' groups

- Swimming clubs

Using his list as a guide, Ken contacted local clubs and associations *after* he took possession of the island for $500 down. In less than two weeks Ken had four bids for the island and within a month he sold out at a $15,000 profit.

WHY ISLANDS ARE PROFITABLE

You *can* make money from islands because this type of property:

- Is often in rural areas

- Is generally sold by novices who inherited the island

- Seldom is sold creatively

- Is not sought by too many people

- Can be difficult to sell fast because a special type of buyer is needed

But you may move island property fast with the know-how I've given you here. Just be sure the island isn't in the middle of an ocean. The middle of a small lake is fine from an investment standpoint, but the middle of an ocean is bad!

Also remember that you can't act as a real estate broker in most states unless you are licensed. So check out your state to be sure. You can, of course, sell your personal real estate *without* a license—which is what was done in the above two deals. Also, when you hold an option on a property, you do *not* need a license to sell it because it is your personal holding.

HANDLE ONLY VIEW-TYPE PROPERTIES

"I've always wanted a house with a view," said the young woman. "I'd rather live in an apartment for 10 years than to have a viewless cramped house in some little development."

This woman was expressing the thoughts held by the house-with-view set. These people scrimp and save for years so they can buy their dream house—one with a view. And you can earn money by catering to their dreams. You can either offer them land with a view or offer them homes with a view.

KNOW THE VIEWS TO SELL

Basically there are only three kinds of views to sell:

1. Land views

2. Water views

3. A combination of both

Each of these kinds of views can be subdivided.

Types of Land Views

- Mountains

- Valleys

- Plains

- Populated areas

Types of Water Views

- Ocean

- Bay

- River

- Lake

- Swamp or bayou

You can, of course, combine these types of views. For instance, some homes in California have an ocean view from the front and a mountain view from the back. Local zoning laws often recognize the importance of the view to the owner of property and prevent the partial or complete blocking of the view by construction of any type of permanent structure on adjacent land once the land is occupied.

To judge the view value of a property, site, home, or apartment house, visit the area and then the actual property. Try to see the views as the owner of the property would when:

- Standing up
- Sitting down
- Relaxing in an easy chair
- In a garden
- Lounging by a swimming pool
- From any other position

Once you see the view from these and other positions, compare the view with that from other, competitive properties in the area. Then assign a dollar value to "your" view, based on the prices being charged for other view properties nearby.

When pricing a view property, keep this important fact in mind:

The view from a property remains for years. Buildings can rise and fall but the view remains. So price the property more for its view than for its structures. *(Location gives the view and location remains forever.)*

PUSH VIEWS TO THE RIGHT PROSPECTS

Both boaters and nonboaters love water views. Boaters love to watch the boats and the water. Many nonboaters like to watch the boats and water, too. But most nonboaters like to be far enough away so they never risk getting wet!

Hunters, trappers, camping buffs, hikers, and similar enthusiasts like mountain views. Many "just plain folk" also like mountains, valleys, and plains. So your prospects are everywhere when it comes to land views.

To sell view property, push the one feature all prospects for this type of property seek—namely, the *view*. Get to be known as the person who has the inside track on choice view property.

Kurt L. did exactly this in building a big fortune in view properties. Working on the West Coast, Kurt specialized in businesses having a view. Thus, Kurt's first deal was a tavern overlooking the Pacific Ocean in Pacific Beach, California, just north of San Diego.

Kurt took over the tavern using $2,000 of borrowed money he obtained by taking a business loan from his bank. The total price of the tavern and the land was $120,000.

When Kurt took over the tavern, its business was sluggish because the owner was more interested in sampling his own wares than in serving customers. Also, the owner had allowed to building to go to seed—windows were broken, the roof leaked, painting was needed inside and outside. Lastly the tavern lacked "character"—it had no focus for its patrons.

GIVE THE PUBLIC WHAT IT WANTS

Kurt changed the tavern dramatically. "I want to give the public what it wants—a comfortable tavern with a view which has real character." Kurt borrowed $25,000 more from his bank and:

- Installed curved nooks overlooking the ocean

- Changed the bar so people looked out over the water

- Decorated the interior with South Sea island decor

Within weeks the tavern's income jumped from $1,000 a week to $6,000 a week. With business booming, Kurt put his view property up for sale. In a few days Kurt sold out for $300,000, for a total profit of $155,000, plus the money he'd taken in as a profit on the business while he was having the building interior and exterior improved.

Kurt didn't stop when he sold this tavern. Instead, he kept working his way north—buying, improving, and selling—always at a good profit, and always dealing in either ocean- or mountain-view taverns. Using this approach, Kurt has built a sizeable fortune quickly. What's more, he's had great fun along the way!

Of course, there are many other types of view property from which you can make a profit. Taverns aren't the only kind of view property from which a person can earn a fortune. You can also earn *big money* from:

- Apartment houses

- Shopping centers

- Industrial plants

- Mobile home parks

- Recreation parks

- Camping grounds

So don't give up! Keep looking until you find the right view property for your fortune building.

CONCENTRATE ON DISTRESSED-PROPERTY SALES

This land of ours is full of distressed properties—that is, structures and land that were:

- Abandoned by the owners

- Taken over for nonpayment of taxes

- Discarded because of building-code violations

- Left because of fear of new tenants

Distressed properties are *problem* properties. So unless you welcome solving problems while you earn *big money*, stay away from distressed properties.

When you take over any distressed property, you may have to:

- Repair, rebuild, recondition

- Repaint, repave, reroof

- Drain, dredge, dry

- Find new tenants; eject current tenants

- Raise rents; lower rents

So you see, distressed properties not only have built-in problems. They also require a large amount of work on *your* part. Of course, you can hire people to do this work for you. But when you first start, you may not have the cash needed to hire the people you need. So keep in mind at all times Hicks's rules for distressed properties:

1. It will always cost you *more* than you think it will to make big money from distressed property.

2. It will always take you *longer* to make money from distressed property than you think it will.

With these two rules in mind, you'll be able to face realistically the everyday problems that occur in the buying, selling, and running of distressed properties.

YOUR EASIEST WAY TO WHEEL AND DEAL FOR REAL ESTATE FORECLOSURE WEALTH

Thousands of real estate wheeler-dealer BWBs seek foreclosures as a quick, low-cost way to wealth. Foreclosures *can* be *your way* to real estate wealth—if you pick the easiest route. Thus:

- Bidding for property on the courthouse steps using a certified bank check is *not* the easiest way.

- Negotiating with sellers in preforeclosure (after they've been notified of the possibility of foreclosure but before the sale) is *not* the easiest way.

- Buying from successful bidders after foreclosure sales is *not* the easiest way to get good property at a low price.

"So," you ask, "what is the easiest way to buy foreclosures?" The *easiest* way based on lots of experience in foreclosures is:

- Buy from the bank, or other financing entity, *after* the property has been passed over on the courthouse steps—that is, not bought at auction.

- Don't bother to get a certified bank check, don't bother to go to the auction, don't get into a bidding "war" with other BWBs wanting a property.

- Instead, go to the bank—empty-handed—with nothing but a desire to take REO (real estate owned) properties off the bank's hands, helping them. If you do this you may find the bank:

1. Offering you the property for either zero-cash down—or nearly that—say $100 down, which the bank may lend you.

2. Paying *all* closing costs to encourage you to take over the property—that is, get it off their books.

3. Paying *all* legal costs associated with the property. (While it *is* safe to use the bank's attorney for your purchase, we suggest—for your safety—that you have an outside attorney look over the paperwork *before* you buy.)

4. Helping you get a property rented to a dependable and responsible, paying tenant.

5. Guiding you to Section 8 tenants whose rent is fully (or partially) paid to you by the government. See elsewhere in this book for valuable data on Section 8 tenants and how they can help build your riches in real estate.

6. Showing you how to buy multiple properties, so your holdings and income grow as time passes. Result? You're successful, with a steady income and strong assets you built with foreclosures—the easiest way! Keep in mind at all times: Banks do *not* want real estate; instead they want to receive a monthly mortgage payment. That's why they'll help you build your portfolio of income properties.

HOW TO CONVERT DISTRESS INTO PROFITS

The keys to making money in any kind of distressed property are:

1. Buy cheap.

2. Improve at low cost.

3. Sell high.

Now distressed properties are ideal for the BWB because they can be bought either for *zero cash* or just a few hundred dollars. With such a small investment—or no investment at all—you can easily afford the *fix-up* money needed. "But," you say, "how can I afford the fix-up money when I have a poor credit rating, no money in the bank, and three sick relatives to support?" Here's your answer, friend.

BUILD A PAPER ROAD TO YOUR WEALTH

Let's say that the above conditions—or even *worse* ones—apply to you. Is the world still black, with all hope of a fortune for you lost forever? No, good friend, the money desires you have *can* be turned into sweet, green cash. And here's how.

Let's say you take over a distressed property worth $35,000 for *no* cash down. The property is a three-family house having an average rental of $150 per month per apartment, or a total of $3 \times \$150 = \$450$ per month. This gives you a yearly income of $12 \times \$450 = \$5,400$.

You survey the neighborhood and conclude that each apartment should be renting for at least $225 per month. Since there are no rent controls in your area, you raise the rents immediately. The tenants grumble a little but know that they're getting bargain. So they agree to pay the higher rent. This means that your income jumps to $3 \times 12 \times \$225 = \$8,100$ a year.

Using this as your rental income, and your ownership of the building as collateral, you go to your friendly bank and within one day borrow $5,000 for property improvement. While you're applying for the loan you're delighted to note that, just as Ty Hicks has told you in many of his other money books (which are listed at the beginning of *this* book), the bank loan officer:

- Hardly asked you *any* questions

- Was *delighted* to get your business

- Wanted to *lend* you more than you needed, and

- *Asked* you to hurry back for more money!

Thus, you've started your paper road to wealth, using sweet-smelling greenbacks.

CONVERT OWNERSHIP TO FUTURE INCOME

Next you take $3,000 of your borrowed $5,000 OPM (other people's money) and:

- Have the apartments painted

- Fix up leaks, broken windows, etc.

- Have the exterior spruced up.

Figure 2

Distressed Property Rehab Project

Price of property	$35,000
Down payment	0
Annual income: 3 units @ $150/mo ea	5,400
Rent increase after rehabbing gives an annual income of	8,100
Property value after rehabbing	60,000
Bank mortgage offered on rehab	48,000
FHA mortgage offered on rehab	54,000
Accept bank mortgage with net to you	= 12,000
Less $3,000 for rehab	= 3,000
Final net to you	= $ 9,000

Note: Pay to have this work done. Don't do it yourself unless you're a first rate mechanic!

With the building nice and shiny, you go back to the bank and tell your good friend that you'd like to refinance the mortgage—that is—get a new mortgage for 15 to 20 years. He sends an appraiser around to look at the building while you prepare a simple financial statement for the building. (I've prepared one for you and shown it in Figure 2. You can use this as a general guide.)

Your friendly appraiser sets a fair value of $60,000 on your improved property—for which you put up no cash. And your friend at the bank tells you that the bank will lend you 80% of the appraised value of the property, or 0.80($60,000)=$48,000 instantly. Or, he says, you can easily get an FHA 90% guarantee, giving you $54,000. This will take a little longer—say 4 weeks.

GET YOUR MONEY WHILE YOU CAN

You decide to *mortgage out* fast. So you accept the bank's $48,000 mortgage. You owe $35,000 on the building—that is, the price you "paid" for it. Since the mortgage gives you $48,000, you mortgage out with $48,000 − $35,000 = $13,000, less your closing costs of about $1,000. Thus, you net out with $12,000 cash, tax-free!

"But I still owe that $5,000 I borrowed to fix the place up," you say. True. But you only used $3,000 of that, remember? So you have $14,000 cash and owe $5,000, or a net of $9,000.

Yet several other *nice* things have happened to you since you mortgaged out. These are:

1. Your mortgage payments are probably lower because you *extended* your mortgage.

2. Your *spendable* cash (also called MIF, money in fist) has increased because your mortgage payments are lower.

3. Your net worth has *risen* by $60,000, the appraised value of your property.

4. You converted your no-cost signature to *cash* without putting up a cent!

ANOTHER WAY TO MORTGAGE OUT

There are many ways you can mortgage out—that is, get money when you buy an income property. Here's a reader letter telling how he mortgaged out. This letter arrived while I was working on this chapter of the book:

> Your "three-year" real estate book has been great. I recently started my real estate investment career, about 18 months ago. Since then I bought 17 single-family homes with a value of over $1 million. I've mortgaged out more than $150,000 on these properties and have a positive cash flow of around $4,000 a month.

Analyzing this BWB's income, we see that he paid an average of $58,000 for these houses. And he averaged $8,333 per month mortgaging out money! Add to this his $4,000 per month positive cash flow and he's bringing in enough to take his wife to fast-food restaurants every night! Why don't you plan on how you might do the same as this highly successful BWB? You may find mortgaging out situations—if you pick your properties and deals carefully!

BUILD YOUR REAL ESTATE EMPIRE

You now are in a good position to start building big real estate wealth because you have:

- Cash in your hand
- A steady income
- Property in *your* name

With these assets you're ready to go on to greater things, namely:

- More cash
- More income
- More property

Without putting up more cash of your own! This is how you build your real estate empire.

To start your empire:

1. Find another profitable rental property.

2. Try to get this second property with *no* cash down.

3. If you must put cash down, use the cash from mortgaging out on the first property—now often called a *home equity loan*.

4. Or borrow the down payment using the first property as full or partial collateral for the down-payment loan.

5. Once you take over the second property, try to mortgage out on it, just the way you did on the first property.

6. Continue in this way until you have enough properties to give you the monthly income you seek.

KNOW THE NUMBERS OF UNUSUAL EMPIRE BUILDING

Let's say that the average yearly income from each property you take over is $5,000, after all expenses are paid. This is a rather low annual income but it will give you a good idea of how the dollars can mount up.

We'll say that you own different numbers of rental properties, and that each of them returns you $5,000 a year in profits, or:

Number of Properties	Your Yearly Profit
1	$5,000
2	10,000
5	25,000
10	50,000
15	75,000
20	100,000
100	500,000

And, good friend, 100 properties is *not* a large number of properties to own *and* manage. Just think what you could do with the extra $500,000 *profit* every year of your life! You could live the "Golden Rule," namely: "The guy or gal with the gold makes the rules."

To show you the amounts of income you can get from well-chosen properties, let me share with you a recent reader letter that shows an unusual approach to real estate because this BWB did it while holding an excellent job as a bank executive:

> Thanks for the inspiration your books have provided me in my development as a real estate investment entrepreneur. To this day, when I feel overwhelmed by the demands of property management and development, I refer to the commentaries and passages in your books to recapture the spirit and zeal they invoke in me.
>
> I am very proud and happy to report that my property holdings now produce sufficient cash flow to live on comfortably. I am therefore leaving my banking career as an assistant vice-president to pursue property purchase and management on a full-time basis.
>
> Specializing in small three- to five-family buildings, here's an approximate income statement:

	Building #1	Building #2	Building #3	Building #4
Rent	$20,500*	$44,300	$44,500	$41,800
Expenses	6,000	5,500	8,000	7,500
Mortgage payments	10,750	19,800	19,500	18,500
Net profit	$3,750	$19,000	$17,000	$15,800

*My family and I occupy one apartment rent-free.

Thus, this reader's *net* income from his buildings is $55,550 per year! Not bad, when they were all bought on borrowed money!

This letter, received just weeks ago, puts the end to the helpless wail of readers who really aren't trying and who say:

I can't find positive-cash-flow properties. True, I've only looked a few hours. But I can't find any.

Where I sit, I hear from hundreds of readers every year. And do you know what they report to me—again and again? They report:

I found plenty of positive-cash-flow properties. Of course, I had to look around. But they *are* available to those who look!

So please don't call me and tell me that you can't do this or that! What I want to hear from you is what you *can* do, what you *are* doing! Not for my sake but for *your* sake!

And when you tell me you've spent a few days looking for this or that and haven't found it yet, my curt answer will probably be:

Good friend, I spent *nine years* writing one engineering book. So don't complain to me that you've spent a few days trying to do something and haven't come up with the results yet. Anything worth doing in life takes time. And that's true of real estate and all other worthwhile work!

FIX UP RUN-DOWN PROPERTIES FOR PROFIT

Real estate of all kinds goes through six stages in life, namely:

1. New and shiny

2. Good-looking but not so new

3. Weathered but solid

4. Neglect beginning

5. Major repairs needed

6. Ready to be torn down

A new property is often worth 30% more the day it is finished than it cost to build. Thus, you'll often find that the following is true:

Cost to Build	Value on Day Finished
$20,000	$26,000
50,000	65,000
100,000	130,000
500,000	650,000
1,000,000	1,300,000
5,000,000	6,500,000

On the day the property is finished, it is new and shiny. From this condition to weathered but solid, the value of your property will gradually increase because:

- Inflation is usually pushing property values up, money values down.

- Labor and material costs usually are constantly rising (about 1% per month!).

- Land gets scarcer and scarcer, causing its value to rise (usually by 15% per year!).

- Good properties are almost always in demand by someone for some purpose.

But when neglect begins, the building value often starts to decrease. Why? Because the fix-up costs begin to work *against* the increase in value. So from this condition until the building is ready to be torn down, you can often get valuable property for a song—*if you're willing to fix it up yourself, or pay someone else to fix it up*.

When you're starting with no cash, as many BWBs are, your sweat equity, or the work you do yourself on a property, can put you in the chips when you:

- Sell the property

- Borrow on the property

- Rent the property

- Trade for a better property

But you have to be a special type of person to make money this way. Why? Because:

- Not everyone is a good handyman
- Some people aren't healthy enough
- Time may not be available
- Other work may be more interesting

Knowing that these conditions may exist in your life can really pay off. Why? Because you can decide to have someone else do the fixing up for you, paying for the repair work by using borrowed money. True, the repairs will cost you more this way but you'll have:

- More time for other work
- Less physical strain
- Fewer wealth-building problems

PICK YOUR APPROACH TO FIX-UPS

There are three basic approaches to fixing up run-down properties:

1. Start small; grow big slowly.
2. Start with six or eight buildings.
3. Begin with a very large project and go all out.

If you've never had any previous experience with fixing up buildings, I strongly suggest that you start small. This way you can't go too far wrong if you find that you don't like making money from fix-ups. And if you like the fix-up approach, you can always expand quickly to take over other buildings. This is the way most folks start and move into the big money. Here's a typical example of how one BWB did it.

Spare-Time Wealth in Fix-Ups

Glenn T. is a typical white-collar worker—underpaid, underappreciated, misunderstood, and overbossed. Also, he's best at a desk instead of at a workbench or lathe. So when he first heard of big money to be made in fix-ups, he turned away because of his poor mechanical ability. Yet the more he thought about the unhappiness on his job, the more Glenn felt that the fix-up route to real estate wealth might be his answer. He decided to take the big leap.

Glenn started with a two-family *repossession*—that is, a house that the bank had taken back (repossessed). The bank didn't ask for any cash down and arranged to have its lawyer handle the closing free of charge. So Glenn was able to take over a property for zero cash down. But the property:

- Had *no* tenants

- Was badly run down

- Needed many repairs

- Seemed ready for the house wrecker

But a bored man such as Glenn is also a desperate and "hungry" man. And desperation will often drive us to take action that we might not take otherwise.

Once Glenn had the house, he offered a contractor half the future rental income and half the profit on the sale of the property if the contractor would make the repairs free of charge. The contractor turned him down. So Glenn tried a second, then a third, and a fourth contractor, using the Yellow Pages of the phone book as his source of names. The eleventh contractor Glenn asked finally agreed to do the work.

Once the building was repaired and repainted, Glenn had no trouble renting both apartments. Thus, Glenn had gone from a condition of *no* property to the *owner* of *income-producing property* without investing anything other than:

- Some time

- Some energy

- His signature on a few papers

Sensing that his fortune wasn't far away, Glenn began buying repossessions all over town—*with no cash down*. In a year Glenn took over

33 multiple-family dwellings. In the same time he raised his assets from zero to some $363,000.

During his second year Glenn did much the same, taking over zero-cash properties in his own city and in nearby ones. By the end of the second year, Glenn's assets had risen to $981,000.

Glenn's third year was his big one because it was during this year that he began to trade his improved properties for bigger, newer buildings. When he closed out his third year, Glenn was worth more than $1 million—$3,872,000 to be exact!

You might do the same by wheeling and dealing in fix-ups. Just start, using the above ideas, and you'll soon be on the road to the big money!

MAKE EDUCATION YOUR REAL ESTATE "CASH COW"

Do you live in, or near, a college or university town? If you do, you can make big money renting rooms and/or apartments to college students. Why is this? Because:

1. Student enrollments in colleges and universities continue to rise throughout the world. And enrollments will increase.

2. Chronic student housing shortages exist in almost every college and university in the world today.

3. Student rents are rising because student enrollments are increasing, offering you a substantial income from your rooms or apartments.

4. Year-round courses ensure a 12-month rental of your rooms and apartments in almost every college and university.

How can you get started building real estate wealth on borrowed money from the booming student market? Here are easy steps you can take:

1. Determine if there's a need for student housing in your area or in a nearby college town.

2. Check with local colleges and universities to see if there is a need for clean, well-kept student housing. You will be welcomed if there is a need for such housing.

3. Decide, based on the data from steps 1 and 2, if you can earn a profit in your area by serving the student market.

4. Look for suitable properties if you decide to offer student housing in your area, or a nearby one.

5. Get the word out to operators of buildings near the campus that you're searching for non-school-owned multiunit properties. Contact real estate brokers, giving your requirements. Getting the word out this way will—sooner or later—get you information on properties available for purchase by yourself.

6. Work the numbers of each property that becomes available. Figure your income and expenses, including your monthly mortgage principal (Principal & Interest) payments. *You must have a positive cash flow (PCF)!* And the larger your PCF, the better—in general—the property will be for you in your fortune building. *As a general guide, aim for a minimum of $1,000 per month ($12,000 per year) PCF from each small student housing property.* Large properties will, of course, show much higher PCF on a monthly and annual basis.

7. Make your offer on each student housing project that meets your income and profit requirements. Put down as little cash as possible to get the property you want. Use the buying tips given elsewhere in this book to convince the seller of your honesty, reliability, and hardworking dedication to making the student housing property more successful than ever.

8. Take over enough student housing projects as you need to give you the income you seek. Get rich on the student boom!

If you have any questions about using the steps above, give a phone call, fax, or e-mail me. And if you're a subscriber to either of my newsletters, I'll be happy to analyze any building for you from a business standpoint—free of charge. All you need to do is provide me with a profit and loss statement (P&L) on the building. I'll be glad to show you its potential profit or loss for you!

RUN MOTELS WITH ABSENTEE MANAGEMENT

Motels attract many BWBs because a motel seems to promise:

- Large, steady cash income

- Several sources of income—room rental, restaurant, bar, catering, etc.

- Steady increase in land and structure values

- Interesting and new people every day

- Relaxed working atmosphere

All these features of motels are true and accurate for modern motels that are well managed. But all motels have certain disadvantages, including:

- Motels are a seven-day-a-week business.

- Most motels are a 365-day-a-year business.

- Labor costs tend to be high in motels.

- Labor problems can lead to headaches.

- "Skips" or no-pay customers can cause income losses.

- Expansion of your business may be impossible in crowded areas.

Is there any way to get around these disadvantages? Yes, there is—at least in part. Why do I say in part? Because the famous Ty Hicks's law says:

There is *no perfect business*! Every business has problems of some kind. If you buy, start, or take over a business that earns you a profit, you are *certain* to have problems of some kind!

What's the way *you* can partially get around the disadvantages of motels? There's a relatively simple answer: use a resident or local manager who will allow *you*, the owner, to operate by *absentee management*. In motel ownership, absentee management means that you don't have to be around the place seven days a week. You may even be able to run the motel profitably by spending only one hour a week on the premises!

HOW TO MAKE BIG MONEY FROM MOTELS

You can make *big money* in motels if you:

- Run your motel as a sideline business

- Have a manager who takes care of day-to-day details

- Keep tight financial control
- Cater to lucrative customers
- Watch *all* your expenses
- Hold labor costs down

Let's look at the resident or local manager aspect because, to me, this is the most important feature of absentee management of motels. With this look I think you'll soon see that *you can make big money in motels.*

Who makes a good motel manager? My wide experience in this field shows that some of the best hotel managers are:

- Married people
- In their forties
- Ex-servicemen
- People with kitchen or hospital experience
- Wanting to settle down

Other good candidates for the job of motel manager include former ship stewards, former hotel waiters, bartenders, and similar people. Why do I suggest married people with these backgrounds? Because:

The married person who has professional kitchen, catering, hospital, or similar experience can quickly learn all he or she needs to know about motel operation.

And, of course, being married gives the person greater stability and dependability than a single person. Also, by raising the person's salary by a few dollars a month, you can get the spouse to help with certain jobs, like:

- Registering guests
- Supervising the housekeeping staff
- Hiring new maids, waitresses, and clerks
- Watching over the kitchen, if your motel has a restaurant

Yes, hiring the *right* manager can allow you the freedom you deserve and seek in your business life. Why? Because while you're operating your motel by absentee management, you can be:

- Building another business

- Searching for financing, new partners, or other assistance you might need

- Or just taking life easy

HOW ABSENTEE MANAGEMENT CAN PAY OFF

Let's say you take over a $400,000 motel with the following financing:

- $300,000 first mortgage from a local bank

- $125,000 second mortgage from the seller

You get $425,000 in financing but the motel cost you only $400,000. This means that you have $25,000 tax-free cash for:

- Closing costs

- Miscellaneous expenses

- Capital for buying another business

- Money to pay off existing debts

You take over the motel and have $17,000 left after paying your closing costs and some other small expenses that piled up during the past few months before you found this deal.

The average monthly profit on this motel when run by the owner and spouse is $8,000, or about $2,000 a week, after paying *all* expenses. You decide that you and your spouse would prefer to be married to each other instead of to a motel. So, to "divorce" yourself from the motel, you decide to hire a competent manager.

After doing some figuring you decide that it would be worth $2,000 a month, plus an apartment in your motel for you to be free of seven-day-a-week slavery. Checking around, you quickly find that there are many good managers available for the pay you offer. Why? Because you let the manager hold an outside job, if he or she wants to.

START ON THE RIGHT BASIS

You advertise for a manager and interview more than a dozen. When you finally select your manager, you carefully outline the duties, both in spoken words and in writing, detailing:

- Work hours and work days
- Duties while on the job
- Pay schedule and pay benefits
- Annual vacation allowance
- Emergency procedures
- Other important job facts

With these facts presented to your prospective employee, they have a better chance of deciding if he or she will like your job offer. And you have a better chance of deciding if you will like him or her!

FREEDOM CAN BE CHEAP

Now just look at what you're buying for $2,000 a month, plus an apartment. You'll have:

- Five days a week off
- Time to check out other businesses
- Freedom to travel
- Avoidance of drudgery

While you may think that giving up $2,000 a month, plus the apartment rent, is a high price to pay:

Freedom from routine drudgery can open up new wealth vistas to you, can make you more creative, and put big money in your pocket.

So—if you *can* afford to do so—run your motel by absentee management. The extra income and leisure you'll get will be well worth the price!

RENT OFFICES TO THE POSTAL SERVICE

One of the steadiest bill payers in the world is the U.S. Postal Service. And with postal rates constantly on the rise, it looks as though this fine reputation for dependable bill paying will go on for a long, long time.

You can make big money in real estate by building and renting post offices to the postal service. Why is this so? Because:

With a long-term lease of your property by a highly-rated tenant, you can sit back and collect your rent without lifting a finger.

Or you can take your lease to the bank and borrow against your future income. You won't be able to borrow the full amount of your future rent, of course. But you can borrow a large portion of it, say 80%, on the average.

For example, let's say that you have a 20-year lease for a post office. You go around to your friendly banker who loaned you 90% of the cost of building your post office building. You show him your lease that pays you $10,000 a month rent for two years. "How much can I borrow on this lease?" you ask. "Sit down and we'll figure it out," he replies. He then writes out this column of figures:

Year No.	Percent Loanable	Amount Loanable (dollars per year)
1	100	$120,000
2	95	114,000
3	90	108,000
6	85	102,000
8	80	96,000
10	75	90,000
11 through 20	70	84,000

For 20 years of regular rental of this property, your income would be: (20 years)($120,000 a year) = $2,400,000. But if you borrow against this income, you will instantly receive $1,884,000—the sum of the above annual incomes. Then, as time passes, you will also receive an additional $516,000—the difference between the rent actually due you and the amount of money your bank loaned you. Of course, you'll have to pay interest on money you borrowed. But you can put the money to work earning a higher rate of return than the interest you're paying!

PUT OPM TO WORK

Your borrowed money is OPM—other people's money. You can take your $1.8 million and:

- Invest in other buildings
- Buy property for future developments
- Take over an ongoing business
- Set up other people in business

The big point here is that you can swing freely when you have cash in your pocket. Also, you've converted a long-term payout into instant money.

Can you work this deal with other types of tenants? You can—if they're AAA rated, or better, by credit-rating agencies. But keep these facts in mind:

- Different banks will offer different percentages on leases
- Tight-money times may cut your cash proceeds from a loan because the bank may not have much cash or may require that you leave 20% of the loan on deposit as a compensating balance.
- Some banks may not want to lend on a lease

But never worry! If you look *long* enough, and *far* enough, you're almost certain to uncover a profitable loan deal for yourself. So don't give up—keep looking.

You *can* make money by using unusual real estate techniques. This chapter has mentioned a few unusual techniques you might want to consider using yourself. Why don't you sit down right now and list six more unusual techniques you might use in your local area? Your payoff could be in the millions!

Points to Remember

- Unusual real estate wealth techniques can pay you millions in profits.
- Typical unusual real estate deals can be made in islands, view properties, distressed properties, motels, and post offices.

- OPM can get *you* started in unusual deals with zero cash.

- Run-down properties can be your fortune-maker.

- If you decide to invest in motels, be sure to use absentee management to save yourself from drudgery.

- You *can* find positive-cash-flow properties—you just have to look for them!

- You always have a good friend in your author—Ty Hicks. And I'll try to help you whenever I can!

ELEVEN

BUILD REAL ESTATE PROFITS USING LIMITED PARTNERSHIPS

Real estate is a beautiful business. Why? Because in real estate there are hundreds of chances for you to get started:

- In an activity that's an accepted "borrowing" business
- Without putting up a penny
- Using other people's money
- Keeping control of the deal
- In a hurry

Two of the best ways to consider getting started on zero cash without giving up control of your ideas and income sources is to use either the limited partnership (LP), or real estate investment trust (REIT). Let's see how you can use these forms of business to make your real estate fortune sooner.

We'll look at the limited partnership first. Then, after giving you complete data on how you might possibly get rich with a LP, we'll take a full look at forming, and prospering from, your own REIT.

UNDERSTAND THE LIMITED PARTNERSHIP

Any partnership consists of two or more people who've joined together to do business. You're probably familiar with many such partnerships.

You'll sometimes find lawyers working together in a partnership. The same is true of accountants and some medical doctors.

In the usual partnership, each partner has an equal say in the management of the business. And should the business be sued, each partner has equal liability for debts, court awards, and so on.

With such an arrangement, each equal partner is called a *general partner*. A partnership can, in most states, have as many general partners as it wants or needs.

Partnerships of all types are used in real estate activities. But in recent years the limited partnership and the master limited partnership have become very popular because they:

- Make raising money easier

- Are easy to sell to the "public"

- Give good control of the business

In a limited partnership and in a master limited partnership* you may have two or more *general* partners and a large number of *limited partners*. Your limited partners:

- Have *no* voice or vote in the management of the partnership

- Are limited in their liability—in case of a lawsuit—to the amount of money they put into the partnership—usually $5,000, $10,000, or more, per limited partner

WHAT THE LP OFFERS INVESTORS

"Why," you ask, "do people invest in limited partnerships?" There are a number of reasons, each of which is important to you, if you plan to use the LP as a source of money for building your real estate riches. Thus, people invest in LPs to:

- Earn real estate profits without the daily operating headaches

- Save taxes on real estate income

---

*A *master* limited partnership consists of several smaller limited partnerships.

- Earn future capital-gain profits
- Keep their excess funds working for them

While you may not believe this, there are millions of people in this great country of ours who are looking for good, profitable real estate deals into which they can put their money. And if you can put one or more good deals together, you can get the money you need to:

- Build new structures
- Fix up existing properties
- Buy profitable properties
- Manage profitable properties

Better yet, you don't have to put up a cent of your own. And you can, possibly, get the real estate funds you need:

- Without registering stock
- Without complicated legal documents
- Possibly quickly, easily, and at low cost

Let's see how you can get your LP going.

HOW TO FORM YOUR LP

To form an LP (the master LP is much the same), you *must* have the guidance of an attorney. I expect that you will have the good sense to see an attorney *before* you actually form your LP. However, you will probably find that your attorney agrees with much that is said here. And if he or she is unfamiliar with LPs, he or she may find the following facts a useful introduction.

To form your LP without having to register it with the federal Government,* take these seven steps:

1. Decide that you will be one of the *general partners*.

2. Select one or more other general partners.

---

*You may, however, have to register with your state government. Your attorney will advise you on this *important* matter.

3. Pick the number of limited partners you'd like to have (usually 10 to 20, depending on the amount of money you need and the price per participation).

4. Prepare, or have prepared, the LP description.

5. Sell, or have someone else sell, the LP decision.

6. Invest the proceeds in the real estate activity for which the LP was formed.

7. Go out and earn those profits you planned on!

These steps give you the simplest and least complicated kind of LP because you usually need not register it (under present laws) with the Securities and Exchange Commission (SEC). Later, when you gain more experience, you can sell thousands of participations to the public, provided you conform to the proper SEC rules and regulations. But for the moment, let's take a closer look at each of the steps you'll take in forming the simpler and smaller LP, with the help of your attorney. (For, as I said earlier, you *must* have the help of an attorney when you form a LP.)

SELECT YOUR GENERAL PARTNER

To gain the maximum from your first LP, I suggest that you become one of the general partners (GPs). As a GP you'll get in on the financial and operating management of your LP. This will teach you plenty about:

- Borrowing money

- Handling people

- Running a real estate business

So once you've appointed yourself a GP, pick at least one other GP. Note that by definition a partnership must have at least two members. And, of course, you can have many more if you wish.

Pick your GP—and I suggest that you have only one GP, other than yourself, for your first LP venture—as carefully as you'd choose a spouse, doctor, lawyer, or accountant.

Why should you be so careful in picking your GP? Because the two of you will be working together for a year or longer. You'll be sharing decisions, solving problems, and earning profits together. If you don't see eye-to-eye at the start, your partnership may wreck an otherwise perfect deal. I've seen it happen plenty of times.

To be certain you're picking a compatible, helpful partner for your real estate deal:

- Find out what your prospective GP can contribute to the partnership in:

  Time

  Money

  Ideas

  Energy

- Ask your partner-to-be what *he* or *she* wants out of the deal.

- Then ask what *he* or *she* can give to the deal.

My experience with many LPs shows that unless a prospective GP has something to *give* the LP in terms of himself or herself, he or she is usually an unsuitable candidate. So be careful—don't rush your GP choice.

PICK THE NUMBER OF LPS

In most states you can have a *private* offering of partnership shares to *limited partners*. Such an offering *usually* need not be registered with federal authorities if you sell 35 or fewer participations, in one state. Some states require a simple registration of LPs with the county clerk, attorney general, or some similar official. A nominal fee (which varies from state to state) may also be charged for the registration. You can easily learn if registration of *your* LP is required in *your* state by calling or writing to the attorney general for your state. Or your attorney can quickly answer the question.

To avoid the need for SEC registration of your LP, offer 33 or fewer LP participations to the residents of only *one* state, on a *private* (nonadvertised) basis, where the limit of 35 applies. You may also be able to avoid the need for state registration by having a private offering to 33 or fewer LPs. (I suggest 33 instead of 35 LPs just to keep you on the safe side. In some states you need not register a LP if you have 50 or fewer LPs.) But *be sure to check this out with your attorney before you take any action to offer even one participation!*

FIGURE YOUR CASH FLOW

Let's put *you* into an LP real estate deal. You'd like to buy a two-year-old 250-rental building that is completely modern in every way—swimming pool, tenant garages, electronic security system. The seller wants $550,000 cash down.

You negotiate with the seller using the famous "Hicks Law of Real Estate Buying," namely:

Never pay the asking price on any piece of real estate. Always negotiate a lower price, particularly for the cash portion of the asking price.

You take this advice and go to work. Your hours of wheeling and dealing on the down payment are worthwhile. You get the cash down payment reduced from $550,000 to $470,000. Also, the seller agrees to share the closing costs, which you figure will run some $50,000.

Everything else about the deal is good—that is, the place will throw off a big cash flow to the investors, and you and they will have a sweet tax shelter in the form of depreciation. Here are the figures:

Annual income	**$750,000**
Total price	3,800,000
Cash down	470,000

With these figures in mind, you aim to put together an LP to:

1. Finance the down payment

2. Operate the building

3. Earn a profit from the building

PUT YOUR LP TOGETHER

You need a total cash down payment of $470,000, plus $25,000 for your share of the closing costs, plus an emergency fund of $5,000, or a total of $500,000. Knowing that you want to make a *private offering,* to avoid registration, you limit your LP to 20 limited partners. This means that each limited partner will have to put in at least $500,000 ÷ 20 = $25,000. And, if you can get more, say $28,000 from each limited partner, you will try to do so!

You and your other *general partner* will manage the property. So you can put up *no* cash—instead you sign an agreement to run the building for a stated period, or until the property is sold. (If you wanted to, of course, you *could* put up whatever cash in multiples of $25,000 that you could afford. But I'm trying to show you how to work out an LP on *zero cash*.)

With your plans set, you write an LP description or prospectus. To help you, you'll find a sample LP description included in the IWS *Starting Millionaire Program*. You may want to use this as a guide, or you may want to change it completely. Either way, however, it will give you a starting point. Or it may help your attorney get started on writing the description for you. And you can benefit from a quick reading of the LP description given in this program because it shows you what information such a description usually contains. Also, since this description is for a real estate LP, you can get a good start on what kind of data you'll have to get for the description of your LP.

Have your attorney write the description of your LP as soon as you have enough facts. Or write the description yourself and give it to your attorney for editing and polishing up. Once you have your LP description written, you've "put the deal together" on paper. (And writing the description will have been a wonderfully enlightening experience for you!)

Now you have to find enough limited partners with enough money to make the deal go!

WHERE TO FIND LIMITED PARTNERS

If you have a large group of rich friends, you'll have little trouble in getting the money you need from them. But if you don't have many (or *any*) rich friends, as is the case with most BWBs, you'll have to:

- Find LPs yourself

- Get friends to recommend LPs

- Use any other available sources of LPs such as ads in the monthly newsletter *International Wealth Success*

Let's take a look at each of these potential sources of LPs.

Find LPs Yourself

Most LPs are wealthy people seeking the pluses of real estate investing without any of the drawbacks, other than the remote chance of losing some tax-deductible dollars. So you have to locate such people from local sources like:

- A social register

- Lists of golf, yacht, and country club members

- Expensive-auto dealer lists

- County clerk lists of investors in other limited partnerships

- Rentable mailing lists of high-income people

Before approaching any of these people, *be certain to get the advice of your attorney!*

Get Help from Friends

If you have wealthy friends, they may be able to give you the names of other wealthy people who might be interested in buying participations in your LP. If you do not have wealthy friends, as is probably the case, you'll have to try to meet some rich people.

You can meet wealthy people in the places they usually go, such as:

- Golf clubs

- Country clubs

- Yacht clubs

- University and college clubs

- Expensive restaurants

- Other similar places

The advantages of meeting wealthy people are often overlooked by the not so wealthy. Such people do not recognize the huge potential in networking with successful entrepreneurs. The advantages include:

- Many wealthy people are relaxed and friendly. Why? Because it's easy to be nice when you have a wad of money in the bank!

- One wealthy contact can lead to 10 or more others.

- Once you make money for one wealthy person, your reputation will spread and you may find yourself approached by a number of others with money in hand, trying to get you to invest it for them.

So cultivate good relations with *every* wealthy person you meet. You can benefit enormously from the contacts you make. (As an aside, make a habit of being friendly with everyone. You'll be happier—and you'll make many other people happy. Also, you will eventually profit from such an outlook.)

Use Other Available Sources

To get started in any business, you usually have to spend money. As the saying goes: "It takes money to make money!"

But where does a BWB turn when he or she has little or no money to spend on the advertising he or she wants to do to attract limited-partner investors in a real estate project? One place to turn is the monthly newsletter *International Wealth Success*. This helpful publication gives you: 100%, 110%, 115% financing (money) sources; compensating-balance loan sources; new wealth ideas every month; many, many sources of business loans; part-time moneymaking ideas; mail-order riches opportunities; hundreds of finder's fee listings; worldwide international moneymaking ideas; fast-fortune easy-money wealth deals; franchise riches ideas and methods; capital available for borrowers of many types; monthly Ty Hicks page where I talk to you; financial broker opportunities; hundreds of other ideas, sources, and ways to earn big money and make your fortune today; ways to get money you need; unique techniques to earn big money; successful methods that put cash in your pocket.

APPROACH PROSPECTS CAREFULLY

You are making a *private* offering of your LP. So you must be very careful not to violate any SEC or state rules and regulations. I can't act as your partnership adviser in this book. And I don't intend to try to so act. Only your *attorney* can do so. But in any private offering of a LP, you *must* be careful to:

- Follow *all* SEC and state requirements

- Limit your offer to the number and resident limitations for your area

- Prepare a suitable description (often called a prospectus) for your offer (your attorney can do this, if you can't)

- Be factual and accurate in all your dealings

SELL YOUR PARTICIPATION AND START WORKING

Returning to the LP we were considering earlier, let's see how it stands. With your 20 prospects identified and contacted, you sell each one a participation for $28,000, a price that is acceptable to all.* The LP thus takes in $560,000 in cash. Each limited partner signs the necessary forms, as shown in the LP offering mentioned earlier in this chapter.

With this cash in hand you negotiate the deal and take over the rental property for which the LP was formed. As a general partner you get a negotiated income that is acceptable to you. Also, you may get a portion of the ownership in the property, depending on the deal you worked out. As you get the various aspects of the property organized the way you want them, you can begin thinking of your *next* LP.

BUILD YOUR FUTURE RICHES

By assembling a series of LPs, you can start to build a multimillion-dollar real estate fortune in a few years. And as each LP grows and earns money for its members, you'll find you can sell participations quicker and with less effort. Why? Because your reputation will spread rapidly among monied people. Soon they'll be begging you to sell them participations—sight unseen!

Yes, the real estate LP can be your road to future riches. But to use this way to your wealth, you *must* have the advice of an attorney. Don't try to do it yourself—you can wind up with all kinds of legal problems that can eat away your profits, both present and future.

---

*This $28,000 is a higher partnership price *you* worked out with each prospect to give the LP more starting cash. (No LP was ever hurt—that I know of—by some extra starting cash!)

RELY ON THE INCREASE OF YOUR REAL ESTATE WEALTH

You need not worry about the safety of your real estate LPs, if you invest in well-located properties. The practical experience of real estate BWBs shows again and again that:

- Real estate property values double about every seven years, if the property is maintained properly and kept fully rented. For example, a property you paid $100,000 for could rise in value to $200,000 in seven years or so.

- Real estate rents for single- and multifamily units also double about every seven years. Thus, if an apartment rents for $800 a month when you buy an income property, the same apartment will rent for $1,600 a month about seven years later.

With these "built-in" rises for most income real estate, you really don't have to worry about the success of your LPs. The usual, expected price and rent increases will almost surely make your LPs safe for your investors and yourself!

USE A REIT TO RAISE REAL ESTATE MONEY TODAY

A real estate investment trust—called REIT, for short—is today's way to raise money for real estate. A REIT, which rhymes with "feet," is a real estate business organization that must, by laws governing its formation and taxation, invest in real estate properties or in mortgages on properties. With a REIT you can:

- Raise money from the public and invest this money in buildings, land, or mortgages of your choice

- Pay your investors out of the income the REIT earns from its holdings of buildings, land, or mortgages

- Use a brokerage house to do the actual selling of shares to the public, instead of you doing the selling

- Give yourself the advantage of raising money by going public and doing so in the real estate field

HOW TO FORM YOUR OWN REIT

You can form your own REIT by taking these easy, sure steps:

1. Decide what type of REIT you want to form and run. There are three types of REITs:

   - *Equity REITs* own income properties—such as apartment houses, shopping malls, factories, hotels, motels, hospitals.

   - *Mortgage REITs* lend money to real estate operators. The mortgage REIT's income is derived from interest and fees earned on loans the REIT makes.

   - *Hybrid REITs* own property and make mortgage loans—that is, they're a combination of the first two.

2. Choose the types of properties your REIT will own or lend on. Every type of real estate property that exists seems to have a REIT serving it. So you can form a REIT for the type of property you want to work with. The types of properties a REIT can invest in, or lend on, is enormous. Besides those listed above, REITs invest in or lend on:

   - Golf courses

   - Office buildings

   - Amusement parks

   - Psychiatric centers

   - Ministorage

   - Parking garages

   - Nursing homes

   - Race tracks—horse, auto

   - Marinas

   - Cold-storage buildings

   - Child-care centers

3. Estimate how much money you'll need for your REIT. When making your estimate, keep in mind that most REITs raise money

in the multimillions of dollars. Why? Because the public and institutional investors (who put money into REITs) are not interested in deals of less than $1 million. They're just not worth their time or money. So if a deal you have is less than $1 million, you'll have to get several deals to build up to the $1 million level. To help yourself make a sensible estimate of the number of properties you'll need:

- Count how many properties you want to own in your REIT. If the properties will be smaller ones, figure on at least 10, 20 midsize, or 5 large.

- Get the typical price of a property from real estate salespeople. With small properties at an average price of $500,000 each, you'll need at least $500,000 × 10 = $5 million for your REIT. With midsize properties at $1 million each average, you'll need $20 million for your REIT; with large properties at $5 million each, you'll need $25 million for your REIT. Add another 20% for startup operating costs (rent, salaries, fees) and you'll need $6 million, $22.4 million, and $30 million respectively for the REITs mentioned here.

4. Prepare, or have someone else prepare, a write-up (called a Declaration of Trust) telling what your REIT will do to earn profits from the properties it will hold.* Your profits can come in these ways:

- Equity REITs earn their major income from the rents they collect from tenants. A secondary source of income is the appreciation (rise in value) of their property when they sell it on the open market.

- Mortgage REITs earn their major income from interest and fees on the loans they make.

- Hybrid REITs have a combination of these income sources.

    A declaration of trust (DOT) uses simple language such as, "We will buy apartment houses in good condition and earn

---

*A declaration of trust resembles the charter for a corporation in which you tell the public, and any other investors you may have, what your REIT business will do to earn a profit.

money from the rents we collect." Or, "We will raise money from the public and then lend that money out on real estate projects and earn interest on the money we lend out."

5. If you purchase my REIT kit, my company will prepare for you—at no charge—a proposed declaration of trust for your planned REIT. You provide IWS with complete data on the type of REIT you want to start, how much money you need, and what your expected profits will be. In preparing a sample DOT for you, IWS is not giving investment advice, is not acting as a sales agent, is not providing professional consultation. Instead, IWS is simply writing a sample DOT, which will probably be altered by the brokerage house that will sell your REIT to their private or public investors.

6. Submit your declaration of trust to a brokerage house for having your shares sold to public or private investors. If the brokerage house likes your REIT idea, it will have the remainder of the offering circular prepared and the cost will come out of the proceeds of REIT shares sold to the public and other investors. No money will come out of your pocket for this work!

7. Carefully read your offering circular prepared by the brokerage house. You want to be sure it covers all the types of property you plan to invest in with your REIT. And if you plan to put any of your own existing properties into the REIT, you want to be certain they are included in your offering circular. You can never be too careful with these deals.

8. Give approval to the brokerage house to take your deal public. Watch as they take it to market and get 100 or more investors for your REIT, giving you the money you need to reach your real estate dreams, working with public and investor money!

9. Expand your REIT to cover other areas of the country or other types of property to increase your income and that of your shareholders. Be certain to run your REIT exactly in accord with the rules and, with luck, your income and wealth may grow steadily.

Points to Remember

- A limited partnership and/or REIT can build your real estate wealth steadily over a period of time.

- You *must* have a competent attorney to advise you in any limited partnership or REIT.

- Be sure to follow all national and local laws when setting up and running your limited partnership or REIT.

TWELVE

GO THE CONDO ROUTE TO YOUR REAL ESTATE WEALTH

Real estate wealth builders are among the most creative folks I've ever known, and I've met thousands of them. You'll find that real estate people are dedicated, creative, ambitious, alert, and enterprising folk.

SEE ZERO CASH AT WORK

Real estate people invented the condominium—*condo* for short—because they felt a need to satisfy people who enjoy living in an apartment house and who are seeking:

- A piece of real estate of their own
- Legal tax deductions for their real estate
- A "piece of the action" in a hot real estate market
- Superior housing or office space

In a condo each owner has all the above advantages. And the real estate wealth builder gets the *big* return that can be earned by someone using his or her brain and creative thinking. Let's see how you can put zero cash to work in condos.

WATCH YOUR WEALTH GROW

Let's say that you spot a nice piece of land for an income apartment house. You survey the property and find that you can put up a 100-unit building at an average cost of $50,000 per unit, including the purchase of the land. This means that the total cost of your income building will be: 100 units×$50,000 per unit=$5 million. With the usual real estate financing, you can borrow up to 70% of this amount, 0.70×$5 million=$3.5 million. So, to construct this building on this land, you'll have to raise $5 million−$3.5 million=$1.5 million cash.

But if you decide to make the building a condo and *sell* each of the 100 apartments, here's what happens:

- The land cost remains the *same*.

- The construction cost remains the *same*.

- Your borrowing ability *zooms*.

Let's see how this can happen. You'll quickly see the value of creative financing using *none* of your own cash.

PUT OTHER PEOPLE'S MONEY TO WORK

A condo apartment will usually command a list price of at least twice its cost. This means that the apartments in this building will sell for $100,000. (Your asking price would probably be $99,995.) Thus, your potential revenue from selling 100 apartments would be: 100 units× $100,000/unit=$10 million. With a 70% loan-to-value ratio, as before, you can borrow 0.70×$10 million=$7 million. Since the building and land will cost you $5 million, you could (with the figure we have here) *mortgage out* with $7 million−$5 million=$2 million cash!

"But," you say, "I can get 70% financing for a rental-income building I can put up on this land. Won't that change the deal?" No, it really won't change it that much because you'll still have to come up with the cash for the rental building (30% of $5 million or $1.5 million here) while you'd net out with MIF (money in fist) on the condo. True, it is usually easier to rent an apartment than to sell one, but the whole point is:

With a condo you might get 100%-plus financing from the start. But this is often difficult with a straight rental building. Condo financing is often easier, and quicker, because the lender knows you'll be selling the units before, or on, completion. Thus, you'll repay the loan faster!

LEARN THE FACTS OF REAL ESTATE MONEY

"But why," you ask, "can I get such a better deal on the condo?" There are several reasons:

- With the condo, you sell out all (or almost all) of your ownership of the property.
- You have little rise in value of your condo building because you don't own much (or any) of it.
- Rise in land values are also out for you for the same reason.

If you want to go the cash-on-the-line route, pick the conventional rental building deal, either residential or commercial. But if you're the beginning wealth builder (BWB) I think you *might* be, with:

- Little cash today
- No big inheritances coming along
- Possible credit problems
- Strapped for future loans

then the condo way to wealth is a great way to start. (For even if you never put up your own condo, you'll learn a great deal just by checking out the condo idea.)

CONDOS ARE BUSTING OUT ALL OVER

Recently I made a wonderful cross-country editorial and business trip, stopping along the way to visit many readers of my books and my *International Wealth Success* newsletter. While on this trip I was delighted to see:

- Townhouse-type condos
- Apartment-house-type condos
- Office-building condos
- Industrial-park condos

Here are a few of the more important reasons for putting up so many condos:

- A hundred percent, or better, financing is often possible.

- The land gets "higher use" because the structure on it is worth more.

- Less time may be needed for the financing approval.

- Condos sell faster because they help people and firms make tax savings.

Truly, good BWB friend, the condo concept could put you into the multimillionaire class sooner than you think! And I'd just love to see you in that class within the next year—or even sooner.

PLAY THE CONDO GAME ON ZERO CASH

As many of you who've read my earlier books, taken my courses, or read my newsletter know, I'm a *zero-cash* enthusiast from way back. By this I mean:

It is my firm belief—based on years of actual experience—that you can start and succeed in your own business using very little or no cash at all!

Condos are one zero-cash activity in which you can "get off the ground" quickly and easily. Let's see how.

Two friends of mine moved south recently and soon discovered the condo boom in their new city. Seeing condo apartments advertised for *no cash down* while still in the construction stage, they "bought" several of these condos by just signing a few option papers. Since it would take at least a year for the condo to be finished, these friends thought there was a good chance that the value of each apartment would increase and they could sell out their options at a profit.

And that's just what happened! Each friend realized a $12,500 profit on each apartment in less than a year without investing a penny!

Other people use a similar method for condo apartments requiring a fully refundable down payment. They hold the apartment until they sell the option. Or—if they can't sell the option—they allow the apartment to revert to the building promoter and get a full refund of their money.

Their only loss is the interest the money might have earned for them if they left it in the bank. Deposits required for condos under construction are often nominal—$100 or thereabout. Some developers, however, may require you to deposit $3,000 or more.

There are other ways of playing the condo game on zero cash. These include:

1. Taking over several units in a condo with no cash down by using your relatives and friends. Arrange the order each person gives so that you cover the most desirable areas in the building—such as corners, top floor, penthouse, or any other areas you think will be popular. Sell out these holdings as the demand for space in the building increases. Hold choice spots until the end, when the prices are likely to be the highest.

2. Offer to help sell units for the owner, provided he or she gives you title to one or more units for no cash down. Hold your units until the last and then *sell out* at a high price.

Before using any of these methods, be sure to check them out with your attorney. The rules on condos vary widely from one state to another. You *must* obey the laws in force in your state.

USE THE "NEW" CONDO METHODS

As I mentioned earlier, real estate people are among the most creative folks I've ever met. So a few months ago when I first heard of the "new" condo I was delighted to see that it was another example of creative real estate thinking. Here's how it works.

In many cities some of the older apartment houses and office buildings have been owned by their owners for so long that they have ceased to provide tax shelter. This means that much of the income from the building is taxable, leaving fewer money-in-fist (MIF) spendable dollars. So some of the owners decided they wanted "out." To get out some owners hit on the idea of selling the building to the rent-paying tenants! Here's how this works.

Let's say that you own a 10-unit building having 10 identical units. The building and land are worth a total of $1 million. You decide you want to sell the building to the tenants.

With a value of $1 million for the land and the building and 10 units in the building, each unit is—at first glance—worth $100,000.

But let's look at your building a little closer. When a tenant buys a unit (which is his or her complete apartment plus part of the lobby, land, etc.), he or she gets:

- Ownership of his or her unit

- Tax deductions he or she may not have had before

- Part ownership of the land

- A chance to get in on the rise in value of the property

- Other benefits of ownership

So each unit is really worth more than $100,000. In your opinion, every unit is worth $130,000. You propose to the tenants that the building be converted to condos (after you've had your attorney advise you on the legal aspects in your area). Six tenants agree right off and four tenants refuse.

Depending on the area your property is in, you can start converting right away. (The rules vary from one area to another, so *check with your attorney*.)

Let's say that you sell six units within a month for $130,000 each, giving you $780,000 cash. You then still own 40% of the building.

Two of the four tenants who refused your condo idea soon move out in disgust. If these tenants refuse to move out, you'll have to wait until some natural event such as marriage, divorce, or death occurs, making the units available for sale. You quickly sell these two units and you now have $780,000+$260,000=$1,040,000 in cash and you still own 20% of a $1 million building!

Now you can probably sell out the other two units. Or you can keep one for yourself and sell out the other. If you do this you'll come out of the deal with $1,170,000 in cash and a 10% ownership in the building!

GET IN ON THE "NEW" CONDO YOURSELF

"Ty," you say, "this is a great idea! There's just one catch, man—*I don't have any building to sell to the tenants*. Further, I don't even have the cash to get the building to sell to the tenants! So your idea is a bad one for me."

"Now hold on a moment," I reply. Recall that real estate is:

- A borrowed-money business

- Often a 100%-plus financed business

- A business with billions in lendable cash

- A business in which beginners can win riches

A borrowed-money business can really make your life much easier because it means that:

- There's money available for *you*

- This money is easier to get

- You can probably get 100%-plus financing

Let's see how the "new" condo could work for you.

Let's say you see an older office building in your area that you'd like to buy and convert to commercial condos. The price of the building and land is $500,000. You think you can convert the building to condos and get $700,000 to $800,000 for it. Let's trace the steps you take.

Find the Mortgage Data You Need

In any real estate deal, your initial step, after learning the price of the property you want, is to find out:

1. The first mortgage amount, if any, on the property

2. The amount of any junior mortgages (second, third, fourth) on the property

Once you have the mortgage data, your next steps are:

1. Determine if you can assume (take over) the existing mortgage

2. If you can't take over the existing mortgage, determine how large a new first mortgage you can get on the property

3. Find out how large a purchase-money mortgage (PM) the seller will give you

Using the above steps, you find out that you cannot take over the existing first mortgage. This often happens when the interest rate on the existing mortgage is two or three percentage points below the going interest rates on mortgages at the time you want to buy the property.

While asking about the existing mortgage, you also learn that you can get a new mortgage for 70% of the property value, or $0.70 \times \$500,000 = \$350,000$. This means that if you want to take over the property for 100%-plus financing, and we're assuming you do, you'll have to find $\$500,000 - \$350,000 = \$150,000$ for the junior mortgages. Also, your closing costs (legal fees, taxes, etc.) will probably run about $5,000.

Next, you ask about junior mortgages. (These are second, third, fourth mortgages.) There are various ways you can get such mortgages. The ways used most often include:

1. Borrowing from a second-mortgage lender

2. Getting the seller to give you a mortgage for all or part of the amount you need. (This is called a purchase-money or PM mortgage)

3. A combination of these methods

You ask the seller to give you as large a PM mortgage as possible. He agrees to give you a PM mortgage of $50,000, leaving you with $\$150,000 - \$50,000 = \$100,000$ still to go.

To get this $100,000 you contact a second mortgage lender. After some discussion, he agrees to lend you $105,000: the $100,000 plus $5,000 for closing costs. The term or duration of your loan will be five years.

TAKE OVER THE PROPERTY YOU WANT

You meet with your attorney, the seller, and the mortgage lenders and arrange for the *contract*. This is the usual first step in most real estate purchase deals. In the time between the contract and the closing (called the *passing* in some states), you get the various loans you need.

At the closing there's usually a mad shuffling of papers, a lot of talk in terms you may not understand, and the signing of what seems like hundreds of names on dozens of papers. But after a hectic 90 minutes you finally own your own office building! You're really in real estate—at long last.

True, you now owe various banks, people, and other lenders $505,000.

But you *do* have an income to pay off these loans, plus depreciable property to shelter from taxes all—or almost all—of your income. And you have your plan to convert to condos as soon as possible. Also, your assets have risen by half a million dollars! (So have your liabilities, or what you owe!)

GET YOUR MONEY BACK QUICKLY

Once you have this office building in your own, or corporate, name, you approach the tenants either personally, by telephone, fax, e-mail, or by postal mail, asking them if they are interested in buying their rented space. As is usual when such requests are made, 50% to 60% probably say yes immediately. You sell their space to them and within three months you've taken in $573,000. You use this to pay off the various loans on the building.

Once you have some "financial breathing room"—that is, you've either completely, or almost completely, paid off your loans—you can start concentrating on the last few tenants. In almost every condo conversion, it's the sale of the property to these "end-of-the-line" tenants that puts the big-money profits into *your* pockets.

Selling out to these tenants brings in another $292,000. Here's how the overall deal works out for you:

Total selling price of condo	=	$865,000
Cost of property, including closing	=	505,000
Gross income, excluding interest	=	$360,000
Interest, real estate taxes, miscellaneous	=	68,000
Net profit	=	$292,000

So, starting with *no* cash, you have, in a period of a few months, accumulated nearly $300,000. Of course, you'll have to pay income taxes on this profit. However, if you earn this much in a few months, I'm sure you'll be pleased to pay the taxes due.

ANOTHER "NEW" CONDO IDEA

In some areas of the country that have vacation appeal—such as Florida, California, South Carolina—real estate wealth builders came up with another "new" condo idea. In this one, each of six or more people buys a one-sixth (or less) interest in a condo apartment unit.* Each buyer can

---

*In some condos, as many as 26 people own it, giving each owner two weeks' use per year.

spend two months of the year in his or her condo apartment. Or, if another buyer wishes, he or she can rent his or her apartment out for the two months, instead of living in it. By renting the apartment out for two months, the buyer can usually pay for it (that is, recover his or her investment) in three to four years.

Now what does this mean to *you*, a beginning real estate wealth builder offering such apartments for sale? Well, since you may have difficulty selling an apartment in times of reduced economic activity, this approach can get your cash money inflowing faster. Let's see how.

Say that you build or buy a building having 20 apartment units in a vacation area. Typical values of such vacation units are in the $100,000 range and higher. Using $100,000 each for your units, fully furnished, a one-sixth interest would cost a buyer $100,000÷6=$16,666. Besides his or her one-sixth ownership, the buyer will also get common ownership use of the building's recreational facilities, pool, dock, etc.

To you, as a condo real estate wealth builder, there are a number of big advantages in doing business this way, including:

- It is often easier to sell smaller priced partial units.

- As soon as a portion of a unit is sold, cash becomes available to you.

- You can earn fees handling the rental of the condos during the year.

If you'd like to live in a vacation area while you earn money, think about going the condo route—either full or partial! It might put *you* into the big money soon!

USE "BUILT-IN" FINANCING TO GET YOUR CONDO

With "built-in" financing your condo seller has your loan approved before you buy! Built-in financing can save you years of effort in your real estate fortune building with condos, because you:

- Take over a condo with financing set up for you by the seller. The money is there for you.

- Have *half* the challenge of getting your condo solved for you because the financing is waiting for your acceptance of it. The other half—finding a suitable condo—is already solved when you find the condo you want

- Save time in getting your condo because you don't have to search for a lender to get started

How and where can you find built-in financing for your condo? Look for condos advertised thus:

1. The condo property is described in the ad, followed by: *Financing available.*

2. The condo property is described in the ad, followed by: *Owner will finance.*

3. The condo property is described in the ad, followed by: *Owner financing.*

4. The condo property is described in the ad, followed by: *0 cash down.*

Where can you find such condo deals? They're all around you—just take a look in the following sources:

1. Your large-city Sunday newspaper in the real estate section.

2. Real estate industry magazines—covering the field in which you buy your condo property.

3. Trade associations covering condo real estate in the area in which you want to invest and earn money.

When you find such condo deals advertised—and you will if you look long enough—contact the condo seller immediately. Get the following data:

- Asking price; annual income; annual expenses; annual profit when the condo is rented out

- Time needed to take over the condo real estate from the seller

- What is expected of you to qualify to buy the condo real estate being offered for sale

- Any guarantees offered the buyer in the event the purchase does not work out to be what the seller promises

If all seems positive, go ahead and buy the condo—with built-in financing—and you'll get started earning your real estate fortune fast!

BE A MULTICONDO OWNER

Friends of mine who live on Long Island (where I also reside) aren't in love with cold winters. So they journey to Florida right after their New Year's Eve celebration welcoming in the new year. These good friends stay in Florida off and on through April.

Two of these friends bought several condos each in an older Atlantic Ocean waterfront building. Their business logic told them:

1. The ocean would always be there, attracting renters for their condo units.

2. Being an older building, the price of one- or two-bedroom condo apartments was lower than an equivalent unit in a new building or a single-family home.

3. The building's location—in the center of the entertainment, sports, and dining attractions—made the older condos just as attractive as newer condos and single-family homes farther away from the center of attractions.

4. These friends believed they could rent the older condos for the same monthly charge as newer condos and single-family homes because of their convenient location near the major attractions.

Guided by these four thoughts, these two friends bought several condos each, using borrowed money for the down payment. Today, each condo is rented at an average of $300 per month more than their total mortgage and maintenance payments. Further, the depreciation they are allowed to take on the condos shelters their condo income from income taxes. Income from other businesses is also partly sheltered by the condo depreciation. Both of these friends are delighted with the results of their condo investments.

RENTING CONDOS TO SUBLET

Another friend of mine is a piano-player and singer who performs in Florida nightclubs during the winter months. Three years ago he rented a condo for himself and found—one week later—that he could sublet the condo for a $200 per month profit.

After doing a little market research by reading newspaper ads for apartments wanted and apartments available, he concluded that he could make money subletting rented condos. In a day he was into a new business.

Within a week, he rented and sublet five condo apartments. His income rose by more than $1,000 per month with no ownership responsibilities.

The two real-life examples given here (*multicondo ownership* and *renting condos to sublet*) show that you *can* make money in condos, starting with little cash. So take your pick—multicondo ownership or subletting in a populated area. Either way, you can earn a sizeable income, starting with no cash!

PROFIT FROM THE WORLD'S CONDO CRAZE

Today, condos are selling at higher prices than ever before in history. You should be in on the rapid rise in value of residential condo units throughout the world. For instance, a 5,541-square-foot condo in New York sold for $2,256 per square foot at the time of this writing. Its total price was $12.5 million!

Another condo, in a nearby building, sold a few weeks later for $3,000 per square foot. Maid's rooms for these condos sell for $400,000 to $600,000 each, even though they are only 400 square feet in area. There are private wine cellars for half the 38 condos in this $100,000-million building. Sales of 32 of the 38 apartments in the building produced over $260 million in revenue.

The monthly maintenance charges for high-priced condo apartments can run as high as $12,000!

To cash in on the condo craze, take these easy, quick steps:

1. Look for a condo apartment offered for sale by a troubled owner—divorce, death in the family, child leaving for college, etc.

2. Contact the owner directly. Ask that you be shown the condo so you know what you're bidding on.

3. Get full details on the asking price, maintenance charges, utility costs, real estate taxes, etc.

4. Review the numbers carefully to see if you can earn a profit charging the going rent for the size apartment in the area where the building is located. Your rental income should cover your mortgage and maintenance payments.

5. Check recent condo sales in the area. See if the price you're being asked to pay is in line with the sales price of the units that were sold.

6. Make an offer on the condo if your research shows that you can make money holding the condo for a year or two and then selling it on the open market.

Pick your condo carefully and you're almost certain to benefit from today's condo craze. You should make a bundle when you sell a residential condo you've held for one year or longer. Keep at it for a few years and your name might be listed as the seller of a $12.5-million condo!

CO-OPS ALSO MAKE MONEY

Cooperative real estate—often called co-ops—is probably more common for apartment houses than for any other type of real estate. In a co-op each tenant owns one or more shares of stock in a corporation that in turn owns the building and land. Ownership of one or more shares of stock entitles the tenant to occupy one apartment in the building. Monthly or annual maintenance charges are paid by each tenant for the upkeep of the building. The charge for maintenance is usually based on the area occupied by the tenant's apartment.

Since ownership in a co-op is shared, there is less chance for a beginning real estate wealth builder to hit the big money. For this reason, most BWBs prefer the condo route to wealth.

But if you'd like to try to build your real estate wealth in co-ops, you might want to consider trying the following.

1. Use borrowed money to buy one or more co-op units.

2. Become active in the co-op management group.

3. Push the idea of constant improvement of the property by the management.

4. If you own more than one unit, rent out the units you don't occupy yourself.

5. Try to take over other units in the building so you share in more of the value rise.

6. Sell out when prices reach a level where you can earn a good profit.

7. Work closely with the co-op board of directors to get approval of your renting your apartment on a long-term basis.

8. Pick *all* your tenants carefully. You want each to behave well so the board of directors does not order any of your tenants out of the building.

9. If you need help with any of your real estate financing, and you're a two-year subscriber to my newsletter, feel free to ask for my suggestions.

Points to Remember

- Condos offer owners a "piece of the real estate profit action."

- Condos offer greater profit potentials to many real estate operators.

- OPM (other people's money) is a powerful force in condo wealth building.

- 100%-plus financing is possible with condos.

- Condos are being built in many areas of the country and for many purposes.

- Some condos can be financed with "zero cash."

- Existing buildings are sometimes converted to condos by being sold to their tenants.

- Office and industrial buildings are now being built as, or converted to, condos.

- Junior mortgages can often help you get 100% financing of condos.

- Condos offer quick recovery of your cash investment.

- Vacation condos offer wealth opportunities to real estate wealth builders.

- Co-op buildings can also make money for some real estate dealers.

THIRTEEN

HOW TO COMBINE REAL ESTATE AND OTHER PROFITABLE BUSINESSES

Many beginning wealth builders (BWBs) I meet (and I meet many) are more interested in earning *big* money from a business than from real estate. Yet when they try to borrow money for another business—say, an indoor swimming pool, a boat marina, or a hardware store—they find the money is hard to raise. So when they hear of 100% financing in real estate, they find it difficult to believe. Yet with a little thinking and planning they might get 100% financing for the business they like when they combine it with real estate. Let's see how.

GO THE BORROWED-MONEY ROAD

Ken P. is a swimming "nut." He swims every day of the year he can get near the water. (I think he even swims in his bathtub!) Besides swimming for exercise, Ken gives swimming lessons, teaches skin and scuba diving, and works as a lifeguard at a local beach. Ken's ambition in life—as you might guess—is to own an indoor swimming pool in which he can give year-round swimming lessons while taking a daily dip himself.

"I don't want to go into real estate," Ken told me on the phone one evening when he called me for help. "Yet when I try to borrow money to build an indoor pool, people say: 'Come around *after* you've put up the pool and we'll be glad to help you then.'"

"Ken," I replied, "I've heard stories like this a hundred times. What you have to do is start using some creative financing methods!"

"But how can I use creative financing methods when I can't get the money to start with?" he asked. "You have to go the borrowed-money route," I replied. Then I pointed out to Ken that:

1. Real estate is a borrowed-money business.

2. An indoor swimming pool usually needs land and a building.

3. It is common practice to borrow money to buy land.

4. It is also common practice to borrow money to construct a building.

5. By thinking in terms of real estate instead of the business that will eventually occupy the real estate, the businessperson can often get 100% financing for both the real estate *and* the business.

6. Many businesses eventually earn more from their real estate investments than they do from their regular profit-making activities.

"Sounds good," Ken said. "But I don't want to be a miserable little landlord. I want to make big money so I can really enjoy my life!"

GET ALL THE THINGS YOU WANT

Ken's remark about the "miserable little landlord" really annoyed me. "Ken," I said, "until you're ready to at least listen to what I say, you can try getting free help for yourself elsewhere." Then I hung up.

The reason I was annoyed was because I had just returned from a Caribbean business trip to the beautiful island of St. Thomas. There I'd met one of the biggest real estate men in the world—a man who owned 14,000 rental apartments in a northern city of the United States.

During a friendly conversation in the gazebo overlooking the beautiful Caribbean palms, sand, and water, I did some quick mental arithmetic.

"With 14,000 units and an average monthly net rent of $200 per unit, your monthly net income before mortgage payments is around $2.8 million," I said to the real estate man. "And in 12 months you take in some $33.6 million. That's a nice piece of change to any businessperson."

He laughed. "It sure is! But your average net rent figure is a bit low. My actual cash income—the last time I looked—is about $38 million a year. It keeps me in Caddies and penthouses and big yachts without any problems!"

So this man was no "miserable little landlord." And he started by using borrowed money to take over his first property! Further, he built his empire on borrowed money! Yet here was Ken, a BWB with *no* money who was ready to criticize a successful real estate landlord without any real reason for doing so. Since I admire people who start with little and end up with a big bundle, I also try to protect them from uninformed critics.

As you probably guessed, Ken called back a few nights later, full of apologies. During our conversation I told him about my St. Thomas friend and his $38-million-a-year cash flow. "Now, Ken," I joked, "I know that $38 million a year isn't much money to *you,* but it sure is a lot to most people!"

Ken sputtered and said: "Stop the kidding and tell me how I can get started in real estate—tonight!" I answered by telling him the steps usually taken by businesspeople who combine real estate with another business. The steps they, and you, would take are:

1. Decide what business you want to enter.

2. Determine how much real estate you need.

3. Look for a suitable property and building (if needed).

4. Get a price for the property from the seller.

5. Borrow as much money as you need.

6. Take over the property.

7. Start running your business on the property.

Ken took these steps. The only difference was that Ken had to have a suitable building put up for his swimming pool because none of the properties he found had a building he could use. Because his area needed a recreational facility as well as a pool, Ken added a gym, meeting rooms, a game room, and other facilities to his pool building—all on 100% financing. Here's how he got his financing:

1. He took an option on a suitable piece of land.

2. He prepared a business plan showing what services he intended to offer, his expected yearly revenues for the first three years in business, and the cost of the building he planned to build.

3. He applied to lenders, using his business plan as a guide for their loan thinking.

4. He received firm loan offers from some lenders, showing that these lenders had faith in his plan.

5. He contacted sports enthusiasts who agreed to cosign for him for the needed 25% down payment for the land and building.

Today Ken has a booming pool and recreation business. His customers include thousands of local residents and numerous local Boy Scout, Girl Scout, Sea Scout, and Explorer Scout troops, and high school and college swimming teams.

And of course the pool area is Ken's delight. There are really two pools—one for diving practice and contests and the other for swimming practice and contests. Done in modern decorative tile, the pools are the nicest I've ever seen anywhere.

"Ty," Ken said as we finished our tour, "I'm sorry for my crack about the landlord. You were right to hang up on me. It brought me to my senses. I have to thank real estate for putting me in the recreation business! Thanks again, friend."

UNDERSTAND WHAT REAL ESTATE CAN DO FOR YOU

There are hundreds of other businesses that you can "hinge" and leverage around real estate. When I say hinge and leverage, I mean:

With a real estate–based business you can often borrow the money you need for the business and the real estate by using the real estate as the collateral for your loan.

Typical real estate–based businesses (that is, businesses in which real estate is an important element of the business profit activity) include:

- Marinas, boatyards
- Camps, hunting lodges, theme parks
- Mobile home parks, trailer parks
- Motels, hotels, youth hostels
- Apartment houses, condominiums

- Auto wrecking yards, junkyards

- Factories

- Airports, golf courses, country clubs

- Parking lots, garages, storage yards

- Warehouses, miniwarehouses

There are many others.

Since a number of these businesses require little investment other than that for the real estate, you can often get started or take over an ongoing business on little or no cash. This means that the real estate serves as your collateral or backing for the loan. While you may be much more interested in your business activities (such as a parking lot, a mobile home park, tennis court) than in real estate, it may be the land or buildings that put you into your business!

MAKE YOUR FORTUNE AS A LOAN ORIGINATOR

A *loan originator* is a person who finds real estate borrowers for lenders of many different types—banks, mortgage companies, credit unions, private investors. As a loan originator you:

- Do not need a license of any kind; instead you work as an independent contractor under the lender's license, which covers you and all the work you do.

- Work on a commission basis; you are paid when a deal is completed. If the deal does not go through (a loan is not made) you are not paid anything. Any expenses you have—gas, postage, phone calls—are yours to pay in full!

- Usually work with just one lender. And as a local loan originator you generally work in a named area, such as one city or state your lender services. But this can be a source of good income for you in many areas. Active real estate sales may bring you a commission several times a month.

- Work part-time, usually in the evenings, because almost all loan originators deal in home mortgages. To get a deal closed, you must see the owners at the same time. Generally, the only time they're available is evenings and weekends. This means you work these times to close deals.

"So what," you ask, "is the difference between a financial broker and a loan originator?" Here are the usual differences today:

1. The financial broker usually works with numerous lenders nationwide or worldwide. The loan originator generally works exclusively with just one lender locally.

2. The financial broker works on many different types of loans—industrial expansion, inventory, mortgage, accounts receivable, advertising, personnel. The loan originator usually works only on single-family home mortgages. These may be first mortgages, home refinancing, or home equity loans, depending on the lender you work with.

3. The financial broker is typically paid a fee of 5% of the loan amount up to the first million, 4% on the second, and so on. The loan originator is typically paid 1% of the loan amount after the loan is made. But the loan originator knows the lender he or she works with will make the loan, if the borrower is qualified. A financial broker is never sure a lender will make a loan.

Then why become a loan originator? For several good reasons, namely:

1. You can learn real estate lending quickly, in your local area.

2. You get free real estate loan training.

3. You can close a lot of deals if you work at finding clients.

4. You get great experience at little cost to yourself.

5. You can go on to become a successful financial broker using the experience you gained as a loan originator and work only nine to five!

Call or visit your local banks and mortgage lenders to start successful loan originating as a source of extra income and enormous knowledge and experience about real estate lending. You may even find the real estate loan you're seeking for yourself!

HOW TO GET BUSINESS MONEY THROUGH REAL ESTATE

Since real estate is a borrowed-money business, it is usually much easier to borrow on real estate than on any other type of business. (Yes! real estate *is* also a business.) Knowing this, you can get ready to combine real estate and the business of your choice. For best results, you might want to consider taking these six profit-laden steps:

1. Try to keep your business cash needs as low as possible.

2. Allow time for your business to grow—don't expect the real estate to support gold-painted jet planes at the start!

3. Pay attention to the details of your real estate deals—they may make you a bigger fortune than your business does!

4. Try to get some monthly income from your real estate, besides using it as a source of 100% financing and a place to conduct your business.

5. Hold onto your real estate while prices are rising in your area.

6. Keep accurate records of your real estate expenses, income, and profits.

In most businesses, real estate—either rented or owned—is just an extra expense we have to pay. What I'm suggesting here is that you make this extra-expense item pay for itself and, it is hoped, earn *you* a profit.

RENTED PROPERTY CAN EARN YOU BIG PROFITS

A young friend of mine is a world-recognized computer expert. His firm grew quickly from a borrowed desk in a friend's office to a payroll of more than 500 people because he worked hard and gave good service to his customers. After several expansions of his office, he decided to move his firm into a brand-new, sparkling office building. Since there was a severe shortage of office space at the time (as there usually is, every few years or so), my friend Chuck decided to rent nearly twice as much space as he needed at the moment for his firm. He then sublet the space he didn't need, earning a nice profit on other people's property (OPP).

Today smart real estate wealth builders are renting entire buildings and then subleasing them, or portions of them, to large firms. There are a number of advantages to you if you use such a plan, including:

1. No large down payment required

2. No title search, transfer tax, or other similar fees or expenses

3. Quicker (usually) takeover of the building

4. All rent payments made by you are usually fully tax deductible

5. No need to sell the building when you want to close your business

Renting a building and then subleasing it to others is more of a *business* activity than a real estate investment. So you lose some of the inherent advantages of real estate since in rental property you rent to others there is:

1. *No* depreciation to help offset your rental income (except some minor writeoffs for improvements you may make to the inside of the building)

2. *No* appreciation in value of your land or building since you don't own either

3. *No* chance to refinance your mortgage to give you tax-free cash

Even though rental real estate that you sublease to others *does* have these disadvantages, let's take a quick look at a typical deal to see how you might profit from it.

Rental Sublease Deal

You rent an eight-story office building containing 10,000 square feet of floor area per floor for $18 per square foot per year. Then you rent out various floors at the best rates you can get. Here's how your building rental expense and sublease income might work out.

Rental Expenses:

Building rental cost to you per year	=	$1,440,000
8 stories × 10,000 sq. ft./story × $18/sq. ft.		
Building operating expenses (electricity, labor, maintenance, insurance, etc.)	=	300,000
Total annual cost to you	=	$1,740,000

Rental Income per Year:

10,000 sq. ft. @ $22/sq. ft.	=	$220,000	
30,000 sq. ft. @ $25/sq. ft.	=	750,000	
20,000 sq. ft. @ $28/sq. ft.	=	560,000	
20,000 sq. ft. @ $30/sq. ft.	=	600,000	
Total income	=	$2,130,000	
Total annual cost	=	1,740,000	
Net income to you	=	$390,000	

So, by taking on a big building such as this with no cash down, you develop an income of about $390,000 per year. I say "about" because you might have other unexpected expenses (such as sudden roof leaks, fire damage, etc.) that could reduce your income somewhat. However, I think you now see clearly the method, namely:

You can make money from rented buildings with no cash down if you can rent out the space at a higher rate than you pay for the space.

Note: If you're wondering why the rental rates vary from one floor to another in the above example, it's because the rent *charged* varies with the:

1. Height above the ground

2. View offered by higher floors

3. Services the tenant gets with the rent

So the variations in the rent payment per square foot reflect these differences.

PROFIT WHILE YOU CAN

"But," you ask, "why doesn't the owner rent out the building and make this income, instead of letting me do this?" There are any number of reasons why the owner might rather rent his or her entire building to one person, instead of many, including:

1. Only one tenant to deal with instead of many

2. Fewer leases, tenant credit checks, etc.

3. No maintenance headaches

4. Fewer vacancy problems

Some building owners would prefer to sun themselves in California or Florida while holding only one lease per building than to have the headaches that might come from 50 leases on space in the same building. Such owners are people who've "made it" in life. They have either earned enough for themselves or inherited enough to allow them to live without a struggle.

You can help such people (and there are more around than you might think) while earning big money for yourself by:

1. Running their buildings

2. Providing rental space for others

3. Earning a profit for the owner

To find buildings you can rent out profitably, look at the real estate columns of any large-city newspaper under these as well as other headings:

- Buildings for rent (commercial and residential)

- Buildings for sale (commercial and residential)

- Real estate opportunities

And keep in mind one key fact about rental buildings of all types, namely:

Renting a building can be your fastest and lowest-cost way to get into real estate without the need for a large cash outlay by yourself.

Think about this for a moment. Rental real estate could put millions of dollars into your pocket in three years! And you do *not* need a big bundle of money to get started—less than $100 is often enough! And if you include an option to buy the building as part of your lease, you may eventually own it!

COMBINE THE STOCK MARKET AND REAL ESTATE

With a few investors you can start a real estate investment trust—REIT for short. Once your REIT is formed, you can—with proper legal guidance—sell shares of your REIT to the general public. Some REITs sell $10 million worth of shares before they own a square inch of land or one brick or one nail in a building! Others have sold as much as $50 million in shares *before* doing any business.

Your REIT can, if you wish, specialize in certain aspects of real estate, such as:

- Mortgages (short or long term)
- Construction funds (for two to three years)
- Real estate operation
- Second, or junior, mortgages
- Land and site development

Or, if you wish, your REIT can go into any or all of these real estate activities. The main point to keep in mind is that:

In a REIT you combine the magic power of OPM—other people's money—with the rapid growth of real estate and the potential rise in the value of the REIT shares on the stock market.

One beauty of selling shares in your REIT is that the equity money you receive for the shares is *not* a loan. Hence, you do *not* have to repay this money. Instead, you work hard to make the money grow in value as the real estate you control rises in value. REITs are discussed in greater detail in chapter 11. I've covered them briefly again in this chapter because they are a unique example of how you can combine real estate with another business—in this case, the stock market.

You can get full data on forming your own REIT from *How to Build Your Real Estate Fortune Today in a Real Estate Investment Trust Kit*, described in chapter 15.

MAKE THEATERS YOUR FORTUNE SOURCE

Theaters require space, whether they're movie houses, legitimate theaters, outdoor movies, minitheaters, or multiplex theaters. Many people live comfortable, easy-hour, no-stress lives on the income from theaters. And they get to see the latest shows free in their own theaters and in those of their friends!

As a theater property owner or renter, you can:

1. Operate your theater on the property

2. Rent the property to a theater operator

3. Combine the theater with another business

For example, a theater owner I know runs his outdoor movie theaters at night. But during the day he rents out his theater as a parking lot for commuters who don't want to drive all the way into the city. This owner got a local bus company to stop its buses at his lot to pick up passengers who parked their cars in his lot during the day!

And if you're artistically inclined—or your spouse is—you can run any kind of shows in your theater that appeal to you. If your choice matches the interests of the public, then you'll profit while enjoying the shows free! Also, your real estate holdings in the theater will probably be rising in value at the same time.

OTHER REAL ESTATE–BASED BUSINESSES FOR YOU

There are many other real estate–based businesses that could pay you big profits while your real estate rises in value. These businesses include:

- Health clubs, gyms
- Bowling alleys, billiard parlors
- Golf courses, country clubs
- Motels, hotels, ranches
- Farms, citrus groves, timber lands
- Marinas, fishing stations, hunting lodges
- Ski slopes, ski lodges
- Theme parks, trailer parks
- Indoor tennis, outdoor tennis

Often, people will invest in one or more of these businesses because they are more interested in immediate cash flow than in the long-term rise in real estate values. Yet over a period of years their real estate may pay them a larger return than their daily cash flow!

Friends of mine who like sports own two real estate–related businesses. One is a ski lodge in the West for their winter skiing. The other business is a marina in the East for their summer sailing fun. Other friends own only one real estate business—working at the business about six months of the year and relaxing the other six! While they're off for six months their building is closed, safe and sound from storms and other natural events. Knowing this, they have fun year round.

TRY "MOVING REAL ESTATE" TO BUILD YOUR WEALTH

All real estate—no matter where it is located—has one common characteristic:

Real estate is permanent—it does not move from one spot to another. The land remains where it was staked out on the deed.

Yet real estate often provides a number of common services, such as:

- Shelter from the elements

- Comfort, cover, convenience

- Status, location, enclosure

Certain movable structures not permanently connected to land but offering real estate services (shelter, comfort, etc.) might be termed "movable real estate." The "movable real estate" I'm talking about here includes:

- Boats, such as sailboats, houseboats, yachts

- Mobile homes, house trailers, campers

- Some luxury airplanes

Almost all movable real estate has certain characteristics, namely:

1. Movable real estate tends to go down in value with the passage of time.

2. Movable real estate might be rented only part of the year.

3. Movable real estate may have large insurance costs.

Yet I know plenty of people who own movable real estate who:

- Earn profits *every* year
- Get *big* depreciation tax deductions
- Enjoy their movable real estate regularly

Take Tim, who owns three boats that he rents out an average of 15 weeks a year. His average rental fee is $2,000 per week for a bareboat charter (that is, without a paid captain). Such a charter is one in which the person who rents the boat for a period of time brings along the:

- Needed food
- Bedsheets, tablecloths
- Charts, navigation books
- Other necessities for cruising

So these items need not be supplied by Tim.

Tim's income averages $30,000 per year per boat. Since each boat cost about $100,000, Tim is able to deduct some $10,000 per year in depreciation (assuming a 10-year life for that boat). This means that the first 10,000 of income is completely tax free, for each boat. So Tim has a total of $30,000 a year in income that is free of any federal, city, or state income taxes.

Other legitimate tax deductions shelter more of this income. And since Tim is also a boating enthusiast besides being a businessman, he enjoys having three boats at his disposal anytime he needs one.

And, like myself, Tim is a sun enthusiast. So he keeps two of his boats in Florida and one in the Caribbean during the winter. Any trips south he has to make during the winter from his home in the north to inspect or maintain his business properties are completely tax deductible. "These expenses," Tim explains, "are ordinary and necessary for my business."

GET OTHERS TO PAY FOR YOUR MOVABLE REAL ESTATE

I've done much thinking about and study of actual movable real estate deals. While you can own boats, mobile homes, and campers as Tim does, your expenses can be high. The best way to own such "real estate" is through a limited partnership. This way you:

- Reduce, or eliminate, your investment

- Can buy more income producers (boats, campers, mobile homes)

- Spread the risk among many people

- Have greater ease in proving your business intentions

Yes, you *can* make money with movable real estate. One of the most successful gas station operators I know is a guy who owns a motor home and several campers, along with a slew of trailers and trucks. His income from these often equals or exceeds the income from his gas and repair sales! And he's not fully dependent upon the sale of gas, oil, or repairs. This gives him more independence than he might otherwise have.

MAKE YOUR FORTUNE IN REAL ESTATE–BASED BUSINESS

You *can* make a quick, easy fortune from real estate–based businesses. In this chapter we've mentioned only a few you can try. There are hundreds of other such businesses.

So resolve *today* to find yourself such a business. Then—when you make your fortune—drop me a note telling me how you did it. (I have a great publisher who forwards *all* my mail.) I'll include your successful method in a future book to help other BWBs. (But to keep your success a secret, your name will *not* be used in the writeup.) Now, go out and combine another business with real estate!

Points to Remember

- You can often get 100% financing for a business other than real estate when you tie it in with real estate.

- Some businesses eventually earn more from their real estate investments than from their regular profit-making activities.

- There are seven easy steps to take to combine another business with real estate.

- Hundreds of different businesses can be "hinged" and leveraged around real estate.

- Real estate is a business, much like any other business.

- Always seek to obtain some income from your real estate even though you're more interested in another business.

- You can earn money by renting out rented property.

- You can usually make money from rented buildings with *no* cash down if you can rent out the space at a higher rate than you pay for it.

- To find buildings to rent out, look in the real estate columns of large-city newspapers.

- Renting a building can be your fastest and lowest cost way to get into real estate without a large cash outlay.

- Other potentially profitable real estate-related businesses include REITs, theaters, recreation facilities, motels, and hotels.

- "Movable real estate" might build your wealth while you enjoy it.

FOURTEEN

HOW TO GO FROM PENNIES TO MILLIONS IN REAL ESTATE IN THREE YEARS, STARTING WITH NO CASH

This is the shortest chapter in this book because it gives you the 36 steps—one for each month—to go from pennies to millions in real estate in three years. Each month is numbered and you have a space for entering the date on which you complete a step. So start taking your first step now!* Read the following steps carefully. Then, if you have any questions, refer to other parts of this book covering your question. If you still have questions, call or fax me at the numbers listed at the end of this chapter.

FROM PENNIES TO MILLIONS IN REAL ESTATE IN THREE YEARS, STARTING WITH *NO* CASH

Month No.	Check Off When Done	Your Action
1	_____ Date Done	Start building your real estate empire by reading this book from cover to cover and deciding which type of *income* real estate you'll use to build your fortune.

Important notice: Your 36 steps give you *suggested prices*. Please note: *these are only suggested prices*. The prices in your area may be *higher* or *lower*. *You* will make *your* buying decisions based on local conditions, *not on the suggested prices*!

Month No.	Check Off When Done	Your Action
2	_____ Date Done	Look for, and buy, your first income property using 100% financing. (Such a property will usually be priced at $100,000 to $150,000 and will require $25,000 in borrowed cash.)
3	_____ Date Done	Improve your first property by having it upgraded by making repairs, getting it fully rented, and making plans to raise the rents as soon as possible.
4	_____ Date Done	Buy your second income property, using the upgraded value of property number one on your financial statement. Property number one may now have a value of $160,000 to $220,000, based on the increased income and worth resulting from the improvements you made. Property number two will probably be priced at $250,000 to $375,000 and will require $35,000 in borrowed cash.
5	_____ Date Done	Devote this month to getting property number two into shape so you can raise the rents and increase your cash income.
6	_____ Date Done	Continue working on property number two while you look for number three. Your number-two property will now probably have a value of $325,000 to $450,000. This value will look good on your financial statement.
7	_____ Date Done	Locate property number three and make an offer for it. This property will probably have a price of $400,000 to $525,000 and will require $50,000 in cash, which you will borrow using the equity you have in properties one and two.
8	_____ Date Done	Buy property number three using borrowed cash.
9	_____ Date Done	Improve property number three by making repairs, raising rents, etc.

Month No.	Check Off When Done	Your Action
10	_____ Date Done	Continue working on all your properties.
11	_____ Date Done	Survey your income and cash situation.
	_____ Date Done	Make a summary of your net worth. Thus:

Property No.	Present Worth
1	$220,000
2	450,000
3	525,000
Total	$1,195,000

Month No.	Check Off When Done	Your Action
12	_____ Date Done	Take a month's vacation so you can enjoy your newfound income!
13	_____ Date Done	Look for property number four, which will have a value of $750,000 to $1.2 million. Spend at least four weeks looking for this property because it will put you very close to the multimillionaire class! If you need more time to find your property, take it.
14	_____ Date Done	Take over property number four during this month. Use the increased value of your first three properties to come up with a "beautiful" financial statement.
15	_____ Date Done	Improve property number four, if necessary. Often, a property of this price will not need much improvement because it is in excellent condition at the start.
16	_____ Date Done	Look for property number five. It will be in the $3 million price range. Again, use your excellent financial statement as the basis for borrowing *all* the cash you need.
17	_____ Date Done	Take over property number five. You are now a real estate millionaire, based on your five properties. Thus:

Property No.	Present Worth
1	$220,000
2	450,000
3	525,000
4	1,250,000
5	3,000,000
Total	$5,445,000

Your MIF (money in fist) should be at least $250,000 a year.

Take a vacation and enjoy your wealth.

18 _____
Date Done

Here are 18 more months for you to work to get the money you seek, just in case:

19–36 _____
Date Done

1. You're slower than others.
2. You have trouble finding suitable property.
3. Money tightens up.
4. Your wife or husband objects.

Even so, you can see how easy it is for *you* to make millions in real estate in just three years, starting with no cash!

"CONVINCERS" FOR THE DISBELIEVERS EVERYWHERE

When I talk to people about making money, I sometimes see doubt in their eyes. Yet when one of my readers tells these same people what he or she actually did, I see ready acceptance. Since I can't bring you (my reader) together with other actual readers in the pages of a book, I'm doing the next best thing I can: I'm quoting from actual letters readers write me.

As I mentioned earlier, *all* these letters are available for your inspection in my New York City office (or my Long Island office if that would be more convenient for you). All I need is a few days' notice from you so we can get the letters out of the safe deposit box in the bank. Here are a few of those convincing letters that will show *you* that you *can* get rich in real estate today.

Recently I bought Ty Hicks's How to Make Millions in Real Estate in Three Years Starting with No Cash. *I personally began buying real* estate a year ago when I was 21 and had no credit. Since that time I bought a beautiful home, two co-op apartments, a five-family and six-family, all for no down payment. They appraise for just under $800,000. It still amazes me, a year later, that I am able to own real estate.

And next,

In the past year I have been able to acquire six properties—five single-family houses and one four-unit building—from lists of HUD (Housing and Urban Development Administration) and VA (Veteran's Administration) foreclosures, and have taken over each property with at least a 25% discount. In two cases the VA sold to me at over 30% discount and provided 100% fixed rate financing for 30 years. By best estimate, these properties are worth $435,000 with combined equities of $126,000. Though this effort required some work, I'm amazed at how easy it has been. I'm really pleased with the results.

Again, with *no* money,

I bought several homes over the last several years. But Friday I closed a 12-unit apartment complex for no money down. A $225,000 value for $185,000. I assumed first and second mortgages and the owner gave a third with interest only. Ty, I know I'm on my way now and I just wanted to thank you for the knowledge.

In fewer words,

We, my wife and I, have been using the "0" cash concept for several years to acquire property. We currently own 72 units and are constantly looking for more. The current gross rental income is in excess of $100,000 per year.

A reader who's branching out says,

After reading your books I found myself getting up and going. I bought some apartments and town houses with your no-money-down ideas and they have worked wonderfully. At present I'm working on a private hospital in Europe using your technique.

A big moneymaker writes,

> I received your *Real Estate Riches Kit* and I think it is very good. Many of the ideas in it I have been using for years, and have made several million dollars in land development.

A smaller, but successful moneymaker writes,

> I have purchased one apartment building for only $500 down and $500 at closing (it was a repo) using the Ty Hicks method given in a recent newsletter. I'm now negotiating for four more buildings from the same bank.

Likewise,

> I bought my first rental property after reading your book *How to Borrow Your Way to Real Estate Riches*. This property gives a positive cash flow of $220 a month, which we consider good for a first attempt in this area.

Just 18 months to double her money,

> When I first contacted you, my net worth was $377,856. Today (18 months later) it is $767,106. You can take satisfaction in my pleasure because my contacts with you both by phone and your writings helped motivate and taught me how to achieve what I have.

Also, what this chapter shows you,

> I have read most of your books and just want to tell you that I have been able to make several million dollars in the last four years, following your advice! Thanks millions!

Finally, one of the best letters ever written to me, via fax,

> This letter is a follow-up to the telephone conversation I had with you this morning regarding property/real estate investing. I want to give you (and your readers) a background of how I started in real estate with no money.

My parents divorced when I was 12 years old, which was not a good situation, but it happened. I started working at the age of 14, mostly after school, and held two jobs. The harder I worked, the more money I made. But the more money I made, the more often my car broke down and my school bills grew. It was never-ending!

When I got to college I worked as a waiter at two to three restaurants each week. At the age of 24, still working as a waiter, my step-grandfather, with whom I was living, became ill and his family sold the house. So I had to find a place to live.

I had less than $500 in my checking account, and one credit card with a $5,000 line of credit on it. I was working as a waiter at a large hotel in the morning and at night as a waiter at a fine dining restaurant. I was making about $3,000 a month between both jobs, working 80 hours a week.

My mom suggested I buy a condo to live in. I thought "I can take a cash advance on my credit card and make payments from my income." So I called my credit card bank and asked what the payment would be if I took the entire $5,000 advance. After I explained what I wanted to do, the operator put me on hold. After a few minutes of waiting (which was well worth it) she said "Because you've been with us for four years and have a good payment record, I can raise your credit and cash advance limit to $10,000 and I can also reduce your interest payment by 4%!"

At the time real estate prices were low in my area. I looked at condos for $120,000 but nothing struck me as a nice place to live. After three days of looking the Realtor took me to see a home (not a condo) that was a bank repo for $167,000. It was a wreck. It had a hole the size of a basketball in the garage, insect infestation, overgrown landscaping, broken windows, etc. I told the Realtor I wanted that old house on the corner lot and that I could learn to fix it up on my own. He laughed and said, "You don't want that house. I just wanted to show you what you'd pay for the cheapest house in the neighborhood versus a condo in the same area."

But I did *not* want a condo. And with my $10,000 of borrowed money I could afford an FHA loan at 3% down plus closing costs. That day we made an offer and within 30 days I owned my first home for a purchase price of $158,000. I spent the next six months fixing up that old house, including living in the garage for two months. I took in a roommate for $350 a month rent.

At the end of six months, in December, a mortgage broker called me and asked if I'd be interested in refinancing my home. I said, "I don't have money for that." He told me I could do it for free and pull out $50,000 in cash on a second loan and that my current interest of 8.5% would be reduced to 6.75%. The savings would almost cover the cost of the larger loan! I was so excited. Within a week my house appraised at $225,000. It was now one of the nicest homes in the neighborhood and all my neighbors thanked me for cleaning it up because it was such an eyesore before.

During the next few weeks I searched for other homes to buy. I found my "dream" home, a bank repo that went on the market an hour before I saw the sign. It was on almost an acre of land, a huge house (3,000 square feet) with four bedrooms and three baths. The one drawback was there was no landscaping. I did not mind this as I was into landscaping and gardening. I got this house for $475,000 and it was a steal (about $5,000 under market).

I rented my first house for the monthly payment I was making on it and moved into the new home. I fixed it up like the first one with new paint, carpets, landscaping—all with no money out of my pocket. It all came from refinance money from the first house and I only had to put a portion of the money down on the second home.

Within 10 months, in October, I sold the second home for $735,000 to a cash buyer who needed a one-level home (an elderly lady). I made $260,000, less Realtor fees, commissions, and approximately $40,000 in supplies to fix up the home.

I took my profit and moved up to a new home near the beach. I bought it for $780,000 and within two years sold it for $1.4 million. I kept repeating this process of buying, fixing, and refinancing, pulling out my equity to leverage myself. And it does work!

Last June I bought my current home, which was in a distressed situation, for $2.5 million. The home was being sold as is by a couple getting a divorce. They just wanted out. The home on the left of my home just closed escrow for $2.6 million, without an ocean view. Two doors down, the house on the right sold for $2.8 million in one day!

I feel my house is a good deal because two other houses that just sold were old, but all three (including mine) are one street above the Pacific Ocean in a very highly demanded neighborhood that commands top dollar.

So I am adding four bathrooms and two bedrooms and a large

master closet. I've already cleaned up the yard and upgraded the interior. I will list my house for $5 million in July of this year when it is done and get close to the asking price as this is what newly remodeled homes go for in this neighborhood.

With my approximate $2 million in profit I will do a 1031 exchange and buy income properties of the type we discussed on the phone this morning.* I have always said: *"If you always do what you have always done, you will always get what you have always gotten!"*

I am not a waiter anymore. I am a national sales manager for a financial firm. I started from nothing and I am now making seven figures a year from real estate—*not* my job! I am still frugal and plan on retiring from my job in three years to work full time in real estate. I only wish I could have read your book sooner! But at only 31 I cannot complain. I *did it* and will continue to *do it*! I hope we can meet someday so I can say thank you in person. Until then, please accept my deep gratitude for sharing your knowledge.

You can do what these readers have. Why? Because these real-life letters are just a sampling of the thousands in my files. If they can do it, so can you! Get started—right now!

Points to Remember

- You *can* make millions in real estate in three years starting with *no* cash. But you *must* work at building your wealth. And you *must* have good legal and accounting advice *every* step of the way.

- The steps in this chapter are the keys to *your* wealth.

- You can call me at my business phone number, (516) 766-5850, from 8 A.M. to 10 P.M. New York (eastern) time. Or fax me 24 hours a day, 7 days a week at (516) 766-5919. If you fax me, please include your mailing address so I can contact you by mail, if necessary.

- You can e-mail me at TYGHICKS@AOL.COM. And you can see all my books, kits, and newsletters on the Internet at www. iwsmoney.com. Or you can use www.iws-inc.com. Any of the products shown on the Internet can be ordered by credit card.

---

*A 1031 exchange is a tax-free trade of income-producing property under provisions of Section 1031 of the IRS Tax Code. It is used by experienced real estate investors.

FIFTEEN

HOW AND WHERE TO GET MORE DATA ON REAL ESTATE

Knowledge is power—power to build your wealth faster, with fewer problems and more surely. In this chapter I'm giving you many sources of more data on real estate and efficient business management. By building your knowledge, you will almost certainly build your wealth. For as Aldous Huxley wrote, paraphrased for today's world:

> **Every person who knows how to read has it in his power to magnify himself, to multiply the ways in which he exists, to make his life full, significant, and interesting.**

REAL ESTATE INVESTMENT AND MANAGEMENT BOOKS

The following books are available from Penguin Group (USA), 375 Hudson St., New York, NY 10014-3657. You will find these books useful in building your real estate business to earn your fortune.

Allen, David, *Getting Things Done,* 288 pages
Ambler, Tim, *Marketing and the Bottom Line*
Amis, David, *Winning Angels: The 7 Fundamentals of Angel Investing*
Breuel, Brian, *The Complete Idiot's Guide to Buying Insurance and Annuities,* 352 pages
Brown, Tom, *Business Minds: Management Wisdom, Direct from the World's Greatest Thinkers*
Crainer, Stuart, *FT Hand Book of Management*
Damodaran, Aswath, *The Dark Side of Valuation*

Davis, Evan, *The New Penguin Dictionary of Business*, 400 pages

Davis, Park, *The Complete Idiot's Guide to Running a Bed and Breakfast*, 336 pages

Day, Alistair, *Mastering Risk Modeling*

De Vries, Manfred, *The Leadership Mystique*

Edwards, Casey, *The Complete Idiot's Guide to Being a Smart Landlord*, 252 pages

Edwards, Paul, *Secrets of Self-Empowerment*, 400 pages

Edwards, Paul, *Working from Home*, 688 pages

Epstein, Lita, *The Complete Idiot's Guide to Tax Breaks and Deductions*, 336 pages

Garson, Barbara, *Money Makes the World Go Round*, 352 pages

Gladstone, David, *Venture Capital Handbook: An Entrepreneur's Guide to Raising Venture Capital*

Gratton, Lynda, *The Democratic Enterprise*

Hicks, Tyler, *How to Make Big Money in Real Estate*, 336 pages

Hopkins, Tom, *How to Master the Art of Listing and Selling Real Estate*, 416 pages

Koslow, Brian, *365 Ways to Become a Millionaire*, 192 pages

LeBoeuf, Michael, *How to Win Customers and Keep Them for Life*, 256 pages

Maple, Stephen, *The Complete Idiot's Guide to Law for Small Business Owners*, 352 pages

Matysiak, Gerald, *Real Estate Investment*

McKnight, Thomas, *Will It Fly?: How to Know If Your New Business Idea Has Wings . . . Before You Take the Leap*

Mintzberg, Henry, *Strategy Safari*

Muckian, Michael, *The Complete Idiot's Guide to Finance and Accounting*, 320 pages

Murphy, John, *Think Yourself Rich*

Nofsinger, John, *Investment Blunders of the Rich and Famous . . . and What You Can Learn from Them*

Nordstrom, Kjell, *Funky Business*

Nordstrom, Kjell, *Karaoke Capitalism*

Orman, Suze, *The Courage to Be Rich*, 448 pages

Orman, Suze, *The Road to Wealth*, 608 pages

Pickford, James, *Mastering Management 2.0*

Ramsey, Dave, *How to Have More Than Enough*, 288 pages

Rider, Stuart, *The Complete Idiot's Guide to Investing in Fixer-Uppers*, 384 pages

Rider, Stuart, *The Complete Idiot's Guide to Real Estate Investing,* 400 pages

Roberts, Ralph, *Real Wealth by Investing in Real Estate,* 384 pages

Robin, Vicki, *Your Money or Your Life,* 384 pages

Rosen, Robert, *Leading People,* 400 pages

Shell, G. Richard, *Bargaining for Advantage,* 208 pages

Stutely, Richard, *The Definitive Guide to Managing the Numbers*

Tanzer, Milt, *Real Estate Investments and How to Make Them,* 352 pages

Weisman, Steve, *Guide to Elder Care: Everything You Need to Know to Protect Yourself Legally and Financially*

Weltman, Barbara, *The Complete Idiot's Guide to Starting a Home-Based Business,* 385 pages

REAL ESTATE SUCCESS KITS, BOOKS, REPORTS, AND NEWSLETTERS

The following are available from International Wealth Success Inc. (IWS Inc.), P.O. Box 186, Merrick, NY 11566-0186.

Success Kits

Fast Financing of Your Real Estate Fortune Success Kit shows you how to raise money for real estate deals. You can move ahead faster if you can finance your real estate quickly and easily. The *Fast Financing Kit* concentrates on getting the money you need for your real estate deals. This kit gives you more than 2,500 sources of real estate money all over the United States. It also shows you how to find deals that return big income to you but are easier to finance than you might think! $99.50. 7 Speed-Read books, 523 pages.

Financial Broker-Finder-Business Broker-Consultant Success Kit shows you how to start your private business as a financial broker-finder-business broker-consultant! As a financial broker you find money for firms seeking capital and you are paid a fee. As a finder you are paid a fee for finding things (real estate, raw materials, money, etc.) for people and firms. As a business broker you help in the buying or selling of a business— again for a fee. See how to collect big fees. Kit includes typical agreements you can use, plus four colorful membership cards. $99.50. 12 Speed-Read books, 485 pages.

Foreclosures and Other Distressed Properties Kit shows you how and where to find and buy foreclosed and other distressed properties of all types.

Gives names, addresses, and other data about agencies offering foreclosed properties, often at a bargain price. Includes forms giving examples of actual foreclosure documents and paperwork. $59.95. 150+ pages,
6 audio cassette tapes.

Hard Money Commercial Real Estate Loan Kit shows you how to raise hard
money for commercial real estate—such as industrial and medical buildings, mixed-use properties, mobile home parks, apartment complexes,
townhouse developments, residential subdivisions, shopping malls and
strip centers, hotels and motels, golf courses, nursing homes, and offices. Five-hour videotape and manual with comprehensive loan data
and forms present useful guidance on how to do hard-money deals today. Covers financing from $300,000 to $20 million-plus; close in one to
two weeks; nationwide lending; brokers protected; minimal documenta-
tion required; short form appraisals accepted; flexible loan structures.
$150. 150+ pages.

*How to Build Your Real Estate Fortune Today in a Real Estate Investment
Trust Kit* shows you how to start a REIT to finance any type of real estate you want to invest in and earn money from. Gives you the exact
steps to take to raise money for your real estate from either private or
public sources. Today REITs raise millions for almost every type of real
estate used by human beings—multifamily residential (apartment
houses), factories, marinas, hotels, motels, shopping malls, nursing
homes, and hospitals. REITs can own these types of properties, lend on
them (issue mortgages), or make a combination of these investments.
$100. 150+ pages.

Loans by Mail Kit shows you how and where to get business, real estate,
and personal loans for yourself and others by mail. Lists hundreds of
lenders who loan by mail. No need to appear in person—just fill out the
loan application and send it in by mail. Many of these lenders give unsecured signature loans to qualified applicants. Use this kit to get a loan by
mail yourself. Or become a loan broker and use the kit to get started.
Unsecured signature loans by mail can go as high as $50,000 and this kit
lists such lenders. $100. 150 pages.

Loans by Phone Success Kit shows you how and where to get business, real
estate, and personal loans by telephone. With just 32 words and 15 sec-
onds you can determine if a lender is interested in the loan you seek for

yourself or for your client if you're working as a loan broker or finder. This kit gives you hundreds of telephone lenders; about half have toll-free numbers. Necessary agreement forms are also included. $100. 150+ pages.

Low Cost Real Estate Loan Getters Kit shows the user how to get real estate loans for either a client or the user. Lists hundred of active real estate lenders seeking first and junior mortgage loans for a variety of property types. Loan amounts range from a few thousand dollars to millions, depending on the property, its location, and value. Presents typical application and agreement forms for use in securing real estate loans. No license is required to obtain such loans for oneself or others. $100. 150+ pages.

Mega Money Methods Success Kit covers the raising of large amounts of money—multimillions and up—for business and real estate projects of all types. Shows how to prepare loan packages for very large loans, where to get financing for such loans, what fees to charge after the loan is obtained, plus much more. Using this kit, the beginning wealth builder should be able to prepare effective loan requests for large amounts of money for suitable projects. The kit also gives the user a list of offshore lenders for big projects. $100. 200 pages.

Real Estate Riches Success Kit shows you how to make big money in real estate as an income property owner, a mortgage broker, mortgage banker, real estate investment trust operator, mortgage money broker, raw land speculator, and industrial property owner. This is a general kit, covering all these aspects of real estate, plus many, many more. Includes numerous financing sources for your real estate fortune. This big kit also covers how to buy real estate for the lowest price (down payments of no cash can sometimes be set up) and how to run your real estate for biggest profits. $99.50. 6 Speed-Read books, 466 pages.

Starting Millionaire Success Kit shows you how to get started in a number of businesses that might make you a millionaire sooner than you think! Businesses covered in this kit include mail order, real estate, export-import, limited partnerships, and more. Kit includes four colorful membership cards. $99.50. 12 Speed-Read books, 361 pages.

Zero Cash Success Techniques Kit shows you how to get started in your own business or real estate venture with no cash! Sound impossible? It really is possible—as thousands of folks have shown. This big kit, which includes a special book by Ty Hicks on *Zero Cash Takeovers of Business and Real Estate,* also includes a 58-minute cassette tape by Ty on "Small Business Financing." On this tape, Ty talks to you! See how you can get started in your own business without cash and with few credit checks. $99.50. 7 Speed-Read books, 876 pages.

Multi-Family Home and Multi-Unit Real Estate Riches Success Kit by Tyler G. Hicks focuses on zero-down methods you can use to buy multiunit buildings—apartment houses, town houses, garden apartments, condos, and offices—even though your credit may not be the best. Shows how to squeeze the maximum profit from multiunit buildings while providing your tenants with good-quality housing or office space. This kit shows how and where to find and buy multiunit properties for profitable income. Gives hundreds of lenders for all types of multiunit properties. Comes with four special bonus reports to help you succeed in multiunit properties, including smart methods for creative zero-cash financing of multiunit buildings, a special lender for multifamily apartment house financing, and where to find multifamily properties for sale. $150. 200 pages.

How to Build Riches in Real Estate with Single-Family Homes Using Other People's Money! Success Kit by Tyler G. Hicks gives more than 150 ways to make money in single-family homes using other people's money (OPM) and includes 1,000 lenders who want to finance single-family homes. Explains income streams and financing in clear, everyday language. Actual case examples show how to acquire and use various types of single-family homes for a desired stream of income. Covers types of single-family homes; costs you might have in certain properties; figuring your positive cash flow; kinds of lenders and U.S. government loan guarantee programs; using HUD's Section 8 housing programs to build your income; how to have your renters make your monthly mortgage payments; what to look out for and what *not* to do when buying a single-family property; income from a six-bedroom home; investing in multiple homes; how to get financing; and much more. Comes with four bonus items. $150. 200 pages.

Real Estate Books

209 Fast Spare-Time Ways to Build Zero Cash Into 7 Figures a Year in Real Estate by Tyler G. Hicks gives proven strategies for you to get started quickly in income real estate. Using dozens of actual examples, the book shows you how to acquire single-family homes, multifamily dwellings, condos, townhouses, small office buildings, and many other types of valuable property. Includes hundreds of actual letters showing strategies people are using today to earn a fortune in income real estate. Gives dozens of financing sources for your income real estate. $14.95. 288 pages.

How to Buy and Flip Real Estate for Profit by Rod L. Griffin shows how to buy, hold, and flip real estate for fun and profit while avoiding novice mistakes. The author shows you the importance of buying cheap and selling high. Filled with ready-to-use strategies, checklists, and real-life case studies and success stories, this book shows you how to earn cash in days instead of years. Includes the best-kept secret in real estate on how to get 100% financing. $19.50. 198 pages.

How to Build Real Estate Riches with Low-Cost Properties by Tyler G. Hicks shows both beginning and experienced real estate wealth builders how and where to get preforeclosure and postauction properties at low cost. Covers how to finance any income property, smart steps to getting your down-payment loan, using options to control property, smart mortgage methods, plus much more. $21.50. 100 pages.

Sources of Canadian Financing for Business and Real Estate helps you find loans for Canadian real estate projects. Includes hundreds of selected financing and loan sources in Canada. Describes the largest and most active loan programs. Covers banks, credit unions, factoring firms, finance companies, mortgage lenders, mortgage brokers, government programs, and trust companies. Gives names, type of lender, address, phone and fax numbers, e-mail address, Web site, area where loans are made, loan amounts, types, options, application info, sample loan application, and related documents. $29.50. 90 pages.

Selected Lenders for Commercial and Residential Construction Loans gives data on some 150 construction lenders—name, address, phone/fax numbers, e-mail/Web site addresses, types of loans made, preferred geographic area, and loan amounts. Finding construction lenders was formerly a challenging task. Today, with this big book in hand, you can locate potential lenders that might want to work with you on your real estate deals. Includes typical loan application plus many related documents used when making construction loans of many types. $29.50. Includes lenders in both the United States and Canada. 90 pages.

Comprehensive Loan Sources for Business and Real Estate gives hundreds of lenders' names, addresses, and lending requirements for many different types of business and real estate loans. Does *not* duplicate *Diversified Loan Sources*. $25. 136 pages.

Directory of 2,500 Active Real-Estate Lenders lists 2,500 names and addresses of direct lenders or sources of information on possible lenders for real estate. $25. 198 pages.

Diversified Loan Sources for Business and Real Estate gives hundreds of lenders' names, addresses, and lending guidelines for business and real estate loans of many types. $25. 136 pages.

Guide to Business and Real Estate Loan Sources lists hundreds of business and real estate lenders, giving their lending data in very brief form. $25. 201 pages.

How Anyone Can Prosper and Get Wealthy Trading Country Land by Frank Moss shows how to acquire wealth and have fun doing it in rural land. Covers supply and demand, starting your own home-operated, spare-time, moneymaking business buying and selling woodland, estimating value, time/distance analysis, financing, buy/sell strategies, zero-cash deals, plus much more. $21.95. 100+ pages.

How to Be a Second Mortgage Loan Broker by Richard Brisky gives complete details on how to set up your office, find clients, find lenders, negotiate with clients and lenders, what fees to charge, how to comply with any licensing laws in the area of your business, what files to keep, plus much more. Using this book, a person can get started in this lucrative aspect of today's real estate market. $25. 90+ pages.

How to Borrow Your Way to Real Estate Riches by Tyler G. Hicks shows you how borrowed money can make you rich in real estate; how to earn millions using other people's money; using zero-cash success methods to build wealth; mortgaging out to build your real estate riches; making your borrowed-money automatic fortune the fastest way; sure steps to getting the real estate money you need; how to borrow real estate money from any lender; using creative financing techniques; going fully financed to your real estate fortune; knowing the numbers of your real estate; making your bundle of money by borrowing on real estate. $20. 312 pages.

How to Create Your Own Real-Estate Fortune by Jens Nielsen covers investment opportunities in real estate, leveraging, depreciation, remodeling your deal, buy- and lease-back, and understanding your financing. $17.50. 117 pages.

How to Make Fast Cash in Real Estate Deals with No-Money-Down-Deals by Rod L. Griffin shows how creativity builds wealth; finding a flexible seller; over 50 ways to build property with no money down; profit from real estate in days, not years; starting your fortune on almost nothing; how to get paid for investing while building your wealth; how to handle and tame negative cash flows; plus much more. $22.95. 180 pages.

Ideas for Finding Business and Real Estate Capital Today covers raising public money, real estate financing, borrowing methods, government loan sources, and venture money. $24.50. 62 pages.

Rapid Real Estate and Business Loan-Getting Methods by Tyler G. Hicks gives innovative techniques to get loans, ways in which real estate can make you rich, declaring your independence from the "nine-to-five grind," new steps to getting venture capital, smart-money ways to get loans, plus many other methods for getting business financing you seek. $25. 90+ pages.

Real-Estate Second Mortgages by Ty Hicks covers second mortgages, how a second mortgage finder works, naming the business, registering the firm, running ads, expanding the business, and limited partnerships. $17.50. 100 pages.

Supplement to How to Borrow Your Way to Real Estate Riches uses government sources compiled by Ty Hicks, and lists numerous mortgage loans and guarantees, loan purposes, amounts, terms, financing charge, types of structures financed, loan-value ratio, and special factors. $15.00. 87 pages.

Real Estate Reports

Here are seven reports on various aspects of real estate finance. Each report presents essential information on getting money for the real estate transaction detailed in the report.

Neighborhood and Convenience Shopping Center Loan Package, M-1 is an example of a typical successful real estate loan package. $12.50. 40 pages.

Downtown Office Building Loan Package, M-2 is an example of a successful loan package for a typical office building. $12.50. 16 pages.

Single-Family Home Foreclosure Business Plan, M-3 shows how money could be raised to buy single-family home foreclosures and rent them out or resell them for a profit. $12.50. 16 pages.

Single-Family Home Income Property Business Plan, M-4 shows how money could be made by owning a string of single-family homes that are rented to tenants at a profit. $12.50. 16 pages.

High-Rise Apartment Building Loan Package and Business Plan, M-5 presents a comprehensive loan package and business plan for the financing and operation of a multifamily apartment building. $12.50. 16 pages.

Refinancing Proposal for a Multi-Family Apartment House, M-6 shows how a large apartment house can be refinanced to enhance its competitive position in its marketplace. $12.50. 61 pages.

FHA Multifamily Building Loan Package and Business Plan, M-7 shows a typical loan package and business plan that complies with agency requirements. $12.50. 14 pages.

Finder's International Network Directory shows how to earn a big income as a finder, how to set up your business, what fees to charge, how to find clients, forms to use to protect your fee, plus much more. Provides an attractive membership certificate and hundreds of up-to-date finder leads usable throughout the world. $28. 52 pages.

Option Wealth Opportunities gives 45 ways to make big money in real estate using options, even though you do not own one square foot of land or buildings. Using powerful options can be your way to get started in income real estate on minimum funds—sometimes as low as $10. Gives lenders from whom your startup money might be borrowed. $20.00. 40 pages.

Real Estate Money Raiser's Quick Guide to Successfully Financing Profitable Projects of All Types shows how to get into real estate on little or no cash; using subprime mortgages; the easiest real estate anywhere; earning big profits from presale buys; how, and where, to get into zero-cash real estate; secrets of 100% financing of real estate; using credit cards for real estate takeover; plus much more. $20. 135 pages.

Newsletters

International Wealth Success, Ty Hicks's monthly newsletter published 12 times a year. This 16-page newsletter covers loan and grant sources, real estate opportunities, business opportunities, import-export, mail order, and a variety of other topics on making money in your own business. Every subscriber can run one free classified advertisement of 40 words or less each month, covering business or real estate needs or opportunities. The newsletter has a worldwide circulation, giving readers and advertisers very broad coverage. Started in January 1967, the newsletter has been published continuously since. $24 per year. 16 pages.

Money Watch Bulletin, a monthly coverage of 100 or more active lenders for real estate and business purposes. The newsletter gives the lender's name, address, telephone number, lending guidelines, loan ranges, and other helpful information. All lender names were obtained within the last week; the data is therefore up to date. Lenders' names and addresses are also provided on self-stick labels on an occasional basis. Also covers venture capital and grants. $95. 20 pages.

INDEX